Consecrated Life } do Outline (summary points)
& Patrimony } for extra credit
or Last Lesson or reflection
Chpt XIII

AF825741

Today

~~Lesson~~ Chpt 11 — Chpt 8

12 A (not Marriage) } Chpt 9

B
C

Next

12 B } Chpt 9 + other reading:
12 C

Next 4/25

Lesson 12 finish

✓ 13 skip.

14 Penal Law — ~~Focus~~ Outside
Focus on Pio. Norms
of Child Protection.
+ Sacra. T.... link

ECTION
IANDBOOKS

PONTIFICIA VNIVERSITAS SANCTAE CRVCIS

2007

COLLECTION
Gratianus
SERIES

A Handbook on Canon Law

Second updated edition

W&L
WILSON & LAFLEUR

ECTION
IANDBOOKS

COLLECTION
Gratianus
SERIES

COFOUNDERS
ERNEST CAPARROS
MICHEL THÉRIAULT (†)

PONTIFICIA UNIVERSITAS SANCTAE CRUCIS

A Handbook on Canon Law

Joseph T. MARTÍN DE AGAR

Second updated edition

W&L
WILSON & LAFLEUR

2007

Bibliothèque et Archives nationales du Québec and Library and Archives Canada cataloguing in publication

Martín de Agar y Valverde, José Tomás

A Handbook on Canon Law, 2nd ed.
(Gratianus series. Handbooks)
Translation of: Elementi di diritto canonico.
Includes bibliographical references and indexes.

ISBN 978-2-89127-804-1

1. Canon law. I. Title. II. Series.

KBU2212.M3713 2007 262.9'4 C2007-942071-0

English translation by Lawrence Feingold of the Italian *Elementi di Diritto Canonico* by J. T. Martín de Agar (Editorial consultant for the 1st edition: Rev. Jerry Jung).
Translation of the updates for the second edition: Mindy Emmons

Nihil obstat quominus imprimatur, Marianopoli, die 19ª Septembris 2007,
Michaël Parent, P.H., I.C.L., vicarius episcopalis, cancellarius,
Censor deputatus, Curiæ diocesanæ.

Imprimatur, Marianopoli, die 19ª Septembris 2007,
Ioannes Claudius cardinalis Turcotte, archiepiscopus Marianopolitanus,
N.P. 7/2007

ISBN 978-2-89127-804-1
Legal Deposit 4th Quarter 2007 Bibliothèque et archives nationales du Québec
Legal Deposit 4th Quarter 2007, Library and Archives Canada

Orders to:
Wilson & Lafleur Ltée
40, Notre-Dame Est
Montréal (Québec) Canada H2Y 1B9
Tel.: (514) 875-6326 / 1-800-363-3227
Fax: (514) 875-8356
www.wilsonlafleur.com

USA:

www.CanonLawBooks.com
2662 East Allegheny Avenue
Philadelphia, PA 19134-5115
Tel.: (215) 634-2355
Fax: (215) 634-2373

Midwest Theological Forum
1420 Davey Road
Woodridge, IL 60517 U.S.A
Tel.: (630) 739-9750
Fax: (630) 739-9758
e-mail: mail@mwtf.org

Table of Contents

Abbreviations xiii

Foreword xv

General Basic Bibliography xix

Chapter I. Canon Law 1

1. The Meanings of *Ius* 1
2. Basis of the Right 2
3. Church and Law 4
4. Divine Law and Human Law 5
5. The History of Canon Law 7
   - A) The First Millennium 8
   - B) Classical Canon Law 10
   - C) The Modern Era 11
   - D) The Contemporary Period 13
     - The Second Vatican Council 14
     - The *Code of Canon Law* of 1983 15
     - The *Code of Canons of the Eastern Churches* (CCEO) 18

Chapter II. The Sources of Canon Law 21

1. Norms and Juridical Acts 22
2. Canonical Norms 25
3. Law 27
   - A) Types of Law 28
     - Divine Law and Human Law 28
     - General and Particular Laws 29

Territorial Law and Personal Law 30
Invalidating and Incapacitating Laws (c. 10)............. 31
B) Promulgation 31
C) Retroactivity 32
4. Custom 33
Types of customs 34
5. Administrative Norms.................... 34
A) General Executory Decrees (cc. 31–33)...... 35
B) Instructions (c. 34) 35
6. Statutes and Rules of Order 35
A) Statutes 36
B) Rules of Order 37
7. Singular Administrative Acts 38
A) Singular Decrees 40
B) Singular Precepts...................... 40
C) Rescripts 41
Privilege 42
Dispensation......................... 42
8. Judicial Acts.......................... 43
9. Private Juridical Acts (cc. 124–128) 44

Chapter III. Who Are Subjects in Canon Law? 47
1. The Physical Person (cc. 96–112)............. 48
2. The Juridical Person (cc. 113–123) 49
A) Corporations and Foundations (c. 115) 51
B) Public and Private Juridical Persons 52

Chapter IV. The Constitution of the Church 55
1. Constitutional Principles.................. 56
A) The Principle of Equality 56
B) The Principle of Variety 57
C) The Institutional Principle 58
2. The Fundamental Rights and Duties of the Faithful.......................... 60
3. Power and Its Exercise in the Church 65
4. Canonical Regulation and the Power of Governance 69

A) Distinction of Functions 70
B) Ordinary Power (Proper or Vicariate) and Ordinaries 71
C) Delegated Power 72
D) Competence 73
E) External Forum and Internal Forum 73
F) The Habitual Faculties.................... 74
G) Substitution of Jurisdiction............... 74

Chapter V. The People of God. Its Social Structure 77
1. The People of God.......................... 77
2. The Lay Faithful............................ 81
3. Principal Obligations and Rights of the Laity... 83
4. Personal Status of Sacred Ministers 86
A) The Formation of Clerics.................. 87
B) Incardination of Clerics.................... 90
C) Rights and Duties of Clerics............... 91
D) Loss of the Clerical State 94
5. Associations of the Faithful 95
A) Types of Associations 97
B) Public Associations 98
C) Private Associations of the Faithful......... 99

Chapter VI. The People of God. Its Hierarchical Structure (Government and Organization of the Church).... 103
1. The Concepts of Ecclesiastical Organization.... 103
A) Ecclesiastical Office 104
B) The Conferral of the Office 105
2. The Universal and Particular Dimensions of the Church 107
3. The Supreme Power in the Church............ 109
A) The College of Bishops 109
The Ecumenical Council 110
B) The Roman Pontiff....................... 111
4. Institutions for the Government of the Universal Church........................... 113
5. The Particular Churches..................... 116

A) The Diocese 117
B) Other Ecclesiastical Circumscriptions Similar to the Diocese 118
6. Government and Organization of the Diocese .. 120
A) The Diocesan Bishop (cc. 381–402) 120
B) Institutions and Offices for the Government of the Diocese 123
Coadjutor and Auxiliary Bishops (cc. 403–411) 123
The Diocesan Synod (cc. 460–468) 124
The Diocesan Curia (cc. 469–474) 124
The Diocesan Vicars (cc. 475–481) 125
The Finance Committee (cc. 492 and 493) . 125
The Diocesan Financial Administrator (c. 494) 126
The Council of Priests (cc. 495–501) 126
The College of Consultors (c. 502) 127
The Chapter of Canons (cc. 503–510) 127
The Pastoral Council (cc. 511–514) 128
C) The Parish (cc. 515–552) 128
D) Vicars Forane (cc. 553–555) 131
E) Rectors of Churches (cc. 556–563) 131
F) Chaplains (cc. 564–572) 132
7. Organisms Above the Diocesan Level 133
A) The Ecclesiastical Province 133
B) The Ecclesiastical Region 134
C) Particular Councils 134
D) The Conferences of Bishops 135

Chapter VII. Consecrated Life 139
1. Institutes of Consecrated Life 142
A) Religious Institutes 145
The Religious 146
B) Secular Institutes 150
2. Societies of Apostolic Life (cc. 731–746) 151

Chapter VIII. The Means of Salvation.
The Word of God 153
1. The Teaching Function 154
A) The Ecclesiastical Magisterium of the Church 155
Obligations Concerning Catholic Doctrine 157
B) Ecumenism 159
C) The Ministry of the Divine Word 160
Preaching (cc. 762–772) 161
Catechesis 163
Missions 164
D) Catholic Education 166
The Teaching of the Catholic Religion 167
Catholic Schools 168
Catholic Universities and Other Institutes of Higher Learning 169
Ecclesiastical Universities and Faculties . . . 170
E) Means of Communication and Books 171

Chapter IX. The Means of Salvation. Divine Worship . . . 175
1. The Sanctifying Office in the Church 175
2. The Sacraments 176
A) Baptism 178
B) Confirmation 181
C) The Holy Eucharist 183
The Holy Sacrifice of the Mass 184
Eucharistic Communion 186
Conservation and Veneration of the Most Holy Eucharist 188
Offerings for the Celebration of the Mass (cc. 945–958) 189
D) The Sacrament of Penance 190
Collective Absolution (cc. 961–963) 193
Indulgences (cc. 992–997) 194
E) The Anointing of the Sick 194
F) The Sacrament of Orders 196

3. Marriage 199
A) General Concepts 202
B) Matrimonial Consent 204
Incapacity 205
Ignorance 207
Error of Law 208
Error of Fact 208
Deceit (c. 1098) 210
Simulation (c. 1101) 210
Conditions (c. 1102) 211
Violence and Fear 212
C) Impediments 213
The Impediments in Particular 215
D) The Form of Marriage 218
E) Effects of Marriage 220
F) Dissolution of the Marriage Bond 221
Dispensation of Non-Consummated Marriage (c. 1142) 221
Dissolution in Favor of the Faith (cc. 1143–1150) 222
G) Separation of the Spouses 223
H) Convalidation of the Marriage 223
Simple Convalidation (cc. 1156–1160) 224
Retroactive Validation (Radical Sanation, cc. 1161–1165) 225
I) Pastoral Care and Preparation for Marriage (cc. 1063–1072) 225
4. Other Acts of Divine Worship 227
A) Sacramentals (cc. 1166–1172) 227
B) The Liturgy of the Hours (cc. 1173–1175) 229
C) Church Funerals (cc. 1176–1185) 229
D) Veneration of the Saints, of Sacred Images and of Relics (c. 1186–1190) 231
E) Vows and Oaths (cc. 1191–1204) 232
5. Sacred Places and Times 234
A) Sacred Places 234
Various Sacred Places 235
B) Sacred Times 238

Chapter X. The Temporal Goods of the Church. Patrimonial Canon Law 241
1. Goods 242
2. The Acquisition of Goods 244
3. Administration of Ecclesiastical Goods 248
4. Alienation of Ecclesiastical Goods 251
5. Pious Dispositions and Pious Foundations 252

Chapter XI. Penal Canon Law 255
1. Offences 255
2. The Offender 256
3. Ecclesiastical Penalties 257
A) Censures 257
B) Expiatory Penalties 258
C) Penal Remedies and Penances 258
4. The Application of Penalties 259
5. Cessation of Penalties 260
6. Specific Offences 261

Chapter XII. Procedural Law 265
1. Judicial Organization 266
2. The Process 269
A) The Parties 270
B) The Competence of the Tribunal 271
3. The Carrying Out of the Process 272
A) The Introductory Stage (cc. 1501–1525) 273
B) The Evidentiary or Probatory Stage: Proofs (cc. 1526–1586) 274
C) The Publication of the Acts, the Conclusion of the Case, and the Pleadings (cc. 1598–1606) 278
D) The Judicial Decision (cc. 1607–1618) 278
4. Challenging the Judgment 279
A) Appeal (cc. 1628–1640) 279
Adjudged Matter (*res iudicata*) 280

B) Complaint of Nullity (cc. 1619–1627) 281
C) Total Reinstatement (*restitutio in integrum*) (cc. 1645–1648) 282
5. The Execution of the Judgment (cc. 1650–1655). 282
6. The Oral Contentious Process................ 283
7. Special Processes.......................... 283
A) Penal Processes (cc. 1717–1731)............ 287
8. Administrative Justice (cc. 1732–1739) 288
A) The Administrative Recourse 289
B) Contentious Administrative Recourse...... 290

Chapter XIII. Relations Between the Church and the Political Community 291
1. Christian Dualism.......................... 292
2. Historical Interpretations of Dualism 293
3. The Second Vatican Council 303
Religious Liberty 308
4. Various Aspects of the Mission of the Church with Regard to the World 309

Index of Particular Canons 311

Subject Index.................................. 321

Abbreviations

AAS	*Acta Apostolicæ Sedis*
CCC	*Catechism of the Catholic Church*
CCEO	*Codex Canonum Ecclesiarum Orientalium* (*Code of Canons of the Eastern Churches*)
Congr.	Congregation
CIC	*Codex Iuris Canonici* (*Code of Canon Law*)
CCLA	E. CAPARROS, H. AUBÉ, *Code of Canon Law Annotated*, commentary prepared under the responsibility of the Instituto Martín de Azpilcueta (Pamplona), 2nd edition revised and updated, Gratianus Series, Wilson & Lafleur, Montréal, 2004. Includes the *Responses of the Pontifical Council for the Interpretation of Legislative Texts*, (Appendix II), the *Complementary Norms to the Code promulgated by English-Language Conferences of Bishops* (Appendix III) and *Tables of Correspondence* (Appendix VI)
EV	*Enchiridion Vaticanum*
ExComCIC	A. MARZOA, J. MIRAS, R. RODRÍGUEZ-OCAÑA (eds.), *Exegetical Commentary on the Code of Canon Law*, V Vols. (E. CAPARROS, General Editor, English Edition), Gratianus Series, Montréal/Chicago, Wilson & Lafleur/MWTF, 2004
M.P.	*Motu proprio*
PCLT	Pontifical Council for Legislative Texts

Documents of the Second Vatican Council

AA	Decr. *Apostolicam actuositatem*
CD	Decr. *Christus Dominus*
DH	Decl. *Dignitatis humanæ*
DV	Const. *Dei Verbum*
GE	Decl. *Gravissimum educationis*
GS	Const. *Gaudium et spes*
LG	Const. *Lumen gentium*
OE	Decr. *Orientalium Ecclesiarum*
OT	Decr. *Optatam totius*
PO	Decr. *Presbyterorum ordinis*
SC	Const. *Sacrosanctum Concilium*
UR	Decr. *Unitatis redintegratio*

Foreword

One could be tempted to consider law as foreign to the Church, since the Church is a community of a spiritual nature based on faith and charity—virtues which should be sufficient to order relations among brethren. In fact, there are examples in the history of the Church of spiritualist currents which have interpreted canonical discipline as an element of rigidity, an obstacle to the development of charisms, or even as an instrument of oppression in the hands of ecclesiastical authorities.

This is incorrect. These errors derive from a deformed vision of the nature both of the Church and of law, not infrequently confusing spirituality with sentiment. They end up juxtaposing a series of irreconcilable opposites: institution and charism, law and spirit, nature and grace, canon law and pastoral care. In reality, however, these opposing aspects are inseparable, although distinct. Perhaps we may forget that faith requires obedience in works, that love for Jesus Christ is shown in obeying his commands, that He told those he sent in his name: Whoever listens to you listens to me (Luke 10, 16). Grace and charity, pastoral care and charism, cannot be realized without the order of justice, which is the channel in which the variety of gifts, tasks, and human qualities collaborate to build up the ecclesiastical community without destroying its unity.

For its part, law should not be understood as a set of arbitrary rules; rather, there is a relationship between norms and life, similar to that of the bed and the water of a river: the bed indicates the limits on the course of the current so that it does not spill into a swamp, but also the force of the water forms the bed, molds it, adapting it to the land, giving life to what otherwise would be a dry riverbed.

The Church has been constituted by the Lord not only as a community of believers who participate in the same invisible spiritual gifts, but also as the People of whom He is the Legislator. Social and visible relations, which must be ordered according to justice, precisely arise from the supernatural bonds and from participation in the same means of salvation (the Word of God and the sacraments). The Church is a visible and organized society which has a mission to accomplish in which all the faithful are called to participate, each one according to his condition. The task of law is also to determine and assign the various roles, and to coordinate them for the common good[1].

Law is not an end in itself. It is an instrument which is used for the realization of justice in social relations. Justice, in its turn, is a virtue necessarily ordered to charity[2], and in this way it is integrated into a higher Justice, which is sanctity. If this connection is not kept in mind, then law could either come to be seen as a mere attachment to norms as if all of life depended on them, or on the contrary, it could be perceived as an arbitrary limit on freedom. These two opposing errors spring from the same root.

Certainly, the elements of a spiritual nature are the most important in the life of the Church, since the mission of the Church is the salvation of souls. All the activities, ways of life, and roles in ecclesial society have to work together for this end, for "the visible social structure of the Church serve

1. Regarding the function and importance of law in the Church, see PAUL VI, *Address* 20.I.1970: *AAS* [1970] 106–111.
2. See SAINT JOSEMARIA ESCRIVA, *Friends of God*, Sinag Tala Publishers, Manila, 2000, nn. 172–173.

the Spirit of Christ, who vivifies it, in the building up of the body" (*LG* 8). From its own perspective, law serves the supernatural mission of the Church.

Although the Lord can directly make every man a participant in His grace, "rather has it pleased Him to bring men together as one people, a people which acknowledges Him in truth and serves Him in holiness" (*LG* 9). Therefore, in the conditions of earthly life, He has willed to make use of His Church. For this reason it has been defined by the Council as "the universal sacrament of salvation" (*LG* 48), that is, as a visible and efficacious sign of invisible gifts.

In this divine economy which is the Church, the Word needs to be preached, grace flows through visible signs of the liturgy of the sacraments, and both have need of validly consecrated ministers of God. Charisms, although personal, are always for the good of all and the hierarchy is also charismatic (tied to the sacrament of orders). Pastoral ministry includes also the juridical power of governance. The communion of faith and sacraments requires that of government and discipline. The various vocations and forms of spirituality subsist in institutional ways of life.

On the other hand, how could the faithful reach sanctity and do their apostolate without the support of pastoral care that is adequate for their needs and which offers them abundant means of salvation? How can the authentic evangelical character of various charisms be recognized without the discernment of the pastors? What lasting fruit could they bear without the possibility of perpetuating themselves through suitable institutions?

The Church, therefore, is both charismatic and institutional. To know it in depth also requires knowing the role of law in its life. This book seeks to give a complete, although not detailed, vision of Latin canon law, to accompany the reading of the juridical texts, especially the *Code of Canon Law.*

General Basic Bibliography

— J. P. BEAL, J. A. CORIDEN, T. J. GREEN (eds.), *New Commentary on the Code of Canon Law*, Paulist Press, New York, Mahwah, NJ, 2000.

— CANON LAW SOCIETY OF AMERICA, *The Canon Law Digest. Officially Published Documents Affecting the Code of Canon Law* (CLD), Washington.

— CANON LAW SOCIETY OF GREAT BRITAIN AND IRELAND IN ASSOCIATION WITH THE CANON LAW SOCIETY OF AUSTRALIA AND NEW ZEALAND AND THE CANADIAN CANON LAW SOCIETY, *The Code of Canon Law* (English translation with Index), W. Collins, London, 1984.

— E. CAPARROS, H. AUBÉ, *Code of Canon Law Annotated*, commentary prepared under the responsibility of the Instituto Martín de Azpilcueta (Pamplona), 2nd edition revised and updated, Gratianus Series, Wilson & Lafleur, Montréal, 2004. Includes the *Responses of the Pontifical Council for the Interpretation of Legislative Texts*, (Appendix II), and the *Complementary Norms to the Code promulgated by English-Language Conferences of Bishops* (Appendix III).

— J. A. CORIDEN, *An Introduction to Canon Law*, Burns and Oates, London, 2004.

— INSTITUTO MARTÍN DE AZPILCUETA (University of Navarra), *Manual de Derecho Canónico*, 2nd ed., Eunsa, Pamplona, 1991.

— P. LOMBARDÍA, *Lecciones de derecho canónico*, 3rd reprint, Tecnos, Madrid, 1991.

— A. MARZOA, J. MIRAS, R. RODRÍGUEZ-OCAÑA (eds.), *Exegetical Commentary on the Code of Canon Law*, V Vols. (E. CAPARROS,

General Editor, English Edition), Gratianus Series, Montréal/Chicago, Wilson & Lafleur/MWTF, 2004.

— T. PAZHAYAMPALLIL, *A Commentary on the New Code of Canon Law*, Kristu Jyoti College Publications, Bangalore, 1985.

— M. THÉRIAULT, J. THORN (eds.), *The New Code of Canon Law. Proceedings of the 5th International Congress of Canon Law*, Université Saint-Paul, Ottawa, 1986.

Particular Law:

— T. J. GREEN, *A Manual for Bishops*, National Conference of Catholic Bishops, Washington, 1983.

— J. T. MARTÍN DE AGAR, *Legislazione delle Conferenze Episcopali complementare al C.I.C.*, Giuffrè, Milano, 1990.

— NATIONAL CONFERENCE OF CATHOLIC BISHOPS, *Addenda to a Manual for Bishops. Specific Legislation for the Church in the United States*, Washington, 1985.

— F. TESTERA, *Canon Law Digest of the Philippine Catholic Church*, 2nd ed., University of Santo Tomás, Manila, 1989.

A basic bibliography on each subject is found in the footnotes.

Chapter I.
Canon Law

1. The Meanings of *Ius*

The Latin word *ius* has two different meanings, which correspond roughly to "right" and to "law" in English. "Right" refers to a reality (*res iusta* = the right thing), whereas "law" can refer to the discipline or science that studies that reality. Right is the object of justice. Justice is the virtue which orders that each one be given what is his (*unicuique suum tribuere*). What—which can consist in very different types of things, spiritual or material—is due to a subject in justice, is called lawful or right: one must give to each one his right or due (*unicuique ius suum tribuere*). *Ius* or right, in reality, is the thing which is just. It is what justice requires be given to each one because it is *his*: what is due to him.

When, on the other hand, we say that someone "has the right" to something, we are affirming that that something (a good) is his and it is owed him (*objective* right), therefore he may claim it (*subjective* right). Clearly the objective right is the cause of the subjective right and not the other way around: for someone to be able to claim something, it must be his and owed to him; on the other hand, what belongs to someone cannot stop being his because he does not claim it (for whatever reason).

However, in order to be able to give each one what is due to him, it is necessary to determine what that consists of.

Therefore, the science that studies and determines what is just in the concrete is also called law or jurisprudence. The jurist is that man who knows or studies what is just, so that justice may be accomplished. His profession is to state what is lawful (*ius dicere*). Therefore, *ius* (law) denominates both what is just (due in justice) as well as the practical *science* of what is just. Furthermore, while law frequently plays an important role in determining what is just, law also refers to the collection of laws which regulate the juridical order of a society. However, laws determine what is right or lawful, but they are not to be equated with it.

In every society or organized group, relationships are created which have to do with the ends and means of society. These must be governed by justice so that each one is given his due. In every society there is a code of law which is meant to establish in practice what is just in that society.[3]

2. Basis of the Right

Because the right is the just thing, the *suum* owed to someone in justice, it seems clear that *the right exists because there are things (goods) that belong to someone and that someone else owes to him* (in the broad sense of giving, respecting, complying). This is the first conclusion one reaches when observing reality: many things belong to someone. This implies two types of relationships only man is capable of: with the things he can possess, dominate, use for his own benefit; and with others who *must* respect his things. The right is the reality of human sociality seen from what is mine and what is yours, of the good that is owed to someone because it is his, from what is just and what is unjust. Only man can have rights, because only he is a personal and social, intelligent and free being; who enjoys a certain self-control capable of conscious, desired acts, for which he is responsible, and through which

3. See S. COTTA, *Perché il diritto*, 2nd ed., Ed. La Scuola, Brescia, 1983; F. D'AGOSTINO, *Filosofia de diritto*, Giappichelli, Turin, 1993, especially the first chapter: "Elementi per una definizione del diritto," pp. 5–22.

he tries to reach his perfection or happiness; his activity is projected outward: toward things and others.

But being able to possess and dominate things is not enough for these things to belong to someone. When a good belongs to someone, it means that it has been attributed or granted to him by someone for some reason (title) and in some way (measure).

The primary and original source of the attribution of goods is nature (God). Each one has "what is his" that precedes law and creates it: it is what is naturally just, the attribution of goods that arises from the fact of being a person. Any other source of attribution of goods is secondary and depends on the former.

He who enjoys a right is called the holder thereof; the *title* is the reason why a thing belongs to a subject. The fact that it is owed to him means that others must respect that specific relationship between a good and its owner.

But that relationship is not a one-to-one relationship. In many ways, it can be said that a thing belongs to someone: saying "this is my son" is not the same as saying "this is my house"; the rights and obligations involved are very different; and even my house can be mine because I am the owner or because I am the tenant.

Giving each one what is his requires correctly specifying the terms under which the thing is his, that is, the measure of his right. However much it is said, every right has limits, a measure: its nature, duration, conditions on its exercise, its prevalence or lack thereof over other rights, etc., constitute its measure. Returning to the previous example, the owner may do things in his home that the mere tenant may not.

In every society or organized group of men, relationships arise, which concern the nature, purposes, and means of the whole, which must be regulated by justice, seeking to give each what belongs to him *in that* specific congregation of persons. That is, in every society, there must be a right, intended to establish in practice what is just in that society, *ubi societas ibi ius.*[4] The right then is a function of the nature, purposes, and means of the society that it helps order.

Societies are specified by their purposes, as a function of which they are organized and ordered, such that each member may enjoy the goods he sets out to obtain.

3. Church and Law

As in every organized human group, there is also law in the Church. The Church is not a simply human society. She is a mystery that can be defined in various ways, each of which emphasizes a different aspect of her being. The Church is the mystical Body of Christ, the People of God, the assembly of believers in Jesus Christ, etc. She is also the society founded by Christ to continue His work of salvation in the world.

The mystery of the Church is the image and reflection of the mystery of the Incarnate Word. As the divine nature and human nature of Christ mysteriously unite in the one Person of the Word, so in the Church the divine and the human are merged, in such a way that, as the Second Vatican Council states, "the society structured with hierarchical organs and the mystical body of Christ, the visible society and the spiritual community, the earthly Church and the Church endowed with heavenly riches, are not to be thought of as two realities. On the contrary, they form one complex reality which comes together from a human and divine element." In this way, "the social structure of the Church serves the Spirit of Christ who vivifies it, in the building up of the body (cf. Eph. 4:15)" (*LG* 8).

It is important to keep in mind the mystical nature of the Church in the study of canon law, since it is the reflection and expression of that nature (*OT* 16, CCC 770–780). What is just

4. See J. HERVADA, *Critical Introduction to Natural Law,* Gratianus Series, Montréal, Wilson & Lafleur, 2006.

(or unjust) in the ecclesiastical society is primarily determined in consideration of the origin, structure, finality, goods, and means given by God to His Church. All of these elements reflect the complex unity of the divine and the human that exists within the Church, and the same is also found within the juridical relations which are derived from these elements.

It is usually said that *societates sunt ut fines*, societies are defined by the objectives proposed. The Church is not a *necessary* society for the natural subsistence of man; he does not belong to it just because he is born, as it occurs with the political community, but enters in it through baptism and remains in it through the grace of God and through his own will; it is a *voluntary* society. Moreover, his existence and his activity find their raison d'être in the spiritual mission the Lord has assigned him; it is a society with specific *purposes*. It is also *homogeneous*: based on the communion of the faith, of the mission, and of the goods in which its members share.

This makes it very different from any civil political community, and this is also reflected in its organization and in its law. One important manifestation is the different scope that the categories *public* and *private* have in the Church, because in fact any initiative that arises in ecclesial life, even when it is private, must be directed towards and contribute to the mission of the Church: the salvation of souls; were it not so, it would make no sense, it would be out of place. On the other hand, in the State, the distinction between the public interest and the private interest is more distinct, because the state common good consists to a large extent in making possible in an orderly way the different, and often opposed, interests of private individuals.

4. Divine Law and Human Law

Since the Church is a society of men founded by Jesus Christ, the first and principal attributions of laws (and duties) in her have their basis in the will of her Founder, and pertain to *divine law*. For example, Christ formed the College of Apostles, placed Peter at its head, and entrusted them with the mission to diffuse, guide and govern the Church. They are succeeded by the college of bishops and the Roman Pontiff who is its head, which are thus of divine institution. The laws and duties which derive from this also are, in their essential nucleus, of divine law. In the same way, Jesus Christ instituted the sacraments of the New Law for the worship of God and the salvation of men. Thus the juridical consequences which immediately follow from that event are of divine law also. In short, Christ has conferred on His Church certain characteristics, ends, means, and rules of operation which are unchangeable and which form the fundamental nucleus of canon law. These we call *divine law.*

It must be remembered that this nucleus also includes the juridical consequences of the fact that the Church was founded for men and is formed by men. Therefore, the demands of justice which derive from the human condition, insofar as they relate to the social life of the Church, also pertain to divine (natural) law. Thus, for example, the right to one's good name, to privacy, to free choice of a state of life, which belongs to natural law, must also be recognized in the Church as in every other society.

We find this fundamental nucleus of canon law in Revelation (the Word of God, written or handed down by tradition). "Yet even if Revelation is already complete, it has not been made completely explicit; it remains for Christian faith gradually to grasp its full significance over the course of the centuries" (CCC 66). Therefore, our knowledge of divine law is always capable of being perfected. In this constant deepening of our understanding, a principal role is played by the ecclesiastical Magisterium, which, with the aid of the Holy Spirit, authentically interprets and expounds the Word of God. However, the progress of theology and canonical science, the liturgy, and the life itself of the Church through history also contribute to this development. To the extent that we gradually know better the plan of God for His People, we can express more faithfully the demands of justice that this plan carries with it.

Nevertheless, divine law indicates to us what is just in the Church in its fundamental features, but it does not explicitly and directly resolve all questions about what is just in every individual case. For this purpose it is necessary to formulate, develop, interpret, and apply the divine law, taking the particular circumstances into account. Hence there arose responses concerning what is just, which are the fruits of human effort, sometimes borrowed from civil juridical culture. In this way, canon law also contains elements of *human law* which interpret and apply divine law in every historical moment.

For example, the duty of sanctifying holy days is of divine law, a commandment of the Law of God. The ecclesiastical authority has then specified this commandment in the precept of participating in the Mass, which is a commandment of the Church pertaining to human law.

Human law is mutable and always capable of being perfected. What human reason judges to be just today, may become unjust tomorrow because of a change in the circumstances. However, human law cannot go against the divine law. In such a case it would certainly be unjust. On the contrary, it must seek to interpret the demands of the divine law ever more perfectly and to draw out all its consequences. Therefore, the divine law is the inspiring principle and the limit of human law, which in turn is the means whereby divine law is embodied in historical reality.

5. The History of Canon Law

Through the centuries the law of the Church has been forged in this framework: by means of legislative acts and decisions of the authority (Popes, councils, bishops, synods, judicial decisions), but also by means of the customs that express the sense of justice in the Christian people, and by the teachings of the jurists.

Four periods can be distinguished in the history of canon law, each with their own characteristics: the *first millennium*, the *classical* period (1140–1325), the *modern* age which extends up to the First Vatican Council, and the *contemporary* period. The latter is above all defined by the codification of canon law, and by the Second Vatican Council, whose juridical directives have been received into the canonical legislation now in force, especially in the two Codes which currently govern the Latin Church and the Eastern Churches.

It is not possible to present in this book—neither here or in the following chapters when the various juridical institutions are considered—a lengthy discourse on the historical evolution of law in the Church, nor on the influence of canon law on legal culture.[5] Nevertheless it is necessary to keep in mind that an understanding of the current juridical order depends in a large measure on understanding its history. Although the codification has marked a certain rupture with the past, this break is more formal than substantial. The Church evolves in tradition and so does its law.

A) The First Millennium

The first Christian communities took the rules of their social life from Sacred Scripture (principally from the New Testament) and from the teaching of the Apostles passed on by tradition: for example, the Pauline commands on keeping

5. Fundamental bibliography on this subject: P. ERDÖ, *Introductio in historiam scientiæ canonicæ*. Prænotanda ad Codicem, Editrice Pontificia Università Gregoriana, Rome, 1999; B. E. FERME, *Introduction to the History of the Sources of Canon Law I—The Ancient Law up to the Decretum of Gratian*, Gratianus Series, Wilson & Lafleur, Montréal, 2007; J. GAUDEMET, *Église et Cité. Histoire du droit canonique*, Cerf, Paris, 1994; L. MUSELLI, *La storia del diritto canonico*, Giappichelli, Torino, 1992; J. MARTÍNEZ-TORRÓN, *Anglo-American Law and Canon Law—Canonical Roots of the Common Law Tradition*, Duncker & Humblot, Berlin, 1998; C. VAN DE WIEL, *History of Canon Law*, Peeters, Louvain, 1991; W. M. PLÖCHL, *Storia del diritto canonico* (2 Vols.), Massimo, Milano, 1963; A. M. STICKLER, *Historia Iuris Canonici Latini. Institutiones accademicæ*, I: *Historia Fontium*, Pontificio Ateneo Salesiano, Turin, 1950.

certain errors in check, on the liturgical celebrations, on the conditions of life (bishops, presbyters, deacons, virgins, married persons, widows), or on the obligation to earn a living through work. The bishops also issued norms and decisions for their communities, in which customs and particular traditions originated as well.

Evidence of these beginnings of canon law can be found in the documents of that time, in the writings of the apostolic Fathers (the first generation of Christian authors after the Apostles), and in those of the Fathers of the Church (from the second to the eighth centuries). They reflect different ways of understanding Christian life, especially between the East and the West. On the other hand, not a few Jewish and Roman juridical institutions were received by the Church and Christianized. Once the Church, with the Edict of Milan (313), achieved the freedom and recognition of the state authority, a more complex organization became necessary that was adapted to the vigorous growth and social influence of the Church.

The law of the communities were given a certain unity by the councils, in which the assembled bishops fixed common rules or canons (hence the name of canon law). Even if the synods were regional, their canons were frequently accepted by other local Churches, and sometimes by the Bishop of Rome, the Pope, who approved them for the entire Church, considering the council which issued them to be ecumenical.

On their part, the Roman Pontiffs, either by a *motu proprio* (on their own initiative), or to respond to concrete questions, addressed the various Christian communities by means of decretal letters. In this way precedents were established which served to solve similar cases also in other communities. In every Church, collections of canons and *decretals* were made which were held to be in force. The collections sometimes passed to other Churches. The many ancient collections which we know of today are the subject of studies concerning their date, authorship, the origin of their elements, the area of their influence, etc. In the beginning, these collections simply followed a chronological criterion, but as early as the seventh century some appear which follow a systematic order.

As the prestige of the papacy grew, even with regard to the secular power, a centralizing tendency developed which implied the ascendancy of the collections made under the auspices of the Popes over other particular collections. An important moment in this process was marked by the Gregorian reform (11th–12th centuries).

B) Classical Canon Law

Towards the middle of the 12th century the classical period began, in which canon law received a systematic and scientific or scholarly development, encouraged in part by the Roman Pontiffs and realized by the masters of the first universities. The fruit of this was the *Corpus iuris canonici*, which constitutes the principal written source of the law of the Church until the first *Code of Canon Law* (1917).

The foundation stone of this process is the *Decretum Gratiani* (*Gratian's Decree*, circa 1140). This was an ample compilation realized by Gratian, the master of Bologna, in which he intended to bring together a great mass of canonical texts, frequently contradicting one another, in a coherent and unitary manner, on the basis of his doctrinal commentaries. He entitled his work *Concordia discordantium canonum* (*The Harmony of Discordant Canons*). Although it was a private work, it had a wide circulation. Its use became so widespread that it superseded the preceding compilations, which remained operative only in the measure in which they were summarized in the *Decretum*.

The collections following upon the *Decretum* gathered only the *ius novum*, the law posterior to it. Those which combined with the *Decretum* of Gratian to form the *Corpus iuris canonici* include: a) the *Decretals of Gregory IX* (1234), also called the *Liber Extra*, which is a compilation in five books made by

Saint Raymond of Pennafort; b) the *Liber Sextus* (1298) promulgated by Boniface VIII to complement the *Decretals*; c) the *Decretales Clementinas*, a collection begun under Clement V, but promulgated by John XXII in 1317.[6] The subsequent decretals were called *extravagantes*; the most important of these decretals are the *Extravagantes of John XXII* and the so-called *Common Extravagantes*, both of which were included in the official edition of the *Corpus iuris canonici*, called "Roman" (1582).

These collections, especially the *Decretum* of Gratian and the *Decretals* of Gregory IX, were glossed and commentated by various jurists and university masters. In this way a scientific literature and method was born which survived also after the codification of canon law.

C) The Modern Era

During this period, the *Corpus* continued to be the central nucleus of the current law. Other collections of norms and doctrinal commentaries were added to it, developing and adapting it to the new circumstances.

Among these enlargements there should be first of all included the Decrees of the Council of Trent (1545–1563), which initiated a profound reform of the ecclesiastical discipline. In addition, the acts of the Pontiffs were gathered in chronological series called *bulls*, to which were joined the ever more numerous dispositions and decisions of the dicasteries of the Roman Curia, organized by Sixtus V in 1588. Among these collections can be mentioned the *Decisions of the Sacred Tribunal of the Roman Rota* and the *Resolutions of the Sacred Congregation of the Council.*

6. Each of these collections was divided into five books, according to the common subject matter division at that time (*iudex, iudicium, clerus, connubia, crimen*).

In this way there developed a growing mass of written norms which were poorly systematized and difficult to use. The canonists continued using the *Corpus* as the basic object of their commentaries, incorporating subsequent innovative norms into them.

On the other hand, the end of the Middle Ages marked the political and religious fragmentation of Christianity, and the ascendancy of the Catholic and Protestant national States, which, both for theological reasons (the Protestants) and simply for historical reasons (the Catholics), considered themselves to be competent to intervene in the organization and life of the national Church. In order to respond to this intervention of the State, the Holy See frequently had recourse to bilateral agreements or concordats, which initiated the creation of a particular canon law in every nation.

The revolutionary period which began at the end of the 18th century led to the abolition of absolute monarchies and the triumph of Enlightenment liberalism. The revolutionary misdeeds and the new ideas produced a great commotion in the life of the Church: the liberals denied the presence of religion and of the Church in social life, considering them to be obstacles to the liberation of man and to the sovereignty of the State. On various occasions, the Popes condemned the errors of liberalism and the revolutionary excesses, which threatened even the temporal sovereignty of the Roman Pontiff in the papal States.

In the juridical field, rationalism and egalitarianism gave rise to the phenomenon of constitutionalism and to the codification of civil law, as an expression of the supremacy of law, in continental European countries and in those of Latin America, which acquired their independence during this period.

The First Vatican Council, convoked by Pius IX, defined the dogma of papal infallibility. This fact, together with the weakness of the national Churches with regard to the liberal jurisdictionalist State, determined a strengthening of the unity of the Church around the Pope. Already in the Council itself, which was subsequently interrupted in a brusque way by the siege of Rome on the part of the Italian troops in 1870, proposals were put forward for a codification of canon law, supported by a good number of conciliar Fathers.

D) The Contemporary Period

This initiative did not then have any concrete realization, but little by little the idea of reordering into a code the immense quantity of canonical norms dispersed in various sources made headway. Some private authors presented projects along this line. It was Saint Pius X who, in 1904, decided to develop a code for the Latin Church, similar to civil codes. The protagonist of the project was Cardinal Gasparri, president of the Commission entrusted with the codification. Benedict XV, the successor of Pius X, promulgated the *Codex Iuris Canonici* (CIC) in 1917, which is also known as the Pio-Benedictine Code. The Eastern codification began during the pontificate of Pius XI, as it will be seen below.

In accordance with its underlying juridical postulates, the Code claimed to be, at least fundamentally, the only source of law, capable of furnishing concrete responses regarding what is just and unjust in individual cases. Legislative progress was to proceed by means of successive revisions of the Code itself. The teaching of canon law was to follow, as before, the exegetical method (gloss and comment), now centering on the canons of the Code.

Even if reality overtook these expectations, it is nevertheless certain that the CIC marked a turning point in the law of the Church. The *Corpus* and the subsequent legislation—to the extent that it was not received into the Code—became old law, although it remained a criterion of interpretation.

The Code of 1917 theoretically remained in force until the promulgation of the Code of 1983, but before that time already many of its precepts were considered having been modified by the Second Vatican Council.

The Second Vatican Council

The Council was convoked by John XXIII on January 25, 1959. On the same occasion, the Pope announced the reform of the *Code of canon law*. The conciliar sessions took place between October 1962 and December 1965. It soon became obvious that it was necessary to await the results of the Council in order to be able to prepare the reform of the canonical legislation. A simple updating of the Code then in force would not be sufficient.

The conciliar teaching, in effect, constitutes the principal source of inspiration for the current Code promulgated by John Paul II on January 25, 1983.

The Second Vatican Council dealt with a great variety of themes, but it can be said that at the center of its reflection there stands the mystery of the Church. In this perspective, fundamental aspects were brought out, regarding the constitution and mission of the Church, which formerly remained latent or were considered to be secondary. The Council itself took care to indicate the most important practical consequences of this in-dept reflection, whose full application to ecclesial life has marked the period following the Council. For what regards canon law, the fundamental guidelines can be summarized as follows:

a) The consideration of the Church as the People of God in which all the members share the same dignity and responsibility of children of God and the same vocation to sanctity. This requires an underlying juridical status common to all the faithful, in which their rights and duties, their initiatives and contributions to the building up of the Church, are defined and guaranteed; on this basis, then, they must construct the different personal statutes that are derived from the diversity of functions, charisms, and ways of life.

b) The reflection on the college of bishops as a subject of the supreme power of the Church alongside the Roman Pontiff, the Supreme Pastor and Head of the college. This brought about a search for new modes of exercise of collegiality with corresponding juridical consequences.

c) The teaching on the sacramentality of the episcopate and the ministry of bishops, which implied a clarification of the various paths and modalities of participation in ecclesiastical power, has emphasized the nature and role of the particular Church in the building up of the universal Church, and has led to a greater autonomy of the diocesan bishop in his pastoral task.

d) The conciliar study of the Church as a priestly community (every member of the faithful already participates in the priesthood of Christ in virtue of baptism), whose organic structure is realized on the basis of the sacraments, the virtues and the charisms, calls for a canon law that is built on these foundations. Canon law, therefore, is to establish the relationships between hierarchical and personal charisms, so that both cooperate for the good of the entire ecclesial body.

e) The affirmation of the role that belongs to the laity in the mission of the Church—principally with regard to their apostolic initiatives in the midst of civil society—demands an adequate pastoral organization capable of maintaining and guiding Christian life immersed in secular realities.

f) The teaching of the Council on the relationship between the Church and civil society affirms a reciprocal independence between Church and State and centers their relationship on the dignity of the person and on the defense of his fundamental rights (especially that of religious liberty). This teaching, furthermore, has repercussions on the relationship of the Church with other religious communities, particularly with those that are Christian, whose members are recognized certain rights of partial communion with the Catholic Church.

The Code of Canon Law *of 1983*

These ideas, among others, were taken into consideration in the phase of development of the new canonical codification.

This was a long process, whose stages can be summarized as follows.[7]

As we have seen, on January 25, 1959, John XXIII convoked the Council and announced the revision of the CIC. In March 1963, shortly before dying, he constituted the Commission charged with this revision. However, it was soon decided that it was necessary to wait for the results of the Council to launch a profound reform of canon law. Therefore, the work of the Commission really began in November 1965, a few days before the closing of the conciliar sessions.

The Commission was composed of cardinals and bishops who were gathered to decide the most important points. The development of successive projects was entrusted to an ample task-force of consultors divided into study groups for each subject. Paul VI indicated the objectives and the directions to be followed.

In order to unify the criteria, the *Guiding Principles* for the revision of the CIC were developed, organized in 10 points and presented for approval to the Synod of Bishops of 1967. These points synthesized the guiding principles derived from the teaching of the Council.[8]

On the basis of these principles and taking the canons of the Code of 1917 as their starting point, the study groups developed—between 1972 and 1977—10 partial schemas which were to complete the new Code. The schemas were sent to all the bishops, to the dicasteries of the Roman Curia and to the faculties of canon law so that they could present their observations and proposals.

The many responses received were ordered and distributed to the groups of consultors, who proceeded to develop a

7. See J. HERRANZ, "Genesis and Development of the New Code of Canon Law", in ExComCIC I pp. 121-168.

8. These guiding principles, as the entire *iter* of the Code, are set forth in the *Preface* to the Code.

new project for the Code. This is the *Schema of 1980*, presented to the Supreme Pontiff, who submitted it for study to the Commission, which at that point had 74 members.

The amendments and suggestions of the individual members of the Commission were discussed and weighed by the Secretariat of the Commission, which in 1981 sent them a report (*Relatio*) giving a reasoned opinion concerning the acceptance or rejection of each proposed amendment.

This *Relatio of 1981* was discussed in the Plenary session of the Commission in October of the same year. The amendments and modifications that were to be introduced into the project of 1980 were then decided upon. The result was the *Schema of 1982* presented to the Holy Father in April of the same year.

John Paul II reviewed the proposed Code twice, first with the collaboration of a group of experts and then with that of three Cardinals. With the modifications introduced in this session, the definitive text of the *Codex Iuris Canonici* was realized, and promulgated on January 25, 1983 with the Ap. Const. *Sacræ disciplinæ leges*. In it, the Roman Pontiff explains "that the Code is in no way intended as a substitute for faith, grace and the charisms in the life of the Church and of the faithful. On the contrary, its purpose is rather to create such an order in the ecclesial society that, while assigning the primacy to faith, grace and the charisms, it at the same time renders easier their organic development in the life both of the ecclesial society and of the individual persons who belong to it."

The CIC consists of 1752 canons divided into seven Books, which deal with: a) *general norms*; b) *the People of God*; c) *the teaching office of the Church*; d) *the sanctifying office in the Church*; e) *the temporal goods of the Church*; f) *sanctions in the Church*; and g) *trials and other processes*. This Code is in force in the Latin Church.

The Code of Canons of the Eastern Churches *(CCEO)*

The 21 Eastern Catholic Churches have always enjoyed a particular law which respects the liturgical and disciplinary traditions of each of them. The codification of their law was seen to be called for shortly after the promulgation of the CIC of 1917. In fact, the work in order to develop a common Code to all these Churches began in 1929. The fruits of this work were four partial texts (laws) promulgated by Pius XII between 1949 and 1957, but which did not succeed in completing a Code.

The Second Vatican Council emphasized the legitimacy of the discipline proper to the Eastern Churches in the Decree *Orientalium Ecclesiarum*, also referring to many of their typical institutions: "this variety in the Universal Church, so far from diminishing its unity, rather serves to emphasize it" (*OE* 2).

In 1972, Paul VI instituted a Commission to which he entrusted the development of a Code of Eastern canon law, which was also to be drawn up in the light of the Council. As for the Latin Code, the hierarchy of the Eastern Churches intervened in the process, as well as the relevant dicasteries and the centers of specialized studies in theology and Eastern law.

The various study groups developed a *Schema* which was sent to the members of the Commission in 1986. With the amendments and corrections proposed by the Commission, the *Schema novissimum* was redacted and presented to the Holy Father. After having reviewed it and introduced the necessary modifications, he promulgated the *Codex Canonum Ecclesiarum Orientalium* (CCEO) on October 1, 1990.

The Eastern Code contains rules of law (canons) common to the 21 *sui iuris* (autonomous) Churches of Eastern rite which belong to the Catholic Church. It is divided into 30 titles ordered according to the importance of the subject, with a total of 1546 canons.[9] Within this common

9. For an introduction to Eastern canon law, see I. ZUZEK, *Understanding the Eastern Code*, PIO, Roma, 1997; see also T. J. GREEN, "Reflections on the Eastern Code Revision Process," *The Jurist* [1991] 18–37.

framework, each Church must then develop its own particular law corresponding to its own traditions.

Finally, it should be added that parallel to the post-conciliar work of codification, the development of a type of Code common to all the Churches (Latin and Eastern) was initiated, which was to gather the fundamental norms of canon law for the entire Church. At least two successive projects were made for this *Fundamental Law of the Church*. However, the theological and practical problems that were raised over such a "Constitution of the Church" led to a suspension of its execution. For the most part the articles of it were introduced into the two promulgated Codes. For this reason, the canons of both Codes coincide with regard to these fundamental matters, often even in their redaction, for example, the basic rights and duties of the faithful (cf. CIC cc. 208—223, CCEO cc. 11–26).[10]

To the two Codes, one must also add the Ap. Const. *Pastor Bonus*, which is the law of the Roman Curia, promulgated by John Paul II in June 1988. On various occasions the Holy Father has emphasized that the three laws (the two Codes and the *Pastor Bonus*) constitute a unitary whole, a *Corpus* of canon law, and he has expressed the desire that in the edition of each of the codes there be included the law on the Roman Curia which is the body the Roman Pontiff uses in the exercise of his ministry of primacy over the whole Church.[11]

This *Corpus* constitutes the central nucleus of ecclesiastical legislation, but is not *all* of the ecclesiastical legislation. Alongside of it there are many other laws intending to regulate specific matters, for example, the election of the Roman Pontiff, the tribunals of the Rota and of the Apostolic

10. For detail tables of correspondence between the two codes, see C. G. FÜRST, *Canones Synopse zum Codex iuris canonici und Codex canonum Ecclesiarum orientalium*, Herder, Freiburg im B., 1992; also in a concise way in CCLA Appendice IV.
11. See Ap. Const. *Pastor Bonus*, Prœmio, n. 11.

Signatura, the Synod of Bishops, the causes of canonization.[12] Furthermore, in the area of ecclesial law there have always been *particular* laws for a given geographical area or for certain communities of the faithful. The Corpus rather constitutes the principal point of reference of the canonical order, to which one must have recourse to clarify the questions that are not regulated by a specific law.

Therefore, one must not confuse the notion of *canon law* with the collection of *written rules* of the Church, of which in turn the *Corpus* represents only the central portion.

12. Besides the *Acta Apostolicæ Sedis* and the other official publications of the Holy See, there are private collections of laws and documents of the Church: the *Leges Ecclesiæ post Codicem Iuris Canonici editæ*, published by the *Istitutum Iuridicum Claretianum*, which gathers the norms posterior to 1917; the *Enchiridion Vaticanum*, Edizioni Dehoniane of Bologna, which begins with the documents of the Second Vatican Council; *The Canon Law Digest*, published by the CLSA; *Origins CNS Documentary Service*, published by the Catholic News Service.

Chapter II.

The Sources of Canon Law

We have said at the beginning of the first chapter that in order to be able to give to each one what is one's due (right) according to justice, it is necessary that it be *determined*. The concept of juridical *source* makes reference precisely to the acts that establish or determine what is just.[13] But in the determination of what is just, it is necessary to distinguish the subject (who) from the activity whereby what is just is established.

We have already seen that the basis and foundation of law is human nature. In this regard, the first *Source* of law is God Himself, the ordainer of creation and of Redemption (divine law). Man is the only creature that God wants for Himself, calling him to communion with Him; in this sense, he has in himself the reason for his existence, he is the owner and purpose of himself; he dominates his own being: he is called, through his actions, to maintain and perfect the image and likeness of God that he possesses through the act of his being. All other beings are the means whereby man may achieve his perfection; they have been created for his service, and they reach their greatest value in this. Nature then

13. In the determination of the right, there are other factors that are absolutely and relatively independent of human will, such as natural events (birth, death, time, age, kinship, and other circumstances). They determine or modify rights but are not juridical sources because they do not depend on human will.

attributes to man, because he is endued with spiritual faculties, the capacity for self-control and for dominating things: he is owner of himself and of all those goods that he needs in order to develop his capacities and his transcendent vocation. The projection of this personal autonomy and of this dominion over things in relations with other men is what constitutes the origin of law: each has what is his which others are called to respect.

In exercising dominion over himself and over things man, through his actions and behavior, determines in various ways what is just in a society or in a specific relationship. In this regard, the source of law is the *person*: individuals or groups, public authorities or private persons, the human legislator, the Church itself and its communities, judges, and any subject capable of exercising rights and meeting obligations. It can be said that the source of law is any human act, to the extent that it is capable of determining what is just.

But although any human act can originate juridical situations, sources of law in the stricter sense are *juridical acts*, that is, those human acts whereby one *tries* to establish what is just (that is, create, modify, extinguish rights); in this sense a source of right is a law, a contract, a judgment, a decree, etc. They are usually *typical* to the extent that their characteristics, requirements, effects, etc. are determined in advance, and they are usually the object of study, classifications, and doctrinal specifications. The first book of the Code concerns sources of law in general and in two complementary meanings: establishing the elements, requirements, and efficacy of the various juridical acts, and also who may perform them, especially those acts that involve the exercise of authority or power.

1. Norms and Juridical Acts

Precisely, a first classification of juridical acts is the one that divides them into *normative and non-normative acts* or simply between juridical *norms* and *acts*. Another important distinction is between acts of the *authority* and acts of *private individuals*.

These four categories combined with each other represent, in the abstract, the entire picture of human sources of law. So we can classify them as:

- normative acts of the authority;
- non-normative acts of the authority;
- normative acts of individuals (or of a community or group);
- non-normative acts of individuals (or of a community or group).

Note that the common basis of these sources is the fact that they are juridical acts; but bear in mind that the first sources of law are human nature (which involves relational life and natural societies), and with respect to canon law, the juridical demands that arise from baptism and belonging to the Church (ecclesiastical communion). The human sources operate on this basis.

The distinctions are always relative: an act of the authority is always an act of someone, as individual as anyone else; the authority does not exist, someone who exercises authority does.

A norm in the generic sense is a rule (written or unwritten) which seeks to determine the law for *a collection* of similar situations, relations, or cases; whereas a juridical act is what defines what is just *in a concrete case*.

The norm predetermines the juridical requirements and effects of other future acts (also of the same norms, because there are norms on norms).

The first fundamental norms or rules of what is just come from human nature or from the divine will, manifested with respect to man, to society or to his Church. Thus for example, the commandments, in that they refer to relationships between men, are rules of law (they determine what is just in social relationships), and likewise the sacraments, because they give rise to rights and obligations in the Church.

On other occasions, it is men (the authority or individuals) who determine what is just among several possibilities in accordance with divine law: these are human norms.

There is a big difference between the two: the norms of divine law are nothing else but the reality of things to the extent that they are a source and measure of the law; they are just in themselves, universal and invariable regardless of their formulation in human norms (which may vary and are never perfect): *what they establish is just and that is why it is ordered.*

Human norms operate within the limits of divine law, defining it according to the circumstances and expressing man's freedom to determine his own activity and to decide what is under his dominion for the future also. On certain occasions, they set forth and try to formulate the divine law into rules, and to that extent they share in its stability; on other occasions they represent mere options of the one who is called to establish what is just: *in that sense, what they establish is just to the extent that it is ordered.* They are mutable, and, as they lose their adaptation to divine law they are no longer saying what is just and are not binding.

In fact, the distinction between divine and human law, being fundamental and real, is never a separation: any rule of divine law needs human mediation to be applied effectively, and any norm of human law has a more or less direct relationship to the postulates of divine law (with the personal and social reality of man).

Everyone may establish rules or norms on those goods that are theirs (their right) establishing rights and obligations with respect to them to the extent that they deem it suitable. A normative act may or may not involve the exercise of the authority; what matters is that it establishes what is just in a multiplicity of similar cases. He who has authority to lead a social group may exercise it (if it is in his power) attributing goods (rights) and duties and regulating the various (present and future) situations in order to achieve the purpose of that society, that is, he can give norms.

Law does not consist of rules only, because together with them, there are other elements or factors that serve to specify the right. Even less does canon law consist of the Code, we should stress. The Code is only an organic set of written norms. Even so the study of the normative sources of law has particular importance, given that experience leads man to establish rules so that what is just in one case will help determine what is just in similar cases. Also bear in mind that from a certain point of view, the norm is also a juridical act.

2. Canonical Norms

Here we are referring to human rules that establish what is just in the Church for a variety of cases.

The norm can be defined, following Saint Thomas, who speaks of law as a *rational ordination promulgated by the authority for the common good*. This concept contains the characteristics of the norm:

a) *Rationality* is the principal note of the norm; in fact, it is for any juridical act, because what is irrational is unjust; in fact, it is established as a cause of nullity or the invalidity of acts in which the object is impossible, unlawful, without cause, harmful to third parties, contrary to the common good, etc.; in any event, doctrine usually pauses to specifically consider the rationality of the norm. Rationality means above all that it must be consistent, compatible with divine law, that is, it must not establish anything contrary to the revealed fact of the Church, on its mission or on the nature of man; and it must also have a reason for existing. In this regard, the norm must be *possible, necessary or fitting* for the common good, and must command things which are *licit*. An irrational norm is always unjust and therefore does not obligate in itself, even if sometimes one must observe it in order to avoid a greater evil.

A norm would be irrational if it commanded or permitted what is impossible or immoral, or if it limited liberty without sufficient reason, or if it unjustly favored some individuals at the expense of the community, or if it was confusing. Irrationality could occur due to a change of circumstances that make it prejudicial.

b) Norms must be made by the competent *authority*, which means someone who has sufficient *power* to bind those to whom it is given. Furthermore, every type of norm requires a specific power and competence; the Pope, and also the Episcopal College, can make laws for the entire Church on any subject, whereas the diocesan Bishop can legislate only for his diocese, and an Episcopal Conference can give norms only on certain matters.

Is the one who issues a norm bound by it as well? In state law, yes. However, in the Church, because of its constitution and the way in which power is exercised, the issue requires some distinctions. It can be said that he who dictates the norm can also modify, suspend, or derogate it. Unless he does so, one presumes that he is also bound to observe it.

c) The norm must serve the *common good*, or that specific end for the sake of which the members of a society are gathered together. The end or goal of the Church and her supreme law (c. 1752) is identified with that of Redemption: the salvation of souls. The aim of the canonical order is the establishment of the conditions of just and peaceful ecclesial life in which all individuals (and groups) can best develop their own capacities (the gifts received) with regard to the goal of the Church, and every norm must contribute to this goal and not pose an obstacle.[14]

Precisely because canon law must contribute, according to its proper nature, to the common ecclesial good, no activities

---

14. See J. HERVADA, *Coloquios propedéuticos de Derecho canónico*, Servicio de Publicaciones de la Universidad de Navarra, Pamplona, 1990, p. 147.

or institutions can find a place in it which are not in conformity with the goal of the Church (still less if they are contrary to it).

The fact that the norms aim to procure the common good does not mean, however, that they must be the same for all, especially if we bear in mind that the salvation of souls is done one by one and that the good of one benefits the good of everyone. Justice demands that each one must be given what is his due, but not the same to each. Furthermore, the Church is a reality in the supernatural order, and an instrument of salvation, because the Holy Spirit acts in it. He works according to His divine will and His multiform action with regard to souls, and institutions must be accepted and respected as a good for the entire body (common good). For this reason, canon law always remains attentive and open to the variety of particular situations and charisms, by means of specific formulas and juridical mechanisms. This effort to create harmony between the action of God and that of men enables the law of the Church to have a greater flexibility and richness than that possessed by state law.

d) *Promulgation*. In order to be able to be obeyed, the norm must be able to be known with exactitude. Promulgation is the way in which a norm is officially made known to its recipients. A written law is promulgated when it is published by the authority who issues it.

3. Law

The most common type of juridical norm is law, so much so that it is frequent in common language to call any type of juridical rule a law. In the technical sense, however, law is the *general written norm, promulgated by someone who has legislative power.*

In the Church, legislative, executive or administrative, and judicial power are distinguished (c. 135 § 1), even if frequently the three powers can be exercised by one and the same organ of power (individual or collegial). For example, the Pope, a Council, or the diocesan bishop can issue laws, put them in execution, and judge on their basis. Other organs do not have all three powers. In any case, laws can be made only by one who has legislative power; and law constitutes the typical expression of legislative power.

Law is the most important canonical norm which regularly prevails over all other norms. The Code deals with requirements and characteristics of the canonical law in cc. 7–22, which shall be examined below.

A) Types of Law

Divine Law and Human Law

We have already said that the fundamental nucleus of canon law is constituted by the rules of divine law (natural and positive) that concern the Church. In the measure in which a human law gathers and formulates a command of divine origin, it participates in the superior and universal binding force of the latter. Sometimes the legislator declares the divine foundation possessed by the law which he has made (for example, c. 207 § 1 indicates that the clergy exists in the Church "by divine institution"; likewise, c. 1084 § 1 says that impotence in certain cases "by reason of its very nature invalidates marriage"); but there are many other canons which translate a divine precept into law even though this is not expressly indicated. In any case, their binding force is the same.

On the other hand, laws which have their origin in the authority of the human legislator are called "purely ecclesiastical laws" and have the binding force that the legislator has established (and always under the condition that they do not contradict the divine law).

For this reason c. 11 establishes that merely ecclesiastical laws bind those: a) who are baptized in the Catholic Church or received into it after baptism; b) who have a sufficient use of reason; c) and who have completed their seventh year of age, unless the law expressly provides otherwise. Therefore, baptized non-Catholics are not bound by ecclesiastical laws.

General and Particular Laws

According to the extent of their application, a law is *general* (common, universal) or *particular* (peculiar, special). This classification is relative, because the scope of a norm may be considered according to various aspects. This depends in the first place on who the *legislator* is. Only the Roman Pontiff and the college of bishops (ecumenical council) can give universal laws (for the whole Church), whereas a particular council, the diocesan bishop or a conference of bishops can only issue particular laws (within their territory).

But in another sense, laws are general or particular according to who their recipients are. If the legislator directs a law to all the members of a community, it is *general*, or *common*; if, on the other hand, he addresses it only to a group within the community, the law is *particular*, or *special*.

There is also usually a distinction between a *general* norm and a *singular* norm, depending on whether it refers to a generality of similar cases or to a concrete particular case.[15]

One must also distinguish between the *recipient* of a law and the subjects that are effectively *bound* by it; these are only those who enter within the situation foreseen by the law itself. The Sunday precept is a universal norm for the entire

15. However, these concepts or types of law (common, general or universal, on the one hand, and particular, specific or special on the other) are relative with regard to the point of observation. What is common in a certain area can be particular in another, if one takes a larger area as a point of reference. In fact, we have seen that the *Code of Canon Law* is universal or common law of the *Latin* Church, but if one takes the *universal* Church into consideration, it is only the *particular* code of a part of the universal Church. Likewise, a bishop can make laws which are general (common in the entire diocese) or particular (for a part of it); and finally the norms of the CIC that deal with the institutes of consecrated life are common law for all of these institutes, but each institute has its own rules of particular law. In return, a Province or House of the institute can have its own particular law with regard to that of the entire institute. The determination of what is understood by a specific or concrete case as opposed to similar cases in general is also relative (it depends on the degree of abstraction).

Church, but it binds only those who are over seven years of age. Laws on marriage are also universal, but effectively regard those who desire to marry or are married. The fact that a law is for all does not necessarily mean that it is applicable to every person, at least with the same intensity.

With regard to the relation of supremacy between common or general law and particular law, it is necessary to consider their respective authorship: particular law has precedence over general law if both proceed from the *same* authority (unless otherwise stipulated: c. 20). On the other hand, common law given by a legislator has precedence over particular law made by *another* who is inferior, who "cannot validly make a law which is contrary to that of a higher legislator" (c. 135 § 2).

Territorial Law and Personal Law

With regard to the way in which the recipients of a law are determined, it can be *territorial* or *personal*, according to whether it concerns those who live in a given area, or certain persons by reason of their personal condition (military, religious, emigrants, etc.).[16] In Western state law, the most common criterion is the territorial criterion; this occurs in the Latin Church, so that laws are presumed to be territorial (cc. 12 and 13).[17] In addition to being relative, these (territorial and personal) criteria are not excluded but rather are usually combined (for example, it is common for a norm to be directed to priests of a specific region, or to the faithful of a rite in some place), because place is a circumstance that is hard to disregard.

16. This distinction is, by itself, independent from the type of jurisdiction (territorial or personal) of the author of the norm.

17. Nevertheless, the two codes, the Latin as well as the Eastern, are not territorial. Their application is linked to the rite of each faithful. See E. CAPARROS, "Territoriality and Personality in the Canon Law System", in P. ERDÖ-P. SZABÓ (ed.) *Territoriality and Personality in Canon Law and Ecclesiastical Law*, Budapest, 2002, pp. 315-356.

Invalidating and Incapacitating Laws (c. 10)

A characteristic of canon law with respect to the sanction for failure to comply with law is that the acts contrary to a law, even if illicit, are not necessarily null: for this to be the case it must be expressly stated by the law (c. 10). A law is *invalidating* if it establishes the nullity of a given act (see, for example, c. 1087). A law is *incapacitating* if it establishes the incapacity or ineligibility of someone for something (see, for example, c. 842 § 1). Not infrequently these laws are based on divine law. The ways of expressing the invalidity of acts contrary to a law are, at times, clear (for example, when it is expressly stated that a certain act *is null* or that something is required *for validity)*, but on other occasions they are not as clear: the general rule is that, in case of doubt, the act contrary to law is valid (c. 14).

B) Promulgation

The forms in which laws are promulgated can be various. Normally, according to c. 8, universal laws are promulgated by means of their publication "in the official commentary *Acta Apostolicæ Sedis*," and particular laws in the corresponding official Bulletin (of the diocese, of the Episcopal Conference).[18] However, laws can also be promulgated in other ways (by edict, for example): what is important is that they be made public in a way that allows their recipients to know them with precision.

From the moment of official publication of the law until they come into effect, it is normal that there be an interval (*vacatio legis*): three months for universal laws, and one for particular laws, unless otherwise stipulated. Therefore, the date of a law is distinct from the date it comes into effect.

18. Decrees and other deliberations of the NCCB are published by the United States Catholic Conference, Inc. (Washington, DC); those of the Canadian CBC in *Official Document—Document officiel*; those of the Australian CBC in *The Australasian Catholic Record*, etc. The decrees of 13 English speaking conferences of Bishops are collected in CCLA appendix III.

C) Retroactivity

As provided for in c. 9, laws deal with the future rather than the past; thus normally they are not retroactive. However, they can be retroactive if it has been established. For example, a penal law is retroactive if this is favorable to the delinquent. On the other hand, one must not confuse retroactivity with the fact that the law claims to modify situations that have already matured, which may be precisely its goal. Retroactivity refers to the effects already caused (acquired rights) that in principle are not cancelled by a subsequent law.

In short, as the distinction of functions that exists in the Church is only relative, it becomes difficult to know whether a norm issued by an organ that concentrates legislative and executive power is a law or a decree. C. 29 establishes that *general legislative decrees*, that is, general norms pronounced by he who has legislative power,[19] really are laws, even if they are not called laws; the canons concerning the law apply to those decrees, previous contrary laws are repealed, must be promulgated, etc.

The same rules apply to delegated legislation, that is, to the *general legislative decree* issued by he who, without having legislative power in himself, receives it through express delegation from a legislator for a particular case, pursuant to c. 30.[20] According to c. 135 § 2, only the Pope and the ecumenical council may delegate their legislative power; the other inferior legislators may only do so in cases expressly provided for by a law.

19. Although they are called *decrees*, the general norms, promulgated by the diocesan bishop or a council, are laws.
20. The most significant example is that of decrees having the force of law, that the bodies of the Roman Curia may issue in some cases (see Ap. Const. *Pastor Bonus*, art. 18).

4. Custom

Custom is a *general norm established by usage in a community*. In fact, customs are part of the life of men and of communities, and establish models of conduct commonly accepted as just, which therefore must be respected.

In every juridical order, the rules established by habitual common practice have a certain binding force born from the general conviction that what is always done is just, and manifests common sense with regard to what is to be done. Custom is thus a norm that is born from the people; precisely for this reason, it has great importance as a vehicle for the adaptation of law to life and to concrete circumstances. In the ecclesial society, custom is a normative expression of the common sentiment of the faithful, who are all called to the building up of the Church. It can acquire *the force of law* according to the conditions given in cc. 23–28.

In order for a custom to have the value of a juridical norm, it is necessary:

- that it be *reasonable* (as for every norm); according to c. 24, this cannot be the case for a custom contrary to divine law nor for what is expressly excluded by human law;

- that it be observed in a stable way by a community as a norm of justice. In other words, there must exist the common conviction that it is binding (c. 25);

- that it be approved by the legislator (c. 23), to the extent that the requirements established in canons 24–26 are met and that the legislator has at least not expressly excluded it. This happens, for example, in c. 1076 which reprobates the introduction of new matrimonial impediments and the suppression of those which have been established;

- that it be a usage that has been observed for the required length of time (c. 26) which depends on the type of custom.

Types of customs

Custom is referred to as being "according to the law" (*secundum legem*) when it determines the concrete and legitimate way of carrying out what is established by law; in this regard it is said that "custom is the best interpreter of the law" (c. 27).

Custom is referred to as being "outside the law" (*præter legem*: beyond the law) when it adds things not commanded by the law (extending it to cases or subjects not established in law), so that it completes the legal order.

A custom that is "against the law" (*contra legem*) is what establishes something in contrast with what is determined by a law, and thus tends to substitute it (*disuse*).

The custom is repealed by a law or by another custom that is contrary to it; but, if they are not expressly mentioned, the law does not revoke centenarian or immemorial customs, nor does universal law revoke particular customs (c. 28).

5. Administrative Norms

They are general norms, that is, for a majority of cases, pronounced by administrative bodies with executive power, in order to specify and enforce the provisions of laws.[21] They are norms that are incidental and inferior to law; therefore, they cannot change or contradict it, and to the extent that they do they are invalid (cc. 33 § 1 and 34 § 2). They are divided into general executory decrees and instructions.

---

21. On administrative law, see E. LABANDEIRA, *Tratado de Derecho Administrativo Canónico*, 2nd ed., Eunsa, Pamplona, 1993.

A) General Executory Decrees (cc. 31–33)

General executory decrees are defined in c. 31 as those "which define more precisely the manner of applying a law, or which urge the observance of laws." They must be promulgated and cease when they are revoked by the authority or by cessation of the law to which they refer (c. 33 § 2).

Those who only possess executive power in the strictly sense (because if one also had legislative power, they would issue laws according to c. 29), for example, diocesan vicars, can issue these decrees within the terms of their competence, and in this area they bind those who are subject to the law in question (c. 32).

There also exist *autonomous* decrees, which are not tied to a law, such as those issued by the dicasteries of the Roman Curia on matters of their competence. Not even these decrees (starting with those of the Congregations) can contradict or modify laws.

B) Instructions (c. 34)

Instructions are rules similar to executory decrees; their typical objective is the same: explaining the provisions of laws and developing and determining the ways in which the law must be implemented, but directed to those whose duty is to execute the law, or to see that it is executed (generally to those who hold office); that is why instructions do not need promulgation.

6. Statutes and Rules of Order

Statutes and rules of order are two types of norms which according to law regulate the life and carrying out of the activities of institutions, meetings or assemblies (a council, an association). Although they are classified as administrative, in fact their nature depends on the person pronouncing them (c. 94).

A) Statutes

Statutes are the norms which regulate the internal life of collective entities (associations, institutes, councils, foundations); they define "their purpose, constitution, government, and methods of operation" (c. 94 § 1)[22]; they are the expression of their identity, autonomy, or competence; they constitute their particular internal law, within the framework of common law. They directly bind only those who are part of the entity in question (members) or those who govern it, but indirectly they also concern those who have relations with such institutions (c. 94 § 2).

Frequently the statutes are drawn up and approved by the institution itself as an expression of their proper autonomy, and they constitute their particular law within the framework of common law.

With respect to entities that arise from the initiative of the faithful,[23] it devolves upon them to develop the statutes of the entity that they voluntarily create, that is, the statutes are developed and approved by the same entity whose life they order. They are a typical example of a contractual normative act that is the result of private autonomy. In any event, in order to be "recognized" by the authority, the private entities must submit to the statutes controlling them.

But when it is a matter of entities that are part of the organization or of the ecclesiastical government or, in general, public entities, the authority may create the entity granting its statutes, or, if they are developed by the entity in question as the fruit of its administrative autonomy, they may then be subject to approval by the authority. In both

22. We should distinguish between the *statutory nature* of a norm and the *statutes* of an entity: both have as their objective regulating the life and activity of collectivities; therefore many canons are of a statutory nature (for example, on associations of the faithful), while statutes are statutory norms belonging to a given entity. Here we are referring to these latter in general.
23. This is the case of an association or of a confraternity.

cases, the authority may grant or approve some statutes through law or decree.

In the case of certain entities, it can happen that the legislative authority itself may give them their statutes. In this case they are properly a particular *law* (c. 94 § 3). This occurs, for example, with the Roman Curia,[24] with the Synod of Bishops[25] or with the personal prelature, which c. 295 § 1 says is governed by the statutes given by the Apostolic See.

B) Rules of Order

Rules of order are norms which regulate conferences or gatherings of people (a synod, an election) and which determine the order to be followed (who presides, who must be convoked, the order of the day, how decisions are made, etc.). Those who take part in a session are bound to the ordinance that has been established (c. 95).[26]

As with all statutes, the legislative, administrative, or private nature of these regulations depends on who is pronouncing them. Usually the same entity or organ whose assembly is in question, has an internal norm that specifies in more detail what their statutes provide. But it may devolve upon the person constituting, convoking, or presiding the meeting or assembly in question to establish it, and he may do so through a law or decree.

For example, the Code reserves some regulations for the Pope, such as those of the ecumenical council (c. 338) or the Synod of Bishops (c. 344). It devolves upon the Episcopal Conference to establish the regulations of the plenary council

24. See Ap. Const. *Pastor Bonus*.
25. See M.P. *Apostolica sollicitudo*, 15.IX.1965: *AAS* [1965] 775–780.
26. Also in this case it is appropriate to distinguish between the *regulatory* nature of a norm and the concrete *regulation* of a meeting or assembly. And of course, naturally, the term regulation in canon law does not have the typical normal meaning of a general written norm, subordinate to law, pronounced by the Administration, that is found in state law.

(c. 441, 4°), upon the Metropolitan the provincial council (c. 442, 3°), or the bishop the diocesan synod (c. 462). Nor is there any shortage of canons of a regulatory nature, such as c. 119 or those regulating elections (cc. 164 ff.). The same Ap. Const. *Universi Dominici gregis,* in part two, regulates the election of the Pontiff.

In other cases—also like statutes—the regulations are established by virtue of the administrative autonomy characteristic of the body that meets (when it is a matter of a public entity; for example, cc. 631, 632) or of private autonomy, and they are norms of a contractual nature (c. 309), naturally subordinate to laws and other higher norms. These higher norms, in many cases, will be the statutes themselves of the juridical person whose collegial bodies are meeting.

In principle, the regulations are only binding on those who participate in the meeting in question (c. 95 § 2); but here also the legislative level of a regulation makes it able to affect third parties.

But apart from the regulations of c. 95, the term *regulation* is used at times in the sense of an executory norm, that is, it develops another and establishes the way to apply it; for example, c. 243 requires that in seminaries there be a internal regulations. Moreover, arts. 37 and 38 of the *Pastor Bonus* establish the various regulations of the operation of the Roman Curia.

7. Singular Administrative Acts

We have already seen that, in contrast to norms, juridical acts are a source of law in *individual cases*.[27] Administrative acts are those juridical acts destined to a concrete subject by the executive authority (c. 36 § 2). In other words, they are the decisions or resolutions taken by the authority with regard to

27. Remember that the distinction is relative, because the act whereby a norm is issued is also a juridical act.

particular cases. They are called "singular," to distinguish them from acts of the executive authority that we have called administrative "norms" that have a general nature.

Cc. 35 to 47 establish the common rules for all these administrative acts, but we will see below that not all the concrete types satisfy these rules.

In that they are acts and not norms, they only apply to the case or cases in question (c. 36 § 2). In turn, this requires that their content be precise, and therefore they must be formulated and communicated in writing, a requirement ensuring juridical security (c. 37).

Because they have the purpose of applying the law to an individual case, they cannot contradict the law, unless it is the legislator himself who issues it (c. 38). However, there are cases in which the act is issued precisely so that the law will not apply in a concrete case (we are referring to the example of dispensation, c. 85).

Singular acts are often the result of the activity of different subjects. Thus they have a complex *process of formation*, sometimes regulated by law as, for example, when there is a petition of an interested party, when a college gives its opinion (or its consent), when some documents are presented, etc. The validity of the act which results may depend on the respect for the established procedure.

One may have *recourse* against the singular acts of the authority, except for those directly issued by the Roman Pontiff or by an ecumenical council (c. 1732). *Administrative silence* is important with regard to recourse: if within three months from the time of the request no response has been given by the authority, it is presumed to be negative, and therefore the interested party may have recourse against the denial (c. 57). Should the recourse prove that the act was unjust, the interested party may request restitution for damages (c. 128).

There are many types of administrative acts according to their content (appointments, grants, mandates, licenses, concessions, permissions, etc.). From a *formal* point of view, c. 35 distinguishes three types: *decrees, precepts* and *rescripts*.

A) Singular Decrees

The singular decree is defined in c. 48 as an act which: a) is given by the competent authority; b) to provide or decide a particular case (c. 52); c) according to the norms of law; and d) without need for a petition to be made by someone.

This is the *common* type of administrative act. In fact, making decisions or provisions can include any action (giving, commanding, prohibiting, nominating, electing, authorizing, etc.). For this reason, any administrative act must have the same requirements and be issued in the form of a decree. The fact that a previous petition by someone is not required does not mean that there cannot be one, and therefore it is possible to have recourse against the denial (c. 57).

Before giving a decree, the authority must be well-informed regarding the case and hear, if possible, any persons who may be affected by that decree (c. 50).

The decree must be *notified in writing* to the interested party, indicating the authority that has given it and the reasons for the decision (cc. 37 and 51). Notification is to singular acts what promulgation is to general norms. Thus the decree is not effective until it has been notified (c. 54). In exceptional cases it is sufficient that the decree be read to the interested party in the presence of a notary or two witnesses (cc. 55 and 56), but without infringing on his rights.

B) Singular Precepts

Precepts are decrees which have an *imperative* character, in that they directly command or prohibit a specific person or persons with regard to something established in the law. In saying "above all" (*præsertim*) c. 49 seems to allow autonomous precepts that are not bound or limited by a specific law.

Especially important are *penal precepts*, in which the authority threatens with a penalty those who disobey a precept (c. 1319).

C) Rescripts

Rescripts are singular written acts, by means of which the competent administrative authority concedes a favor (privilege, dispensation, license, etc.) in response to someone's request (c. 59). In principle, anyone has the right to ask and to obtain a favor (c. 60) that adapts the general law to the particular circumstances of his situation. The right to petition, in fact, is a fundamental right (c. 212 § 2). Its juridical nature is difficult to define, because there are different subjects of the power that may grant it, different actual contents, and different procedures for granting them.[28]

The specific characteristics of a rescript are:

a) It responds to a motivated request of an interested party (whose request is called the *preces*). Therefore, the validity of the concession normally depends on whether the motives adduced were true and upright. In fact, the falsity of the motives (*obreption*) or the suppression of essential elements (*subreption*) invalidates the rescript, unless the authority has granted the favor *Motu proprio*, which means independently of the expressed motives (c. 63).

b) It is *an act of favor* with regard to the one who requests it or to a third party. Thus it is the responsibility of the authority to judge whether it should be conceded or not.

A favor denied by an authority cannot subsequently be granted by another inferior authority, although this can be

28. Recently J. CANOSA has also discussed the issue in *Il rescritto come atto amministrativo*, Giuffrè, Milano, 2003.

done by one of the same level, according to the conditions of cc. 64 and 65. This seeks to avoid conflicts between authorities to the detriment of communion.

There are two particular types of favor that are normally conceded with a rescript: a privilege and a dispensation.

Privilege

Privilege is a favor conceded to a particular subject by the legislator by virtue of his power to legislate. It is a type of *singular law* in favor of certain persons which prevails over the general law (c. 76). For this reason some authors (Lombardía, Herranz, Roca) consider that even if the privilege seems to look formally like an administrative act, in substance it is legislative.

A privilege is *personal* if it is conceded directly to certain physical or juridical persons (parish, confraternity, family, individual). It is *real* if it conceded to a place (shrine, church, chapel). In principle a privilege is perpetual, in that it terminates only when the privileged subject or place ceases to exist.

Dispensation

A dispensation is "the relaxation of a merely ecclesiastical law in a particular case" (c. 85).

The peculiarity of the case is what justifies the dispensation, which is not an arbitrary exception. In fact, divine law cannot be dispensed from. Nor do all norms of human law admit of dispensation, since c. 86 provides that "laws, to the extent that they define what essentially constitutes juridical institutes or acts, are not subject to dispensation." These are elements without which such institutes or acts cannot truly exist (thus, for example, consent of the parties to a contract or marriage cannot be subject to dispensation).

Those who enjoy executive (administrative) power and those to whom the power to dispense has been conceded by delegation or by law (c. 85) can grant dispensations, within the limits of their competence.

The competence to grant dispensations is established in cc. 87–89. As a general rule, *the legislator* can dispense from his own laws; the *diocesan bishop* can also dispense from laws issued by the supreme authority of the Church, except for penal and procedural laws and those whose dispensation is especially reserved to the Holy See or to another authority (see, for example, c. 291); the *local Ordinary* can dispense from diocesan laws and from those of regional or provincial Councils or of the conference of bishops; *other clerics* can only dispense in the specific cases determined by law or by delegation (see, for example, cc. 1079, 1080, 1196). In case of urgent danger, any Ordinary can dispense from a law which is subject to dispensation, even if it is reserved to the Apostolic See, "provided that the matter concerns a dispensation which the Holy See is wont to grant under the same circumstances" (see, on the contrary, c. 1078 § 3).

For the dispensation to be valid, it is necessary that there be "a just and reasonable cause" proportionate to the gravity of the law from which the dispensation is given, unless the dispensation is granted by the legislator or by his superior, in which case it is valid but illicit (c. 90).

Dispensation is one of the elements that give flexibility to canon law, preventing that the rigid application of the law in a concrete case might provoke a greater harm than that caused by its temporary exoneration. This requires a balanced judgment of the authority in view of the spiritual good of the faithful (both those directly interested and others).

8. Judicial Acts

The acts of the judicial power are also a source of law in that they determine what is just in a disputed case, on the basis of what is determined in the general norms. Normally, trials end with a *judgment* or with a *decree* of the judge in which the question posed by the parties is decided. However, there are also other acts of the judge through the course of the trial which create or modify the law, and thus are juridical sources (for example, when the judge accepts the request of a petitioner, there originates the right of the respondent to be called in judgment as a party).

9. Private Juridical Acts (cc. 124–128)

We have already stated that the activity of man is the principal source of human law. It is worth mentioning that this includes juridical acts, strictly speaking, which seek to modify the juridical reality.

Up until now we have studied the norms and some acts *of the authority* (legislative, executive and judicial) as typical sources of law. Now we shall discuss juridical acts in general.

In addition to the acts of the authority in exercise of its competence, another source of law are the *acts that members* of the faithful (individuals or groups) perform in the use of their private autonomy, with the purpose of establishing and organizing their relationships with others (for example, contracts, religious profession, marriage, elections). These acts which are born from the will of private subjects are called in general *private juridical acts* or *affairs*.

Juridical acts or affairs, whether of the authority (public) or of individuals (private), can be quite various. Here we do not intend to examine them all, but rather to study their general elements.[29] Among these elements, one must distinguish those that are *constitutive* (essential, substantial), that is, necessary for their validity, from those that are *legal requirements*.

A juridical act is usually defined as *a declaration of will intended to produce certain juridical effects* (canonical effects in our case). This definition already contains the essential elements of a juridical act: a) deliberation (intent); b) form (manifestation); and c) cause (legal object or purpose of the act).

29. It should be noted that the types of acts of the ecclesiastical authority examined up to this point, in so far as they are acts realized by a person (or by a group), are also juridical acts, although their objective result is a law, a decree, etc.

a) It is essential for any juridical act that it be a truly human act, that is, one that is realized by a *capable* subject who acts with *knowledge* and *free will* (c. 124 § 1). An act done by someone who is completely incapable, whether through ignorance or error with regard to the substance, or without free consent, is absolutely invalid; its perpetrator is not responsible for it, regardless of whether it is so provided in a written norm.

b) Free deliberation is the principal but interior element of the juridical act, which—as it has been said—is a *declaration* of will, that is, the will of the subject must be externally manifested. Mere ideas, volition, or intents in themselves are not juridical. For an act to be juridically effective it must be outwardly expressed in some way; otherwise it does not enter the world of law that is necessarily relational and exterior. The manner, means, and vehicle for declaring a will is the *form*. It may be quite various: the spoken or written word, a gesture or an act, i.e., some sign that may be interpreted as a declaration of will.

At times the law for some acts that are more relevant for social life requires a given form to manifest the will (writing, presence of witnesses...); they are formal acts. This requirement may involve the validity of the act or merely its lawfulness or evidence.

Besides these common essential elements, every act can have specific constitutive elements (for example, only someone of the male sex is capable of receiving the sacrament of orders). It should be remembered that constitutive or essential elements cannot be substituted or dispensed by the authority (c. 86).

Nevertheless, it can happen that an essential element be only partially lacking. In this case, the act can be valid but capable of being *rescinded* or *annulled*; this is the case of one who accomplishes an act for which he is relatively incapable either on account of non-substantial error or ignorance (cc. 125 § 2 and 126). The *relative nullity*, or the fact that an act has the *capacity to be annulled*, signifies that it is valid and efficacious but can be annulled by a decision of the judge.

The legal requirements are those established by the law. Their lack may or may not be the cause of the nullity of the act, depending on what has been prescribed in this regard by the law itself, i.e., whether it is invalidating or incapacitating (c. 10). These requirements are normally dispensable (for instance, the form of marriage can be dispensed in certain cases).

As we can see, the principal elements of the juridical act are or may be internal to the subject (capacity, knowledge, intent) and it would be practically impossible to positively prove that they have existed. That is why c. 124 § 2 establishes a common sense rule: *the juridical act duly performed with respect to its external elements is presumed valid.* It is the *iuris tantum* presumption, which allows the persons claiming (despite appearances) that the act was invalid, to be able to prove it. Therefore, in the case of a doubt, the act must be presumed valid unless it is proven otherwise; the burden of proof is on the person claiming invalidity.

Chapter III.
Who Are Subjects in Canon Law?

Subjects of law are all beings *capable* of having rights (of having something that is *theirs*, something due to them in justice), and therefore of having juridical relations. In the canonical legal order, subjects are those who are capable of rights and duties in the Church. However, in order to speak of capacity it is necessary to distinguish between the capacity of being the *titleholder* of rights and duties (juridical capacity), and the capacity to *exercise* rights and duties, which means to realize acts which have juridical value (capacity to act).

Only the human person who enjoys sufficient use of reason is capable of juridical activity, and has the *capacity to act*; we have already said that the juridical act must first of all be a human act, placed by a subject capable of intending and willing. However, the necessary capacity to act juridically is not always the same, depending on the characteristics of the act: marriage does not require the same maturity as receiving the Eucharist (hence the relevance of age and psychological capacity in law).

On the other hand, the unborn, the mentally handicapped, parishes and associations—although they cannot act for themselves—can nevertheless be the titular subjects of rights and duties. They have *juridical capacity,* but they can only act through representatives who are capable of negotiating for them.

Therefore, although it is only the human person with use of reason who can be the *active* subject of law, every human person as well as social entities can be subjects of law in a *passive* sense, enjoying rights and realizing duties according to their capacity. In this larger meaning, two types of juridical subjects are distinguished: the physical person and the juridical person, a distinction made also by the CIC (cc. 96–123).

1. The Physical Person (cc. 96–112)

In the Church, as in every human society, every human person is capable of rights and duties. However, only those who are incorporated into the Church by means of baptism are members of the *faithful*, and have rights and duties proper to Christians (c. 96).

The universality of the Redemption calls all men to the Church, whose apostolic mission is directed to every person. Those who are not baptized have rights and duties in the Church to the degree in which they enter into relationship with her. Examples include the rights and duties of catechumens (cc. 206, 788, 1170, 1183 §3), non-baptized persons married to Catholics (c. 1135), or those who acquire an ecclesiastical property, or more generally the right possessed by every man to be evangelized and therefore to be baptized (cc. 748 and 851).

The difference between the members of the faithful and the non-baptized can be compared to the one between the citizens of a country and foreigners. Both are subjects of rights, but only the former have the rights and duties of citizens. The non-baptized do not belong to the Church, nor are they subject to her laws, but this does not mean that they are not the subjects of canonical rights and duties in so far as they enter into relationship with ecclesiastical society.

The rights and duties of persons are influenced by various circumstances, such as age, domicile, condition (cleric, lay, religious), rite, etc. For example, we have seen that purely ecclesiastical laws bind only Catholics who have completed seven years of age and enjoy the use of reason (c. 11).

According to **age** (cc. 97–98), the person is an *adult* if he has completed 18 years of age. Until this time he is a *minor,* and before he has completed seven years he is called an *infant*. Only adults enjoy the full *exercise* of their rights (capacity to act); minors can only act represented by their parents or guardians. However, we have said that capacity corresponds to the act to which it refers. Therefore, a minor can realize by himself certain acts to which he is admitted by divine or canonical law. Thus he can receive the sacraments (except holy orders), act in certain trials, etc.

Rite determines membership in a ritual Church (we have seen that the CIC is for the Latin Church). Normally the faithful belong to the rite in which they have received baptism. This sacrament, in turn, is received in the Church of the parents, although a baptized person who has completed 14 years of age can choose his own rite. After baptism one can change rite by concession (license[30]) of the Holy See, by marriage contracted with a person of another rite, or in certain cases by choice (c. 112).

Domicile (cc. 100–107) determines the community or ecclesiastical circumscription to which one belongs, and thus also one's ordinary and proper pastor (c. 107). In addition to domicile, one's *dwelling* is important as well in order to determine the rights and duties of the person.

2. The Juridical Person (cc. 113–123)

Physical persons are not the only ones who are capable of rights and obligations. There are also *corporate bodies* of a social nature which have a life independent of that of the individuals who belong to it in a given moment (the parish, an association, an institute of consecrated life, etc.). Thus they are juridical subjects and act by means of their representatives, in the manner of minors.

30. This license is presumed in certain cases: see the rescript of the Secretary of State of November 1992: *AAS* [1993] 81.

These corporate bodies are called *juridical persons* when their juridical subjectivity is recognized in some way by law. However, even if they do not obtain such recognition, they can have certain rights and duties: they are *de facto* corporate bodies or subjects without juridical personality. Therefore, juridical subjectivity is broader and does not always coincide with juridical personality (for example, according to c. 433, the ecclesiastical region may or may not have juridical personality, but from the time it is established, it is already subject to rights and obligations).[31]

Logically, only those corporate bodies and aggregates whose propose finalities and works are in harmony with the mission and life of the Church pertain to canon law: "works of piety, of the apostolate or of charity, whether spiritual or temporal" (c. 114 § 2). Other corporate bodies which have ends or carry out activities foreign to the nature and religious mission of the Church can have civil but not canonical subjectivity.

In the Church, corporate bodies can have the rights and duties which are befitting to their nature, since there are also rights and obligations of which only a physical person can be a titleholder. In fact, only physical persons can, for example, receive the sacraments, fast or obtain academic degrees (c. 113 § 2).

The Catholic Church and the Holy See—in that they are of divine institution—are primary juridical subjects: they have the rights, faculties and powers, duties and prerogatives which they need for the carrying out of their mission. Their juridical subjectivity is primary and independent of any law or human authority (c. 113 § 1), but it has been configured in different ways in the course of history. Today, the Church often acts—through the Holy See—as a subject with international juridical personality, capable of maintaining relations with States and with international organizations.

---

31. A. GAUTHIER, "Juridical Persons in the 'Code of Canon Law,'" *Studia canonica* 25 [1991] 77–92.

Other ecclesiastical corporate bodies, on the other hand, can acquire personality by law or by decree of the competent authority (c. 114 § 1).

Normally, ecclesiastical circumscriptions (dioceses, parishes, etc.) have personality by law (by the very fact of being constituted) and are governed by law. Other corporate bodies can acquire it by singular decree of the authority and must have their own *statutes* (c. 94) approved by the competent authority.

However, there are some ecclesiastical circumscriptions of a *personal* nature (non-territorial: dioceses, parishes, prelatures) which also have their own statutes; in other words, they have their own particular law. Furthermore, as we have said, there are corporate bodies without written statutes, or with statutes that have not been approved, which act as subjects even if they have not acquired juridical personality.

Statutes are the proper particular law of the juridical person. They serve to specifically regulate their life, determine their activity and autonomy, and to safeguard their identity in time. Therefore, statutory law in the Church has the particular importance of bringing together norm and charism, so that these find in it an adequate recognition of evangelical authenticity, a clear social expression and the guarantee of continuity in the service of all.

Juridical persons in principle are perpetual, but they can be extinguished by a decision of the authority (indicating the reason), by inactivity protracted for 100 years, and for other causes provided for in the statutes (cc. 120 and 123). Juridical persons can also unite and divide in various ways (cc. 121 and 122).

A) Corporations and Foundations (c. 115)

Canonical corporate bodies are distinguished between *corporations* and *foundations*. When the titular subject of rights and duties is a *community of persons*, then it is a corporation; when the subject is a *collection of things*, a patrimony, the corporate body is a foundation.

The corporation (community) must be comprised at least of three physical persons. It is *collegial* (college) if its members participate in the most important decisions; otherwise it is *non-collegial*. Examples of colleges include the cathedral chapter, an association of the faithful, and the conference of bishops. Those which are non-collegial include the diocese, the seminary and the parish.

Collegial acts are governed by c. 119, except when the particular law or statutes provide otherwise.

A canonical foundation is constituted by goods and things (spiritual and material). When it has its proper juridical personality, it is called an *autonomous foundation*, and it acts by means of its own organs of government (one or more physical persons or a college). When it does not have its own personality, but belongs or is connected to a corporation, it is called a *non-autonomous foundation* (cf. c. 1303).

B) Public and Private Juridical Persons

One of the novelties introduced by the Code of 1983 is the possibility of *private* corporate bodies existing in the Church, as a result of the initiative and responsibility of the faithful. Before the new Code entered in force, all recognized that corporate bodies were public ones, i.e., constituted by the authority.

Public and private juridical persons are distinguished principally in that the public ones "are so constituted by the competent ecclesiastical authority" and act "in the name of the Church" (c. 116 § 1). Thus they depend to a greater extent on the hierarchy, since the Church is officially involved in their activity. Private ones, on the other hand, arise through the initiative of the faithful, who govern them on their own responsibility albeit under the supervision of the authority. Their activities and ends can frequently coincide; nevertheless, there are activities which belong exclusively to the hierarchy, and thus can only be entrusted to a public juridical person (c. 301 § 1).

Juridical persons act by means of their representatives, i.e., their organs of government to which the law or the statutes attribute such a function of representation. For example, the diocesan bishop by law is the representative of his diocese (c. 393), as the pastor is for the parish (c. 532). Representatives of private juridical persons are designated in their statutes (c. 118).

Chapter IV.
The Constitution of the Church

In the Church there does not exist a written constitution, a fundamental law, as occurs in the great majority of countries. This does not mean that all the elements that make the Church a juridically organized society must be put on the same level or have a like importance. We have seen (in the first chapter) that the fundamental nucleus of canon law is constituted by divine law, to which all the other sources of law must correspond; that the supreme law of the Church is the salvation of souls; that the juridical condition of *faithful* is acquired by baptism. In other words, it is the same supernatural reality that makes us children of God and also confers on us rights and duties in ecclesial society, etc.

In short, if the Church is a society that has an identity and particular characteristics, with its own mission and the adequate means to achieve it, the juridical elements (norms, principles, institutions) which gather and express these fundamental traits in a given historical moment are those which compose the constitution of the Church.[32]

The problem is that since even today there does not exist a fundamental law of the People of God which gathers

32. See in this regard J. HERVADA, *Elementos de Derecho Constitucional canónico*, 2nd ed., Eunsa, Pamplona, 2001.

together and formulates the fundamental elements of the canonical order, it is not easy to individuate the contents of the constitution of the Church, since it is found dispersed and mixed with other elements that are secondary and of an inferior level.

In any case, we can affirm that norms, principles and institutions which express the plan of its Founder belong to the constitution of the Church: divine law. We shall briefly look at the constitutional principles and fundamental rights of the faithful. In the following chapter we will examine ecclesiastical organization, whose principal elements also belong to the constitutional order.

1. Constitutional Principles

Constitutional principles are those around which the social life of the Church is organized. In other words, they are those which translate into juridical language the being of the Church as she has been designed by Christ her Founder. Hervada lists three of these: the principle of equality, the principle of variety and the institutional principle.

Around these principles are determined the common elements and the specific differences between the various categories of the faithful, and the functions that devolve upon each in the edification of the Church.

A) The Principle of Equality

This mans that the Church is primarily a society of equals. The condition of citizen of the People of God is acquired by means of baptism, which incorporates us to Christ as members of His mystical Body which is the Church. Since baptism is one (one sole baptism, as we say in the Creed), there corresponds to it one condition that is received through it: that of adoptive children of God. Therefore, there remains "a true equality among all with regard to the dignity and to the activity which is common to all the faithful in the building up of the Body of Christ" (*LG* 32).

Through this principle *all* the faithful:

- are equally members of the faithful, so that there are no Christians who are more Christians than others;
- are called to sanctity and to the apostolate, so that one cannot distinguish between active and passive members of the Church;
- profess the same faith, participate in the same sacraments and are equally bound by ecclesiastical authority;
- have the same fundamental rights and duties: what belongs to every member of the faithful is essentially equal for all, and all are equally bound to respect this in the others, so that there can be no privileges and exceptions on this regard. For example, all have the same right and duty to receive doctrine and the sacraments.

B) The Principle of Variety

Although the condition of faithful acquired with baptism is one and the same for all, there exist different *modes* of actuating it: "By divine institution holy Church is ordered and governed with a wonderful diversity" (*LG* 32; cf. *AA* 2). The Spirit which guides the Church and her faithful gives different gifts according to His own will, promoting various forms of life and apostolate which are equally good and legitimate.

The principle of variety is manifested in all levels of ecclesial life, giving rise to a rich pluralism that is brought out, for example, in various rites or in different forms of spirituality with the juridical peculiarities that involves.

Of divine right, and therefore of constitutional importance, is the existence of sacred ministries or *clerics* (c. 207 § 1), which are those faithful who have received the sacrament of orders in any of their three degrees: episcopate, presbyterate, diaconate (c. 1008–1009), and form the ecclesiastical hierarchy. The other faithful are the *laity*.

Another particular status in the life of the Church is that of the faithful (clergy or laity) who consecrate themselves to God through the profession of the evangelical councils through some sacred commitment recognized by the Church.

C) The Institutional Principle

In connection with the foregoing, but with its own significance, is the institutional or hierarchical principle, whereby there exist in the Church pastors who exercise, in the name and on behalf of Christ the Head of the Church, the functions, ministries, and powers directly established and attributed by Him to the hierarchy.

All the faithful equally possess and participate, need and enjoy the goods that lead to salvation: faith, the sacraments, the order of the community governed particularly by brotherly charity. Everyone is also called to actively participate in what concerns those same goods because they are common, the object of the mission of the Church (the faithful transmission and spreading of the Gospel, the proper celebration of worship, the ordered edification of ecclesial society); but in this sphere, the roles, powers, and functions are not the same; there is by the will of divine teacher, priests and governors, the ecclesiastical hierarchy, through which the saving goods, the Word of God, the sacraments, the unity in communion, are transmitted and dispensed to the faithful.

The Church, from this perspective of the organization and attribution of the public functions, is a constitutionally hierarchical society; its basic juridical structure is not of human creation, which was established by its Founder when He instituted the College of the Apostles at the head of which He placed Peter, entrusting to him the mission of proclaiming the Gospel to all people, of baptizing and guiding as pastors the People of God, conferring on them (through a particular effusion—gift—of the Holy Spirit) the powers that, for this purpose, they must exercise in His name.

They founded Churches and took care to elect successors (bishops) to whom they transmitted, through the laying on of hands, that gift of the Spirit, that mission and those powers, faculties or abilities, and it has been so ever since.[33] Throughout the centuries, the college of bishops (successors of the Apostles), with the Pope (Peter's successor) at the head, exercises these powers and functions on behalf of Christ (cf. *LG* 18 s., CCE 874–879).

The ecclesiastical hierarchy is linked to the sacrament of orders, which confers upon those who receive it a *share* in the priesthood of Jesus Christ essentially distinct from that received with baptism; a *sacred power* that qualifies them to represent Christ as the head of His Church, to exercise in His name the public functions (*munera*) of teaching (*magisterium*), sanctifying (worship) and ruling (government) the People of God. But this ability varies according to the degree of the sacrament of orders received,[34] and in some regards its exercise depends on each member of the hierarchy of responsibility (office, mission) that is entrusted to them by the authority.

---

33. In turn, they elected collaborators (presbyters and deacons) to have them a share in their office, entrusting to these collaborators (also in a sacramental way) some of the functions entrusted to them with the powers in question.
34. In a particular way in the celebration of the Eucharist, the mystery of the real Body of Christ and of the other sacraments. The bishops receive the fullness of the priesthood, may perform all the sacraments, included in the sacred orders, in this way perpetuating the hierarchy (*LG* 20–21). The presbyters also receive—albeit not fully—the ministerial priesthood to exercise it as collaborators of the bishops: celebrating the Eucharist and the other sacraments, except the holy orders (*LG* 28). Deacons, the lower level of the hierarchy, are not priests nor do they receive powers of a strictly sacramental nature, but rather they are ordained to perform liturgical and charity services in collaboration with the bishop and the presbyters (*LG* 29).

2. The Fundamental Rights and Duties of the Faithful

We have seen that in virtue of the principle of equality, all the baptized have the same rights and duties, which are a juridical expression of the common dignity and responsibility of the faithful. Therefore, these are duties and rights of a constitutional level in that they derive from baptism; they are thus founded on divine law. They belong to each member of the faithful by the simple fact of being members, not by concession from the community nor from the authority. They are equal for all, perpetual, incapable of being renounced, and they prevail over norms of human law. They constitute the common channel within which each one, by himself or with others, lives his Christian life and participates in the mission of the Church.

The CIC has gathered the most important of these rights and duties in cc. 208–222, which constitute a novelty in ecclesiastical legislation. We shall look at them briefly.

Equality as a right (c. 208), which means that from the principle of equality studied above, there flow concrete juridical demands, such as non-discrimination, the right to equal means of protection and juridical guarantees, etc.

The duty of ecclesiastical communion (c. 209), which includes, according to c. 205, "the bonds of profession of faith, of the sacraments and of ecclesiastical governance." The faithful must conform to these bonds not only in their thought but also with their behavior, by means of a coherent conduct and by obedience to the laws and to the Pastors of the Church.

The universal call to sanctity and to the apostolate (c. 210), which means that all of the faithful must equally commit themselves to their own sanctification and to promote the sanctification of others. Other concrete duties are connected to this generic duty, such as receiving the sacraments at the proper time, confession and communion at least once a year, fasting and abstinence, etc. Other rights also derive from these: rights to the means of sanctification, to the apostolate, and to the promotion of apostolic enterprises.

The right and duty to do apostolate (c. 211). Since all have the obligation of spreading the Gospel, they also have the right to give witness to it and to transmit it to others without need of permission or a mandate from the hierarchy (it is a mission that is received with baptism).

The duty of obedience to the pastors (c. 212 § 1) is a consequence of the hierarchical principle. Pastors must be listened to and obeyed as representatives of Jesus Christ in those things which have to do with doctrine, worship and the governance of the Church.

The right of petition (c. 212 § 2) is also an instrument given to the faithful to cooperate in the building up of the Church, making known to the pastors their own needs and desires. The pastors must listen and respond reasonably to these petitions, but they do not have to give their consent to all that has been requested by the faithful, except when it is a matter of a true right for what has been petitioned.

Freedom of opinion and expression (c. 212 § 3). This right and duty extends to those things which are matters of free opinion in the Church, and not to truths of faith or of morals sanctioned by the Magisterium (cf. cc. 209 § 1 and 212 § 1). Within these limits the faithful have the right not to have the opinions of the others imposed on them, and to maintain and manifest their own opinions with responsibility and respect for others, aiming always at the common good.

Right to the means of sanctification (c. 213). In order to be able to respond to the vocation that has been received (c. 210), Christians have the right to receive from the pastors the means of salvation, the Word and the sacraments. The pastoral organization of the Church is not an end in itself, but a means to realize this right of the faithful. Therefore, it must meet their needs and possibilities so that they can make use of them with abundance. Ministers must not adopt arbitrary pastoral criteria which would pose an obstacle to this right of the faithful.

Right to one's own rite and to one's own spirituality (c. 214). This is a consequence of the principle of variety, and has various concrete manifestations: the right to choose, practice, conserve or change one's rite according to the norms of law (see cc. 111–112); the right to pastoral assistance according to one's own rite; the freedom to adopt that spirituality or form of Christian life and of apostolate that one deems suitable for oneself.

The right of association and of holding meetings (c. 215) are projections of the social nature of the person in the life of the Church. Spheres of autonomy which permit the faithful to realize their vocation in a communitarian form, uniting efforts to promote activities and to reach goals included in their condition as faithful. Among these rights are included the right to found, direct or adhere to associations, as well as the recognition and protection of their autonomy. These rights are developed in cc. 298–329.

The right of initiative (c. 216) is connected with the preceding rights. It consists in the freedom to promote, sustain, direct or collaborate in apostolic works (schools, hospitals, volunteer work, etc.), configuring them according to their own statutes, in the area of canon law. Those who are responsible for these undertakings are their own promoters. In order to assume the name of "Catholic" they must obtain the consent of the authority, which then takes on a special competence in their regard.

Initiatives of the same type which are promoted and constituted as being exclusively civil in character do not fall under this canon. These latter initiatives have the same relation to the hierarchy of the Church as do the faithful who promote them. Naturally Christians must not participate in activities, associations, etc. that are contrary to the faith or morals, especially if they have been expressly condemned (cf. c. 1374).

Right to Catholic formation (c. 217). Each member of the faithful has the responsibility to acquire and improve his Christian formation with the goal of realizing his vocation in the most efficacious way. For this purpose he has the right to have access to schools of the Church and to obtain there the corresponding academic degrees (cf. Chapter VIII, d). As we shall see below, Catholic parents have the right and duty to give their children a Christian education.

Scientific freedom (c. 218) is a concrete aspect of the general freedom of opinion and of expression (c. 212), which has for its object questions of the sacred sciences which are open to discussion, and the subjects of this liberty are those who are engaged in these disciplines. Obedience to the teachings of the Magisterium is required from scholars, as from all the faithful. However, in what the Magisterium has not yet determined, scientific debate is free, and particular theories or conclusions of a school cannot be imposed as if they were certain.

At the same time, prudence requires that such debate be maintained in the channel that is appropriate for it (specialized journals, congresses, etc.) in order to avoid confusion or scandal in those who are not specialists. Thus the role of the Magisterium is to be kept distinct from that of scholars; the latter are not to claim to take the place of the pastors in the mission that has been entrusted to them to expound the doctrine of Christ authentically and with authority.[35]

Freedom in choice of a state of life (c. 219) means above all that no one can have imposed on him a state of life that has not been freely chosen, nor should he be impeded from choosing what he considers being called to. However, this does not mean in itself that he has the right to be admitted, for he must have the necessary prerequisites, and in many cases there must also be the consent of others (for example, to receive orders or to marry).

---

35. On this subject, see the Instruction of the CONGR. FOR THE DOCTRINE OF THE FAITH *Donum veritatis*, On the ecclesial vocation of the theologian, May 24 1990: *AAS* [1990] 1550-1570.

Right to good reputation and to privacy (c. 220). These are natural rights of the person which must be recognized also in ecclesiastical society. Among these can be included the right to a secret (natural, professional, of confession: c. 983 and 984, etc.) and the right to defend oneself from injuries and calumnies; inviolability of mail, of one's domicile or office; the presumption of innocence; the right to freely choose one's confessor (c. 991) and spiritual director (cf. c. 239 § 2, 240, 246 § 4), and also that of confessing one's sins with having to reveal one's identity to the confessor (thus, in a confessional suitable for this purpose: c. 964 § 2), etc.

The right to judicial protection (c. 221 § 1) means that those who hold that they have been harmed or threatened in their rights can have recourse to a judicial authority, so that, by means of a trial, their rights can be declared, determined and be respected.

The right to an equitable judgment (c. 221 § 2) is a consequence of the preceding. Those who are parties in a trial must enjoy the procedural guarantees established by law. For this reason procedural laws cannot be dispensed (c. 87 § 1). This right implies, among other things: that judges must act with impartiality and independence; the right to intervene in the trial personally or by means of a defender; that of proposing and presenting proofs and of manifesting all what one considers to be helpful in one's own defense.

The principle of penal legality (c. 221 § 3) means that actions can be considered as offences only when they have been previously described as such by a penal norm, and that these actions can be punished only with the penalties previously established, which will be inflicted in individual cases according to the conditions and following the procedure established by law. Penal laws are not dispensable (c. 87 § 1).

The duty to economically support the Church (c. 222 § 1). The collaboration of all the faithful in the mission of the Church extends also to the seeking of material means that are necessary for it. The canon indicates the ends to which ecclesiastical goods must serve (worship, ministers, apostolate and charity). The faithful normally fulfill this obligation by means of their voluntary offerings (c. 1261 § 2, 1262), but the Church can also establish taxes under certain conditions (c. 1263).

Finally, it should be observed that these rights and duties are not unlimited nor can they be considered to be a sort of treasure for individualistic use, since their exercise must be based on the achievement of the common good. For this reason law and judicial decisions can determine more precisely the extent, limits and conditions of their exercise, but always respecting their special content (c. 223).

3. Power and Its Exercise in the Church

Just as the principle of equality gives rise to the determination of a juridical statute common to the faithful, the hierarchical principle places us before the subject of power in the Church: its basis, transmission, and exercise.

These issues are far from being easy, because of the need to explain that the power to which we refer here is what is exercised in the government of any organized human group, that is, power in the juridical sense, whereby some members may bind others through norms, orders or decisions (establishing rights and obligations). In canon law, this power is called power of governance or jurisdiction, or also government power. C. 129 states that "it exists in the Church by divine institution."

The problem lies in determining the relationship between this power and the *potestas sacra* with which those receiving orders are invested. In the primitive Church, the bishop with his collaborators (presbyters and deacons) exercised both the sacramental and governmental functions. Later, the need to explain facts, such as the fact that the papacy is not a sacrament or that a bishop, without personally quitting, may lose the government of his diocese, or that subjects who have not received the orders may exercise juridical power, led to a distinction between power of *orders* and power of *jurisdiction*, as well as between any hierarchies in which they may result (Lombardía).

The first consists of the powers or functions of a *sacramental liturgical* nature that are personally acquired with the sacrament of orders according to its various degrees. The second includes the powers of *governance and of Magisterium*; this power, according to some, is not personal but institutional (of the Church) and is obtained through strictly juridical channels (the canonical mission or office).

Doctrine has interpreted the distinction and the relationship between both powers in very different ways, especially its entire nature and the channels through which the two are received: from considering them two dimensions of the sole ecclesiastical power to believing them to be two separate things.[36]

These distinctions are quite clear in the Second Vatican Council and in the current Code. *Lumen gentium* (n. 8), in stressing that the human and the divine element of the Church "should not be considered as two realities, but as just one complex reality," concludes that this unique Church of Christ, "established and organized in this world as a society, subsists in the Catholic Church, governed by the successor of Peter and by the bishops in communion with him." The apostolic succession then includes juridical, and not merely sacramental, power.

Moreover, the sacramentality of the episcopate is confirmed and it states that episcopal consecration "together with the office (*munis*) of sanctifying, also confers the offices (*munera*) of teaching and governing, which, by their nature, can nevertheless not be exercised except in hierarchical communion with the Head and members of the College"

36. This distinction has been set forth in several official documents, among them the CIC 17, affirming that in any event, participation in both hierarchies was still reserved for the clergy (see, for example, cc. 108, 109, 118, 219).

(*LG* 21, c. 375).[37] While the unity and sacramental root of the three *munera Christi* that make up the *sacred power* of those who receive the ministerial priesthood is ratified, the hierarchical communion is introduced as a *condition of exercise,* distinguishing it from the power of its exercise.[38]

For its part, the NEP (n. 2) explains that what the consecration confers is "an *ontological* participation in the sacred *functions* (*sacrorum munerum*)" and that "the word *functions* is deliberately used in preference to *powers* which can have the sense of power *ordered to action.* A *canonical or juridical determination* through hierarchical authority is required for such power ordered to action. A determination of this kind can come about through appointment to a particular office or of the assignment of subjects, and it is conferred according to norms approved by the supreme authority." (cf. *LG* 24b)

It seems clear then that the *potestas sacra* does not imply in itself the power of effective government; what the authors discuss is the nature and scope of that "juridical determination" (normally the *missio canonica*) that makes it such. From those who believe that it is a matter of mere assignment of competence, that is, the delimitation of the sphere (territorial,

37. Something similar is stated regarding the presbyters (see *LG* 28, *PO* 2, 4–7, c. 1008).

38. The *Preliminary Explanatory Note* to *Lumen gentium* (NEP) adds that "without the hierarchical communion, the ontological sacramental office, which must be distinguished from the juridical canonical aspect, *cannot* be exercised." (N.B.) The distinction seems necessary and in any event relative: because every power or public ministry is a function of the purpose of the Church, the *salus animarum,* it is pastoral; because there are sacramental powers (such as the power to baptize) which do not require the sacred orders, while in order to exercise the principal functions of the *magisterium* and of governance (those of presiding over a community of the faithful) the episcopate or at least the presbyterate is needed, although its concrete determination is made by an act of the authority such as the canonical mission. At the same time, there are juridical powers that do not depend on nor are transmitted through the sacred orders or another sacrament; as we said, a mission as important as that of the Pope is received through the election as the Bishop of Rome, not because his episcopate is distinct or superior to that of the other bishops.

personal, material) of exercise of the power *already received through the sacred orders*; to those who believe that his sacrament confers (together with the strictly cultural powers) the personal *capacity or ability* to be the subject of government power (c. 129 § 1), but that this latter, being by definition strictly juridical, is only received through the canonical mission or a similar juridical act.

A complete answer demands that we distinguish various situations, methods of attribution and exercise of the power of government. There are cases in which the *missio canonica* does not confer participation in the power of another, and cases in which it does, as we shall see below.[39]

In the first case we find, apart from the college of bishops[40] and the Roman Pontiff[41] (who do not receive the mission from any human power), the diocesan bishops, of whom *Lumen gentium* says that that "they govern as vicars and legates of Christ the particular Churches that are entrusted to them, with their counsel, with their exhortations, with their examples, but also with their authority and with their sacred power [...]. This power that they personally exercise in the name of Christ, is proper, ordinary, and immediate even if the exercise of the latter thereof is regulated by the supreme authority, and even if, with a view to the utility of the Church or of the faithful, it may be circumscribed within certain limits. By virtue of this power, the Bishops have the sacred right and before God the duty to legislate over their

39. In any event, the *missio* also (and preliminarily) fulfills the role of juridical control of the hierarchical communion.
40. The Episcopal College is the subject of the supreme power over the Church. The forms and modalities of its exercise are determined by the Head of the College (the Pope) and with his consent (NEP 3 and 4). Each bishop, having received the episcopal ordination and by his communion with the Head and the members of the College, participates in this power (*LG* 22, c. 336).
41. The Pope obtains the supreme power when accepting his election if he is already a bishop, but if not, he must be immediately ordained, c. 332. The primate in the jurisdiction is linked to the status as the Bishop of Rome.

subjects, to judge them and to regulate everything involved in the worship and organization of the apostolate" (n. 27, c. 381 § 1).

So then, at the fundamental levels of the ecclesiastical organization (universal Church, particular Church) the juridical power is founded on the episcopal order, even if its exercise is regulated by law. On the other hand, at the other levels, what gives the canonical mission is a share in the power of governance of another, positive law regulates the technical channels and recourses whereby this participation takes place, as we shall see in the following section when we consider the ecclesiastical organization.

Lastly, related to the issues we just stated is the question of to what extent and in what way the laity may participate in public functions, especially those involving the exercise of the power of governance. The answer certainly requires taking into account the participation of the priesthood of Christ that all the faithful receive in the baptism (the common priesthood), the mutual ordination between this and the ministerial priesthood (*LG* 10, 33s; *AA* 2b), the pastoral purpose of the public functions.

In fact, speaking of a closer cooperation of the laity in the hierarchical apostolate, *Lumen gentium* states that "they are suitable to be assumed by the Hierarchy to exercise some ecclesiastical functions for a spiritual purpose" (n. 33). On the one hand, the suitability of the laity in the exercise of the power is affirmed at the same time that it is stressed that this exercise constitutes a collaboration to tasks characteristic of the hierarchy.

4. Canonical Regulation and the Power of Governance

C. 129 states, as we saw, that the power of *governance* or *of jurisdiction* exists in the Church (*est in Ecclesia*) by divine institution; it does not specify whether that power is the Church's or the hierarchy's.[42] It also states that qualified subjects are "those sealed by the sacred orders," but that also the laity may cooperate in its exercise, all in accordance with law. Therefore the provision of c. 274 § 1 seems contradictory, because it extends the old privilege that reserves for the *clergy*[43] all exercise of the power of governance (at least with the stability of an ecclesiastical office). As for the rest, this does not reflect reality.

A) Distinction of Functions

The power of governance, according to c. 135 § 1, is divided into the legislative, executive, and judicial power; this division, in addition to a distinct content, means a difference in the juridical governance for each of the three powers, and in principle also the organs called to exercise them; but it does not mean a *separation* of powers, because the constitutional organs (Pope, councils, diocesan bishop) combine the three, and others more than one (dicasteries of the Roman Curia, conferences of bishops).

It is interesting that c. 135 repeats that power must be exercised "as provided by law." Regarding legislative power, we have seen some rules when speaking of the laws. We should add that the Pope and the ecumenical council may delegate them, but not the other legislators except in the cases explicitly provided by law; likewise, through the principle of the hierarchy of norms, the inferior law is null if it

---

42. After the expression "in the Church" it is argued whether the power exercised by the members of the hierarchy established by Jesus Christ is proper and personal or whether it should be attributed to the Church-institution (*of* the Church), in whose name they exercise it (Hervada, Souto, Lombardía).

43. The diaconate has been re-established as a stable (not merely temporary) rank of the Latin hierarchy, at the same time that the so-called minor orders have been eliminated; therefore today *clergy* are all and only those who have received the sacrament of orders, while in the past one became clergy, a member of the hierarchy, even in a stable way, through mere tonsure, without having received any rank of the sacrament of orders (cf. CIC 17 cc. 108, 118, 948–950).

contradicts a higher law. Judicial power is exercised according to procedural provisions and in principle cannot be delegated except for preliminary investigation proceedings (c. 135 § 2 and 3).

B) Ordinary Power (Proper or Vicariate) and Ordinaries

The power exercised by the college of bishops, the Pope and the diocesan bishop is *ordinary*, because "it involves the proper right" (c. 131 § 1) to the office they hold, and it is also *proper* because it is not derived from any other authority. All other organs of governance share in one way or another in their power; they do not have proper power.[44]

Ordinary vicariate power is the power that comes with an office but which is not proper, but rather derived from he who has proper power in whose name it is exercised (dicasteries of the Roman Curia, diocesan vicars). It is personally acquired when the office is acquired; it is suspended when a recourse against the removal or deprivation of the office is pending, and it is extinguished when the office is lost (c. 143). The principal office (for which the power is proper) and the vicariate exercise the same competencies, they are not excluded, and each organ responds to their actions; but the principal may reserve or take over certain issues for itself, limiting the competence of the vicar, whose acts may also be rescinded or confirmed in the case of an appeal.

The concept of *Ordinary* is important in law; it is understood not to mean everyone who exercises ordinary power, but only those enumerated in c. 134 § 1, that is:

- the Roman Pontiff;
- the diocesan Bishop and those who govern, albeit temporarily, a particular Church or community equivalent to a Church pursuant to c. 368: the territorial

44. Except the particular councils and the conferences of bishops, of whom it cannot be said with certainty that they receive power from others.

Prelate or Abbott, apostolic Vicar, Prefect and administrator; also the personal Prelate (c. 295) and the military Ordinary;

- those who in those same communities have ordinary executive power, that is, the general and episcopal vicars;

- the major superiors of the religious institutes and societies of apostolic life, clergy of pontifical right, who have ordinary executive power and only for their subjects.

When one speaks of the *local* Ordinary, all the foregoing are included, except the latter (c. 134 § 2). On the other hand, when a provision speaks of the diocesan bishop, it is understood to mean only him and those equivalent to him, pursuant to c. 381 § 2 (those mentioned above), but not the Vicars of those communities.

C) Delegated Power

Delegated power is defined—in contrast to ordinary power—as the power "that is granted to a person himself and not by reason of his office" (c. 131 § 1). The delegate works in the name of the delegator and his power is limited to the terms of the delegation or mandate received pursuant to c. 133. Recourse to delegation is employed above all to share executive power. It is acquired when one receives the mandate and is extinguished by any of the causes enumerated in c. 142 § 1.

Delegation may be for all cases of a certain type (general) or for a singular case (*ad actum*) or a given set of cases. The rules on sub-delegation are found in c. 137 § 2–4. As a general rule: executive power delegated by the Holy See may be sub-delegated; the delegation given by a lower authority, only if it is general, will allow sub-delegation *ad casum*; the sub delegate cannot sub-delegate. This is all unless it is provided otherwise.

D) Competence

C. 138 establishes the rules for interpreting the subject area of power (which cases it includes), while cc. 139 to 141 regulate the possible conflicts of competence between authorities. He who acts with ordinary or delegated power may continue to act even if someone *later* addresses another competent authority, albeit a higher one. But if the higher authority has *already* begun to handle a matter, the lower authority must refrain, unless there is a grave and urgent reason, immediately informing the higher authority of the situation.

The delegation of more than one subject for the same matter is presumed to be *joint and several*, that is, it grants to each of them the power necessary to perform it by themselves, independent of the others. In this case, he who acts first (even if he was not the first to receive the mandate) rules out the competence of the others, as long as he does not abandon handling the matter (it is usually called first instance of competence). On the other hand, the delegation is *collegial* when given to more than one as a group; then the exercise of that joint power is governed by the provisions that c. 119 establishes for collegial acts, unless the principal has ordered otherwise.

E) External Forum and Internal Forum

Law in its proper dimension of human sociality has its effects in the sphere of external relationships and behaviors; the external nature is a feature of law, while the power of governance has its effects in the external forum (c. 130). But the virtue that leads one to give to each his own (justice) binds the conscience; it is not just exterior. If we also take into account the spiritual nature of the goods and purposes characteristic of the Church (grace, salvation), we understand that the orders and rules of the authority may also reach the internal forum. The internal forum (the forum of the conscience) is called sacramental when the act of power is exercised during a confession (for example, absolution from censure pursuant to c. 1357) or extra-sacramental if it is outside the confession (for example, the dispensation of the impediment pursuant to c. 1079 § 3).

What is exceptional is the fact that power may have effects only in the internal forum and not in the external forum. This occurs when the act lacks the customary public nature for reasons of prudence (danger of defamation, secrecy of the confession). Even so, it can have effects in the external forum as established by law (cf. c. 1082).

F) The Habitual Faculties

In order to validly or lawfully perform certain ministerial acts or acts related to them, at times it is not enough to have received the sacrament of orders; a certain authorization or license from the authority is required (hearing confessions, marrying, preaching, confirming, etc.). It is not strictly a matter of the power of governance, and that is why they are called faculties, and *habitual* because they are received for all cases of one type that arise (not *ad actum).* Faculties are at times possessed by law, by reason of the office, from the ministry received or even the circumstances, thus faculties c. 566 attributes to the chaplains, or those mentioned in cc. 883, 967 § 1, 968, and 976. At other times, they are granted to the person, such as those of cc. 969 and 1111. It is these latter faculties that, according to c. 132 § 1, are governed by the rules of delegated power (they are even called delegation or mandate), although normally they cannot be sub-delegated.

G) Substitution of Jurisdiction

It is a juridical mechanism to ensure the validity of singular acts performed by someone who in fact did not have the necessary power therefore. C. 144 § 1 states that the Church substitutes the executive power (not the legislative or judicial power), in both *fora,* in cases of common error and positive and probable doubt, *de facto* as well as *de jure*. The reason for the substitution is the common good, the need for juridical certainty; more so when the spiritual good or peace of the faithful is at stake. Some explain this device supposing that the canon grants a delegation in the factual situations it contemplates; others a correction, also *a iure*, of those same acts that otherwise would be invalid, in short, an extension of competence. The canon assumes that the power lies in the Church, which substitutes the power in the cases foreseen.

The common error refers to the passive subject of the act of jurisdiction, who receives it from he who erroneously believes he has enough power to perform it; it does not matter that the active subject is or is not aware of his lack of competence. The fact that it is *common* means for some that most of the faithful of the community must commit a mistake; for others that it must have an objective well-known motive capable of inducing the faithful in common into this error. The error is *de jure* when it is due to an incorrect knowledge of the norms affecting the power (for example, whether the parish priest may dispense the impediments); it is *de facto* when it falls on some circumstance that limits power or competence, such as being domiciled in a parish, the term of extinction of a mandate, the situation of danger of death.

On the other hand, the doubt affects he who performs the act of governance, who due to the complexity of the norms (question of law) or of the specific circumstances of the case (of fact), there is uncertainty regarding whether one has enough power to perform the act in question. For there to be substitution, the doubt has to be *positive and probable*, that is, he who acts has objective reasons of certain solidity to believe that he probably has jurisdiction, even if he is not entirely certain.

C. 144 § 2 extends substitution to the habitual faculties for confirming, absolving, and assisting in marriages, cases in which the validity of a sacrament is at stake, without attempting to decide whether, due to the nature of those faculties, those situations will in any event be included in § 1.

Chapter V.
The People of God. Its Social Structure

1. The People of God

The Church can be considered as a *people* and as a *society*. These two aspects are taken up and distinguished in the two paragraphs of c. 204.

As He did in the past with the descendants of Abraham, the Lord has willed to constitute the People of the New Covenant by means of baptism, which incorporates men into Christ and renders them "sharers in Christ's priestly, prophetic and royal office in their own manner." Thus "they are called to exercise the mission which God has entrusted to the Church to fulfill in the world, in accord with the condition proper to each one" (c. 204 § 1; cf. *LG* 9, CCC 758 ff.).

All Catholics—i.e., all those who have been baptized in the Catholic Church or received into it after baptism, and who are in *full* communion with it "by the bonds of profession of faith, of the sacraments and of ecclesiastical governance"—are included by full right in the Church as a visible society.

Baptized non-Catholics are in *partial* communion with the Church insofar as they profess the Catholic faith, celebrate the same sacraments and recognize the hierarchy of the Church. The non-Catholic Eastern Churches (called Orthodox) fundamentally keep the Catholic faith and celebrate the same sacraments, because the apostolic succession is preserved in them; the reasons for separation concern the recognition of the authority of the Roman Apostolic See. The communities that arose from the Reform (called Protestant) only partially (and to varying degrees) maintain the faith, sacraments, and ecclesiastical structure.

Catechumens are those who "under the influence of the Holy Spirit [...] ask to be incorporated into the Church by explicit choice." The Church responds to this desire, guiding them in the path towards baptism, teaching them Christian doctrine and the Christian life, and granting them "various prerogatives which are proper to Christians" (c. 206).

When studying the constitutional principles, we saw how in the Church, the fundamental and equal dignity and participation which all have in virtue of baptism, is exercised according to a diversity of functions, charisms and vocations which determine the *condition* proper to each one, and the *modality* in which they are to cooperate in the building up and development of the Kingdom of God. An essential expression of the different functions that exist in the Church is those that are proper to the hierarchical ministry.

In fact, the People (to which all men are called) that is comprised of those who are baptized (sharing one dignity and mission) is not simply the collection of believers, an uncoordinated mass of those who have been called together. On the contrary, this People has been constituted by God as a "Church, constituted and organized as a society in this world," which "subsists in the Catholic Church, governed by the successor of Peter and the bishops in communion with him" (c. 204 § 2).

The hierarchy consists of the group of the faithful who, because they have received the sacrament of orders, participate in the ministry of the Apostles, of Christ as the Head of the Church: they are the sacred ministers or *clergymen*. The other faithful are *laypersons*. Thus, by divine will, in the

Church we have the distinction between members of the hierarchy and the other faithful, that is, between clergy and laity (c. 207 § 1).

Depending on the rank of the order, the distinction is:

- *structural,* because the sacred order, by establishing some faithful as pastors, it supports and perpetuates the basic principle of the institutional organization of the Church;

- *functional,* because it assigns to certain faithful the functions required by the pastoral care of the ecclesial society;

- *social,* because the particular configuration with Jesus Christ, Pastor and Master of the Church, which is received with ordination, places those who received it in a special ecclesial condition; it assigns them a proper way of living the Christian vocation and of participating in the mission of the Church, a peculiar and permanent personal statute.

In fact, these properties lie above all in the episcopal order, as we have seen; Jesus Christ entrusted his Church to Peter and to the other Apostles, and it is guided throughout history by their successors: the Pope and the bishops in communion with him. Incidentally, the order of the presbyters structures and assigns functions in the Church, because they also receive the priesthood to collaborate in the ministry of the bishops. The diaconate, still of divine institution, does not confer any ministerial participation in the priesthood. Its functionality is not sacramental or governmental, but of service to the worship and to charity.

Beyond this structural distinction, there exists a third class of faithful, comprised of those who embrace the state of consecrated life, whether they are clerics or lay persons. Their life is characterized by a special consecration to God "through the profession of the evangelical counsels by means of vows or other sacred bonds recognized and sanctioned by the Church" (c. 207 § 2).

The state of consecrated life belongs to the life and sanctity of the Church, to whose salvific mission they greatly contribute (cf. *LG* 44), either through the variety and richness of charisms that it receives and organizes as an institution, or because it determines a *cœtus,* a category of faithful whose dedication and service to the Church contribute fruits from which the entire community benefits. However, they do not belong to its hierarchical structure, which means that those who are consecrated are assigned neither cultural, teaching, nor pastoral government roles in the Church in virtue of their consecration alone (c. 207 § 2).

Laity, clerics and consecrated faithful constitute the three *principal* specific conditions that the faithful can have, and which determine a *modality* of realizing the common Christian vocation, as well as fundamental rights and duties. Thus there is a specific juridical status for each type of faithful: clerics, consecrated persons, and laity. However, some things must be kept in mind:

a) This categorization is rather generic and it is obsolete in some cases. It is hence relative.

b) In the first place, within each of these groups, we can find diverse situations: consider, for example, the many forms of consecrated life, the different statutes of the three orders of clergy, or between married and unmarried laypersons.

On the other hand, the strict separation that in the past could characterize the distinct types of faithful no longer exists: they are not groups that do not communicate with each other. This is proven by facts such as the fact that some consecrated persons are at the same time diocesan clergymen, while others are consecrated as laypersons, to the sanctification of the secular realities; or the fact that permanent deacons enjoy in part the statute of clergymen and in part that of laypersons.

c) The clerical and the consecrated state are *ecclesiastical states* (status), ways of life that emerge from specific ties assumed in the Church, regulated by canon law with great detail, which even have certain consequences in the civil order (the prohibition of carrying out certain types of work, exemption from military service or from jury duty, support, etc.); whereas the life of the laity is carried out for the most part in civil society, so that canon law affects them with a lesser range and intensity.

2. The Lay Faithful

From what has just been said it is understandable that there is no definition of the laity in the Code. C. 207 § 1 only says that the laity are those faithful who are not clerics; § 2 of the same canon explains that both clerics and laity can assume the consecrated life.

The Const. *Lumen gentium* is placed not on a constitutional, but on a functional level, in n. 31 when it states: "The term 'laity' is here understood to mean all the faithful except those in holy orders and those who belong to a religious state approved by the Church. That is, the faithful who by baptism are incorporated into Christ, are placed in the People of God, and in their own way share the priestly, prophetic and kingly office of Christ, and to the best of their ability carry on the mission of the whole Christian people in the Church and in the world." Therefore, from this point of view the laity are the faithful who are neither clerics nor religious, *but may be consecrated non-religious.*

Furthermore, *Lumen gentium* is more explicit in that it immediately refers to what is the specific note of the laity, their secular character: "Their secular character is proper and peculiar to the laity." In this sense their being in the world acquires a vocational significance (calling and mission): "by reason of their special vocation it belongs to the laity to seek the kingdom of God by engaging in temporal affairs and directing them according to God's will."

Here we have the coordinates of the lay condition: baptism and secular character. The laity are members of the faithful called to realize their participation in the priesthood of Christ received with baptism, precisely in the reality of secular life. As citizens, they are called to be concerned with the affairs of the earthly city, as Christians they are called to do so "being led by the spirit of the Gospel."[45]

Therefore, it is not surprising that the norms of the Code concerning the laity are always few in number with respect to those concerning clerics and religious, since the vocation of the laity is not to be occupied with ecclesiastical affairs, but rather with secular affairs, which are governed by state law. For this reason, the Council exhorts: "the faithful should learn to distinguish carefully between the rights and the duties which they have as belonging to the Church and those which fall to them as members of the human society" (*LG* 36). This does not mean that they are to conduct a double life. On the contrary, they are called to harmonize—without confusing—the spiritual and the temporal orders, "remembering that in every temporal affair they are to be guided by a Christian conscience" (ibid.).

Canon law affects the life of the laity on account of their condition as faithful who—like all—must maintain communion in the faith, in worship, and in the discipline of the Church. Therefore, in the first place, they are subject to the same rights and duties "which are common to all the Christian faithful" (c. 224). Thus the canons which make particular reference to them do not have the function of adding new rights and duties, but rather of indicating the *specific way* in which the

45. In addition to the conciliar texts, a specific development of this theme is found in JOHN PAUL II, Apostolic Exhortation *Christifideles laici* (December 30, 1988): *Origins* 18 [February 9, 1989] 561–595.

laity—because of their secular character—are called to live the Christian vocation in the Church and in the world.[46]

3. Principal Obligations and Rights of the Laity

The principal rights and duties which are specific to the laity are listed in cc. 224–231, but one must also keep in mind that these have implications in other areas of canon law.

The right and duty to carry out apostolate. In confirmation of what has been said above, c. 225 notes that this is a task that is common to all the faithful, because it flows from baptism (see c. 211); but in the case of the laity it acquires particular reference to the world of secular realities, which they are to animate and perfect with the spirit of the Gospel, as their proper task (CCC 898–900).

The rights and duties of spouses and parents (c. 226). As in civil society, the family is the cell of ecclesial society (the domestic Church); spouses and Christian parents precisely find in marriage and in family life the first reality that they are called to sanctify, aided by the grace of the sacraments. By natural law, parents are the first educators of their children. This is a role which also has a sacramental significance for Christian parents, especially in their children's religious education.

The right to freedom in temporal affairs (c. 227). The sanctification of temporal realities, which is the ecclesial mission proper to the laity, does not mean that the governance of these realities pertains to the Church. On the contrary, it

46. On the juridical status of the laity, see A. DEL PORTILLO, *Faithful and Laity in the Church*, Ecclesia Press, Shanon, 1972; E. CAPARROS, "Les notions juridiques de fidèle et de laïc", *Studia canonica* 6 [1972] 79-98; J. HERRANZ, "Le statut juridique des laïcs dans l'Église: l'apport des documents concilaires et du *Code de droit canonique*," *Studia canonica* 19 [1985] 229-257; J. MARTÍN DE AGAR, "Il diritto alla libertà nell'ambito temporale," *Lex Nova* (now *Fidelium Iura*) 1 [1991] 125–164; L. NAVARRO, *Il fedele laico*: "Il diritto nel mistero della Chiesa" II, 3rd ed., Pontificia Università Lateranense, Rome, 2001, pp. 138–167.

requires respect for their autonomy, their laws and proper values. Therefore, the faithful have the right to conduct their temporal affairs in freedom (whether in politics, work, or the family), guided by an upright Christian conscience.

In these matters, the faithful must enjoy the same autonomy as other citizens: the State cannot discriminate against them for the fact of being Christians, nor can the Church claim to make herself the representative or *leader* of Catholic citizens in the choices that have to do with civil life. The faithful, however, have the duty of making these choices in accordance with the principles and indications *of a moral order* proposed by the ecclesiastical Magisterium, within which there is room for a great variety of solutions and projects.

In consequence, each of the faithful acts in secular life on his own initiative and assumes his own responsibility, without involving the Church in his temporal options nor claiming to present his own opinions as if they were the doctrine of the Church.

Participation of the laity in ecclesiastical organization (c. 228). This is not a matter of a precise right, but an affirmation of the *capacity* of the laity to occupy certain positions in the Church if they are called by the pastors or by law (catechist, judge, financial administrator, adviser; cf. CCC 910–911). We shall look at them more specifically when we treat these various matters. It should be remembered, however, that the laity are excluded from offices and positions whose exercise requires the sacrament of orders (cc. 129 and 150).

Right and duty to a doctrinal formation (c. 229). The laity, as all the faithful (c. 217), have the duty—and thus the right—to acquire a formation adequate to their particular circumstances and which enables them to develop their proper mission in the Church and in the world.

In this case it is specified that this right includes the possibility to deepen their formation also at the university level and to obtain the corresponding academic degrees (§ 2), which renders them capable of teaching the sacred sciences with a mandate from the authority (§ 3).

The capacity to fulfill certain ministries and functions of worship (c. 230). We are not speaking here of the right and obligation—of baptismal origin—of all the faithful to be called to actively participate in the worship of God, each according to his situation in the Church (c. 835). It is rather a matter of some liturgical functions and ministries that the laity have the capacity to assume in virtue of the common priesthood received with baptism.

The *stable* ministries of lector and acolyte are reserved to laity of the male sex, according to the conditions established by the conferences of bishops, and without this giving them any right to remuneration (§ 1).

Any of the laity (man or woman) can carry out by *temporary* deputation the functions of lector, acolyte,[47] cantor, commentator, and other functions according to the norm of law (§ 2).

Finally, there are liturgical offices which the laity can fulfill in cases of *necessity,* in order to compensate for a *lack* of clerics or in special circumstances that warrant it, pursuant to law (§ 3).[48]

In any case, none of these possibilities we have examined constitute functions that are *proper* to the laity, which they can take up on their own initiative. They are tasks which they have the *capacity* to carry out, if they are called by the

---

47. An authentic response of the PCLT (June 30, 1992) has admitted that a woman can serve at the altar, if the diocesan bishop deems that it is appropriate: *AAS* [1994] 541–542; see the Letter of March 15, 1994 from the CONGR. FOR THE DIVINE WORSHIP AND THE SACRAMENTS, in *Origins* 23 [April 28, 1994] 771–779. For a comment: L. NAVARRO, "Il servizio all'altare delle donne," *Ius Ecclesiæ* [1995] 382–395.

48. For example, baptizing (c. 861 § 2), preaching (c. 766), distributing the communion (c. 910 § 2), assisting marriages as a qualified witness (c. 1112).

authority or by law, and for which they must also have the necessary preparation. It belongs to the diocesan bishop, according to the universal law, to order these matters in his diocese.[49]

Laity who devote themselves to the service of the Church (c. 231). This canon refers to laity who work, full time or part time, in the service of ecclesiastical institutions (teachers, executives, doctors, leaders of associations, etc.). On the one hand, it is stipulated that they must acquire the necessary preparation. On the other hand, there is a recognition of their right to a fitting remuneration which takes their personal situation into account, as well as the right to appropriate health benefits, pension, social security, etc., with respect to the corresponding state laws.

4. Personal Status of Sacred Ministers

The reception of the sacrament of orders and the roles which it determines in the Church have a powerful impact in the personal life of those who receive them (sacred ministers or clerics), also on a juridical level.[50]

In fact, holy orders are a sacrament of service which, in its different grades, implies:

- a special participation in the priesthood of Christ, essentially different from the common priesthood of the faithful;
- a peculiar consecration and deputation to divine worship and to the pastoral service of the brethren;

49. Important in this matter is the *Instruction on Certain Questions Regarding the Collaboration of the Non-Ordained Faithful in the Sacred Ministry of Priests*, issued by eight Dicasteries of the Roman Curia on August 15, 1997: *Origins* 27 [November 27, 1997] 397–409.

50. R. R. CALVO, N. J. KLINGER (eds.), *Clergy Procedural Handbook*, The Catholic University of America Press, Washington, 1992.

- the participation of clerics in the sacred power, integrating them in the ecclesiastical hierarchy, which exists in the Church by the will of God (cc. 129 § 1 and 207 § 1).[51]

The dignity of their vocation and mission implies that clerics, called to take care of ecclesiastical affairs (*negotia ecclesiastica*), have to lead a particular type of life. This, although not removing them from the world, limits in large measure their involvement in secular affairs (*negotia sæcularia*), to which, on the contrary, the laity are called.

All members of the Church (especially the pastors) must be aware of the importance of the sacred ministry, and promote and foster vocations to it (c. 233).

The canons defining the canonical statute of the clergy use the diocesan presbyter as the paradigm. They are applied to the rest depending on the circumstances.

A) The Formation of Clerics

In the first place, the sacred ministry requires a specific formation of candidates, such as it will enable them also to verify their suitability and to mature their vocation. C. 232 confirms that the duty and the right of selecting and forming candidates to sacred ministries belong to the Church. It is an important aspect of the freedom of the Church, in which no other authority may interfere.

The preparation of the candidates for *priesthood* is ordinarily conducted in the *major seminary,* where they are to live for the entire time of their formation (normally six years), or at least for four years according to the judgment of the diocesan bishop (c. 235).

51. According to the official statistics, at the end of 2004 there were 4,784 bishops, 405,891 priests (268,833 diocesan, 137,058 of the religious clergy), and 31,809 permanent deacons in the Church (SECRETARIA STATUS, *Statistical Yearbook of the Church 2004*, LEV, 2006, p. 101).

The preparation of the candidates for the *permanent diaconate* includes a formation program of three years, prepared by the conference of bishops, which the younger candidates must follow "in some special house" (c. 236).[52]

In every diocese, if possible, a major seminary must be erected by the bishop. Interdiocesan seminaries can also be constituted for various dioceses by their respective bishops, or also by the conference of bishops if it is for the entire territory of the nation. The erection of an interdiocesan seminary, as well as the corresponding statutes, must receive the approval of the Holy See (c. 237).

The diocesan bishop must carefully watch over the functioning of the seminary and the formation of the seminarians in its various aspects. It is his responsibility to supervise it, to appoint the rector and to fill the other positions, to approve the statutes and the regulations, and to provide for its economic needs (for which he can impose a special tax in the diocese; cc. 259, 263–264).

The seminary is a public juridical person once it has been erected. It is ordinarily represented by the rector (c. 238), who directs it under the guidance of the diocesan bishop and according to the statutes approved by him. Furthermore, the seminary is exempt from parochial governance, so that the rector also functions as pastor for all those who live in the seminary (c. 262).

In addition to the rector, there must be a financial administrator and at least one spiritual director. There can also be a vice-rector, other moderators or providers of formation, and teachers if the seminarians carry on their studies in their own seminary. All, under the guidance of the rector, collaborate in the formation of the candidates (c. 239). There are also ordinary and extraordinary confessors who hear the confessions of the seminarians in the seminary.

52. See CONGR. FOR CATHOLIC EDUCATION, "Basic Norms for the Formation of Permanent Deacons," *Origins* 28 [August 27, 1998] 181–191.

In order to safeguard the seminarians' freedom, they must be allowed to follow the spiritual direction of other priests designated by the bishop, and to have access to any confessor, inside or outside of the seminary. The confessors and the spiritual director are bound to secrecy, and therefore they are never authorized to give an opinion with regard to the admission of a candidate to orders (cc. 239–240). For his part, the rector, because he is bound to give this opinion, must not hear the confessions of the seminarians, unless in individual instances they request it of their own accord (c. 985).

The formation imparted in a seminary follows the Program of Priestly Formation (*Ratio institutionis sacerdotalis*) issued by the conference of bishops, on the basis of the norms given in this regard by the supreme authority of the Church,[53] and approved by the Holy See (c. 242). Every seminary then has its own regulations approved by the diocesan bishop (c. 243).

The goal of the formation is to render the candidates suitable to the requirements of priestly life and to the pastoral ministry, by means of a life of union with Christ and through doctrinal and human preparation (cc. 244–258). This includes: the exercise of natural and supernatural virtues, devotions (especially to the Eucharist and to the Blessed Virgin Mary), liturgical and personal prayer, love for the Church and for her pastors, zeal for souls, study of the sacred and profane sciences, etc. Seminarians must also complete the civil studies necessary for entrance into higher studies (c. 234 § 2).

The members of institutes of consecrated life and societies of apostolic life, who are candidates to holy orders, must receive, in their institute, the same formation as seminarians.

---

53. The most important is the *Ratio fundamentalis institutionis sacerdotalis*, of the CONGR. FOR CATHOLIC EDUCATION, of March 19, 1985.

B) Incardination of Clerics

Every cleric must be inscribed in that community for whose service he is ordained. This relationship of inscription is called *incardination*. The community can be a hierarchical structure (particular Church or personal prelature) in the case of the secular clergy. Otherwise it can be an institute of consecrated life or a society that has the faculty of incardinating its own clerics (c. 265).

Incardination is an institution with a long tradition, by means of which a concrete pastoral relationship of service and discipline is established between the cleric and the Church. In fact, although holy orders (as all the sacraments) have an essential universal implication, this destination must be made concrete in stable pastoral service to a given community. No one in the Church has the right to be ordained for personal motives only; there must be a reason of service. Therefore, unattached or transient clerics are not admitted, i.e., those who are ordained without being inscribed in any corporate body and thus, are without a superior.

In order to be ordained it is necessary to be called to orders by the diocesan bishop or by the prelate of the personal prelature to whose service one is admitted, or by the superior of the institute or society of whom the subject is a member. With ordination to the diaconate, a member of the faithful becomes a cleric and is incardinated (c. 266).

Incardination, however, is not an indissoluble bond. There exists the possibility of obtaining excardination from a particular Church, but incardination in another particular Church must simultaneously occur. This can happen in various ways (with the written consent of the two bishops, or by legitimate residence for five years in the new diocese without opposition of the bishops). Also the definitive admission of a cleric in an institute of consecrated life or a society of apostolic life determines excardination from the diocese and incardination in the institute or society (cc. 267–269).

Furthermore, to facilitate the mobility of the diocesan clergy so as to respond to situations of scarcity in certain places, c. 271 provides that a cleric can be temporarily transferred to another particular Church, remaining, however, incardinated in his own. This transfer must be accomplished by means of a written agreement between the bishops of both the particular Churches and the interested party.

C) Rights and Duties of Clerics

As we have seen, the clerical condition implies specific functions, relationships and bonds, which necessarily have a profound effect on the personal life style of sacred ministers, determining particular rights and duties or modifying those that are common to all the faithful. The principal aspects are laid down in cc. 273–289.[54]

It should be stated in advance that these define the *personal* status of clerics. However, every cleric will also have the rights, obligations and faculties of the concrete office he exercises (diocesan bishop, parish pastor, canon, chaplain, professor, etc.). The condition of *pastor* has a particular importance. The term "pastor" is frequently used in the canons to refer to clerics who have a precise task of the care of souls, or to those to whom the pastoral care of a given community of faithful has been entrusted (diocese, parish, association, convent, etc.).[55]

Obedience to the hierarchy (c. 273). Like all the faithful, sacred ministers must also obey the pastors of the Church. For them, however, this duty entails a special obligation with

54. For the permanent deacons see CONGR. FOR THE CLERGY, "Directory for the Ministry and Life of Permanent Deacons," in *Origins* 28 [August 27, 1998] 191–204.

55. All clerics are to exercise the task assigned to them with the pastoral spirit that is proper to their vocation, but not all offices carry with them the direct care of souls.

regard to the Supreme Pontiff and their own Ordinary in what also has to do with the exercise of their ministry.

Availability for service and fidelity in the ministry (c. 274). Holy orders are a sacrament which consecrates and destines the cleric to the service of the Church. Therefore, he is bound to accept and faithfully fulfill the offices he receives from his Ordinary.

Fraternity and collaboration (c. 275). The duty of contributing to the building up of the entire Church falls in a special way on clerics, so that they are to live among themselves and with the laity in a spirit of fraternity and collaboration.

Holiness of life (c. 276). All the faithful are called to sanctity, but the special consecration and mission of clerics commits them in a particular way to seek it, through a life of piety and through the generous accomplishment of their pastoral ministry.

Chastity and celibacy (c. 277). In the Latin Church, the sacred ministry also demands complete freedom of heart and dedication to the Kingdom of God. Following an ancient, deeply-rooted disciplinary tradition, the clergymen promise to observe complete continence and to remain celibate. Therefore, clerics must observe perfect continence and remain celibate. In consequence, they must avoid, with prudence and fortitude, those situations in which their continence could be put in jeopardy or which could arouse scandal among the faithful. They must also follow the dispositions given by the diocesan bishop in this matter. Logically, married deacons must make a holy use of marriage.[56]

Right of association (c. 278). Like all the faithful, clerics also have the right to set up and participate in associations, whose aim is in harmony with their state and compatible

---

56. The voluntary assumption of continence has specific canonical reflections, including the impediment of the sacred order (c. 1087) and others of a penal character (cc. 1394 § 1 and 1395).

with their ministry. Associations approved by the authority which facilitate their life of piety and priestly fraternity are especially recommended.

Permanent formation (c. 279). The improvement and deepening of their own formation is a "professional" duty of sacred ministers, so that they may become ever more fitted for pastoral service. Particular law must establish a program of permanent formation for the clergy.

Common life (c. 280). Unlike the religious state, clerical state does not require common life. Nevertheless, it is highly encouraged for clerics also because of the fraternal support that can be found in it. Furthermore, life in common among priests can be facilitated and realized in many ways (gatherings, conferences, retreats).

Right to support (c. 281). Their dedication to ecclesiastical ministry gives clerics the right to a fitting remuneration which will enable them to provide for their own needs and those of others whose services they require. An adequate social assistance is included in this right.

With regard to the remuneration of married deacons, one must take into account their dedication to the offices of the Church, their family needs, and the income that they have from their civil profession.

Detachment from temporal goods (c. 282). In social life, clerics must be exemplary for their simplicity and detachment from material things. This does not mean that they make a vow of poverty like the religious, but they are encouraged to contribute to the needs of the Church according to their means.

Duty of residence and right to a vacation (c. 283). There are offices that entail a particular duty of residing in the place where they are carried out. Therefore, the availability for service to which all clerics are bound requires that they not be long absent from their diocese without permission (see

c. 1396). However, they have a right to a period of vacation established by general or particular norms.

Clerical attire (c. 284). Clerics have a public ministry to accomplish and are at the service of all by their vocation. Therefore, it is reasonable that their condition and dignity should be capable of being recognized by all so that it may be respected. Therefore, they are bound to wear the clerical attire established by the conference of bishops and according to the local customs. Permanent deacons are not bound by this obligation—although they are sacred ministers on the ontological level—since they partially retain their lay condition (c. 288).

Abstention from secular commitments, offices and activity (cc. 285–289). The availability for service and detachment from material goods that are required of clerics, as well as the fact that they are occupied with ecclesiastical affairs, mean that they are normally to avoid everything that is not proper to their state (worldliness, armed service, jury duty). Without permission, they are not to take on commitments and offices of a secular nature (economic, professional, political, or in relation with labor unions) which can involve the Church in these matters, distract them from their mission, or at least give rise to a confusion between the sacred ministry and secular activities (see c. 1392).

Permanent deacons are not bound to these limits to civil participation, since they act as the laity in these matters. Nevertheless, whenever a cleric is legitimately occupied with secular affairs, he does so on his own account.

D) Loss of the Clerical State

The sacrament of orders imprints an indelible character, and therefore it is never lost or annulled. However, one can lose the clerical *state*, which means a loss of the obligations and rights proper to clerics.

The loss of the clerical state can happen: a) by a judicial decision or administrative decree in which it is declared that the ordination was invalid (cf. chapter XII, 7); b) through the penalty of dismissal from the clerical state (cf. chapter XI); c) by a rescript of dispensation conceded by the Apostolic See for truly grave reasons (c. 290). Likewise, only the Apostolic See can readmit to the clerical state those who have lost it (c. 293).

However, the loss of the clerical state by penalty or by dispensation (cases b and c), does not entail a dispensation from celibacy, which is granted solely by the Roman Pontiff (c. 291).

In addition to the loss of the rights and duties of clerics, the loss of the clerical state entails the prohibition to exercise the sacred order that has been received (celebrate rites)[57] and the loss of offices and functions previously received (c. 292).

5. Associations of the Faithful

It is proper to the nature of man to freely unite himself with others in order to combine and coordinate efforts for the attainment of common interests. The Church recognizes, therefore, that the faithful have the right of constituting, directing, and participating in associations, in order to promote activities and goals that are in harmony with the mission of the Church, such as those which are listed in c. 298 § 1.

Thus it is logical that there be mention in the canons of the associations of the faithful that are the result of the exercise of this right.[58] This section, however, does not deal with institutes

57. This does not mean that the rite celebrated by one who has lost the clerical state would always be invalid (for example, the Mass), because sacred orders remain if it has been validly received; moreover it should be recalled that any priest can absolve a member of the faithful in danger of death (c. 976).

58. See L. NAVARRO, *Diritto di associazione e associazioni di fedeli*, Giuffrè, Milan, 1991; J. R. AMOS, *Association of the Christian Faithful in the 1983 Code of Canon Law,* The Catholic University of America, Canon Law Studies, Washington, 1991.

of consecrated life and societies of apostolic life, which are associations of singular importance, in that their members assume a particular state of life recognized by the Church.

An association is a corporate body by means of which a group of the faithful comes to an agreement to accomplish an activity in a stable and ordered way, and to reach common goals which in themselves exceed the possibilities of an individual person. The characteristic elements of an association are varied:

a) *Voluntary character.* An association always exists in practice as the fruit of the freedom of those who decide to participate in it. The bonds that result from it have their origin in the commitment that is voluntarily assumed.

b) *Stability and order.* The activities and ends of an association require the ordered cooperation of all and have an importance and duration that transcend the possibilities of individual members. As a consequence, every association must have its own *statutes* that define it as a subject in itself: name, social objective, finality, modes of action and participation, government, discipline, goods, etc. (c. 304).

c) *Ecclesiality.* According to what we have seen, a canonical association, as a collective entity, is subject to rights and duties. Among these, the first is that of ecclesiastical communion. This means that its project, activity, and life, must be integrated in the ecclesiastical communion. As a consequence, associations, like the individual members of the faithful, are subject to ecclesiastical authority, to which it belongs:

- to issue the necessary norms (such as the norms which we are studying here) to regulate the exercise of the right of association in the Church, norms to which the individual associations must conform;
- to judge on the ecclesiality of every new association, so that an association will not be recognized in the Church if its statutes have not been examined by the competent authority (c. 299 § 3);

- to see to it that the fullness of Catholic doctrine be preserved and the discipline of the Church respected. In particular, this task belongs to the Holy See for all associations, and to the local Ordinary for diocesan associations and for the others in so far as they act in the diocese (c. 305).

The authority, on his part, must respect the legitimate autonomy of the associations, in so far as they are expressions of the initiative and freedom of the faithful who take part in them.

Members of an association are those who promote it on their own initiative and those who, wishing to join it, are admitted according to the statutes (c. 307). Thus there is always an act of will by which one joins an association and acquires the rights and duties that are proper to it.

A) Types of Associations

Associations can be classified in various ways. From the point of view of law, the most relevant classification is what distinguishes them between *public* and *private* associations. These can be further distinguished into other types:

- *clerical* associations are those which are recognized as such by the authority, are directed by clerics, and have the goal of fostering the exercise of holy orders (c. 302);
- *lay* associations are those which intend to form and support the laity in their own proper mission to animate temporal realities with the Christian spirit (cc. 327–329);
- *third orders* are associations promoted and directed by a religious institute, with the goal of having the laity participate in the charism proper to the institute, adapting it to their secular circumstances (c. 303);
- according to the area to which their activities extend, associations can be *diocesan, national, international* or *universal* (cc. 312 and 322). This determines the authority to which they will be subject.

B) Public Associations

Public associations are those that are *erected* by the ecclesiastical authority to act *in the name of the Church,* for the purpose of achieving the ends assigned to them by the authority itself (cc. 301 and 313). Thus they are associations of which the hierarchy makes use as an instrument for the accomplishment of its mission.

There are, in fact, activities and ends which enter into the proper and exclusive competence of the hierarchy of the Church, such as teaching Christian doctrine in the name of the Church, and public worship. In certain cases the authority can erect an association, assigning some of these activities to it (c. 301 § 1). However, it can also happen that certain necessities of an apostolic or charitable nature, which could be met by private associations, are in fact not resolved in a satisfactory way by them. In these cases the ecclesiastical authority can substitute for the private initiative, erecting associations for that purpose (c. 301 § 2).

The authority that is competent to erect a public association is:

- the Holy See for international or universal associations[59];
- the conference of bishops for those which are national;
- the diocesan bishop for diocesan associations (c. 312).

By the very fact of erection, a public association becomes a public juridical person in canon law.

---

59. The Holy See exercises its competency over international associations of the laity by means of the Council for the Laity (cf. Const. *Pastor Bonus*, art. 134; See PONTIFICAL COUNCIL FOR THE LAITY, *Repertorio:Associazioni Internationali di Fedeli*, LEV, Rome, 2004, with a short presentation of 123 International Associations approved by the Council); for the clergy, through the Congr. for the clergy (*id.*, art. 97); and for the third orders, through the Congr. for religious institutes and societies of apostolic life (*id.*, art. 111). The International Catholic Organizations (OIC) are also under the competence of the Secretary of State (*id.*, art. 41 § 2).

Since they act in the name of the Church, and thus they involve the Church in their operation, public associations are subject to the control and guidance of the ecclesiastical authority which constituted them, to whom their "higher direction" belongs (c. 315). Concretely, it belongs to the authority who erects a public association:

- to approve the statutes and the successive modifications or changes of them (c. 314);
- to intervene in the nomination and removal of the president and of the chaplain (cc. 317 and 318 § 2);
- to decide to appoint a commission or trustee to govern the association when circumstances require it (c. 318 § 1);
- to control the economic activity of the association (c. 319);
- to suppress it according to the norm of c. 320;
- to decide recourse against the acts of the directors of the association (c. 316 § 2).

This does not mean that these associations do not have a certain autonomy defined in the statutes that must be respected by the authority (c. 315 and 319 § 1). It must not be forgotten that, although a public association is constituted by the ecclesiastical authority, it is also constituted by the faithful who freely decide to adhere to it, without which it could not exist.

C) Private Associations of the Faithful

Private associations are those which are constituted by private accord among members of the faithful, to promote activities and works which enter into their vocation and ecclesial mission (c. 299).

Logically, these associations that are born of the initiative of the faithful are governed by them and remain under their responsibility. They are autonomous in their internal organization, do not act in the name of the Church, and involve only those who belong to them (c. 321 and 309).

Nevertheless, like every reality that operates in ecclesial society, a private association is subject to the competent ecclesiastical authority.

As for the public associations, the competent authority to which a private association is subject to is the Apostolic See if it is a universal or *international* association; the conference of bishops if it is *national*; and the diocesan bishop if it is *diocesan*.

It belongs to the competent authority to:

- judge concerning the ecclesiality of the association; for it to be recognized by the Church every association must present its statutes for the "*nihil obstat*" of the competent authority (c. 299 § 3);
- watch over the life and the activity of the association with the goal of safeguarding doctrine and ecclesiastical discipline and coordinating the apostolate (cc. 305 §1 and 323 § 2). This supervision also belongs to the Holy See for all associations, and to the local Ordinary for associations operating in his diocese (c. 305 § 2);
- make sure that the goods of the association are used for the proper aim of the association. In fact, although the goods of the private associations are not ecclesiastical goods (cf. Chapter X, a), their destination for ecclesial goals must be respected (c. 325).

In contrast to public ones, not all private associations have juridical personality. They can acquire it by means of a decree of the competent authority. For this purpose, their statutes must have been approved by the same authority (c. 322). For associations without personality, the members act jointly or by means of a delegate or a proxy (c. 310).

Private associations are extinguished according to the norm of their statutes, but they can also be suppressed by the authority, for grave reasons. Their goods will be destined to the ends indicated in the statutes (c. 326).

Chapter VI.

The People of God. Its Hierarchical Structure (Government and Organization of the Church)

1. The Concepts of Ecclesiastical Organization

We have seen that the government of the Church belongs to the hierarchy. But not all the government belongs to every member of the hierarchy nor does the mere fact of being clergy confer functions of government. The various functions of which government is composed are distributed among members of the hierarchy by means of a stable and ordered organization of public functions. The collection of corporate bodies, organs and persons who exercise public functions (of teaching, sanctifying, government), constitutes the *ecclesiastical organization*.

From the juridical point of view, this organizational structure has the goal of maintaining the unity and identity of the social body, the communion in the faith and the sacraments, and guiding, in an ordered way, the realization of the mission of salvation that it has received, which is to represent the Head of the Body.[60]

60. On this subject, see J. I. ARRIETA, *Governance Structures Within the Catholic Church*, Gratianus Series, Wilson & Lafleur, Montréal, 2000; J. HERVADA, *Elementos de Derecho Constitucional canónico*, 2ª ed., Navarra Gráfica Ediciones, Pamplona, 2001, chapters VI–VIII.

There are different concepts of ecclesiastical organization, from those who practically identify it with the hierarchy as a group of persons, to those who see it as a public, institutional structure, subject of attribution of ecclesiastical power and of official activity.

The sacrament of orders determines which persons among the faithful are called to exercise, and are made able of exercising, public functions. The ecclesiastical organization determines the concrete functions that belong to each of them according to the office which has been entrusted to them. This leads us to study some elementary concepts.

First of all, there is a distinction between power and competence. Power is the generic capacity to exercise a certain type of public function, whereas competence is the concrete delimitation of these functions (in a given territory, over these persons or communities, over certain matters, etc.). For example, he who is appointed judge receives judicial power, but may only exercise it in cases within his competence.

A) Ecclesiastical Office

Tied to this distinction is the concept of *ecclesiastical office*, defined in c. 145 § 1 as "any function constituted in a stable manner by divine or ecclesiastical law to be exercised for a spiritual purpose" (cf. *PO* 20b). In other words, it is a stable ecclesiastical function (Pope, diocesan bishop, rector of a seminary, consultor, chaplain...). From this definition, it seems that we can conclude that the constitution of the office or position takes place through a norm or specific juridical act that establishes it as such.

Every office carries with it a collection of functions and the proper and well-defined rights and duties (faculties, competencies, etc.) that are necessary to fulfill it, which can be considered to be independent of the person who exercises them in any given moment: the holder of the office. The rights and duties of the pastor are independent of the fact that it is this or that priest who is named as pastor. The persons change but the offices remain as a stably constituted organizational unit.

Like a piece in a mosaic, the ecclesiastical office or position is the basic element of ecclesiastical organization. The organization of the Church can in a certain sense be defined as the ordered collection of ecclesiastical offices, and also, dynamically, as the ordered functioning of the same offices by means of the exercise of their respective competencies.

Every office, according to the nature of the public functions attributed to it, requires certain qualities or prerequisites in the subject to whom it is entrusted (c. 149). C. 150 is important in this regard. It establishes that "an office entailing the full care of souls, for whose fulfillment the exercise of the priestly order is required, cannot be validly conferred upon someone who has not yet received priestly ordination." This means that only bishops and priests can be pastors in a full sense, and not laity or deacons.

B) The Conferral of the Office

Once the stable position or office is constituted, it must be granted to a given person to be exercised; this is what is meant by the canonical provision. The provision of an office usually includes three steps: the designation of the subject who shall occupy it, the appointment or attribution of the office on the part of the authority, which is called *collation*, and the taking possession of the office.

The designation takes place according to the various methods and procedures enumerated in c. 147, which can be summarized as follows:

a) *Free conferral* on the part of the authority, which means that it is up to the competent authority to freely choose the person who is to carry out the office and to appoint him (c. 148). This provision method is now the general rule (see, for example, c. 157).

b) *Presentation* of one or more candidates to the authority, made by one who has the right to do so. The authority verifies whether the presented candidate is suitable for the office, chooses one if there are many candidates, and *appoints* him as the holder of the office (cc. 158–163). For the nomination of some bishops, the subjects who hold the right of presentation are: civil authorities, the cathedral chapter, bishops of neighboring dioceses. Appointment always belongs to the Roman Pontiff.

c) *Election* is a very frequent form of canonical provision, in which a group or college chooses by voting for a person among various candidates.

d) Also in this case it devolves upon the authority to verify whether the elected person is suitable pursuant to law, in which case the election is confirmed.

One special type of election is the *compromise*: when "the electors unanimously and in writing consent to transfer to a qualified individual or to several qualified individuals [...] the right to elect for that instance," so that these will elect in the name of all (c. 174 § 1).

In order for the election to have effect, the person elected must accept it, but normally it is also necessary that the election be *confirmed* on the part of the competent authority. Elections are generically regulated in cc. 164–179, but each can also have particular norms, as in the case of the election of the Roman Pontiff.[61]

e) *Postulation* is also a special type of election which occurs when the electors desire to elect a certain candidate despite the fact that there is an impediment. In this case they can *postulate* that person, which means that they vote for him together with the request for a dispensation from the impediment which blocks the efficacy of the election. Admission of

61. Regulated in the Ap. Const. *Universi Dominici gregis* February, 22 1996: *AAS* [1996] 305–343; partially modified by Benedict XVI, M.P. *Constitutione apostólica, De aliquibus mutationionibus in normis de electione Romani Pontificis*, June, 21 2007.

the postulation on the part of the authority involves the dispensation of the impediment and the confirmation of the election (cc. 180–183).

The loss of ecclesiastical office occurs:

- through expiration of the *time* established in the nomination (see, for example, cc. 494 § 2 and 522);
- through reaching the *age* limit established by law (cf. cc. 401 § 1 and 538 § 3);
- through *resignation* made for a just cause; in some cases the resignation must be accepted by a superior; in other cases this is not required and it is valid in itself once it has been communicated (cc. 187–189). The resignation of the Roman Pontiff, for example, does not need to be accepted;
- through *transfer* to another office;
- through *removal* from office, which can happen by decree of the authority or automatically. A person is automatically removed "1) who has lost the clerical state; 2) who has publicly defected from the Catholic faith or from the communion of the Church; 3) a cleric who has attempted marriage even if only civilly" (c. 194 § 1);
- through *deprivation*, as a penalty for an offence.

The transfer, removal and deprivation must take place following the procedure established in each case.

2. The Universal and Particular Dimensions of the Church

There exist two fundamental levels of organization in the Church—universal and particular—which correspond to the fact that Christ constituted the College of the Apostles "*after the manner of a college or a stable group, over which He placed Peter chosen from among them*" (LG 19). The College of the Apostles with Peter at the head is succeeded by the college of Bishops, because "*the Lord so disposing, St. Peter and the other apostles constitute one apostolic college, so in a similar way the Roman Pontiff, the successor of Peter, and the bishops, the successors of the apostles, are joined together"* (*LG* 22, c. 330).

The fundamental constitution of the Church—her government and organization—reflects the relationship of communion existing in the college of bishops. Christ entrusted the government of His Church to the college of Apostles and put Peter at its head, giving him the primacy. Thus today the government of the Church is entrusted to the college of bishops with the Roman Pontiff, the successor of Peter in the primacy, at its head.

From its beginnings, the Church spread throughout the world in different Christian communities with an Apostle at their head *"and they passed on this spiritual gift to their helpers by the imposition of hands"* (*LG* 21); at first these communities were headed by that of Jerusalem and then by that of Rome, the see of the successors of Peter. The one Church of Christ is also "a corporate body of Churches" (*corpus Ecclesiarum, LG* 23): the collection of the particular Churches which are in communion with the Church of Rome (CCC 834).

However, this collection of the particular Churches which form the universal Church is not the result of the simple aggregation or federation of self-sufficient subjects, but rather a body where flows the one and only life of the Church among its members. In fact, every particular Church, precisely in so far as it is a part of the one Church of Christ, "makes the universal Church present with all its essential elements." Thus the one and only Church precedes and "gives birth to the particular Churches as daughters, she is expressed in them, she is a mother not produced by the particular Churches."[62]

62. CONGR. FOR THE DOCTRINE OF THE FAITH, Letter *Comunionis notio* (On Some Aspects of the Church Understood as Communion), May 28, 1992, nn. 7–9, in *AAS* [1993] 838–850: *Origins* 22 [June 25, 1992] 108–112. For a commentary, see CONGREGAZIONE PER LA DOTTRINA DELLA FEDE, *Lettera Comunionis notio*, LEV, Vatican City, 1994. Cf. CCC 835.

From another point of view, the Council has expressed this structure of the Church by saying that "the Roman Pontiff, as the successor of Peter, is the perpetual and visible source and foundation of the unity both of the bishops and of the whole company of the faithful. The individual bishops are the visible source and foundation of unity in their own particular Churches, which are constituted after the model of the universal Church; it is in these and formed out of them that the one and unique Catholic Church exists. And for that reason precisely each bishop represents his own Church, whereas all, together with the Pope, represent the whole Church in a bond of peace, love and unity" (*LG* 23).

3. The Supreme Power in the Church

We can distinguish but not separate the constitutional organs to which the supreme government of the universal Church is entrusted: the Roman Pontiff and the college of bishops. "The college or body of bishops has for all that no authority unless united with the Roman Pontiff, Peter's successor, as its head, whose primatial authority, let it be added, over all, whether pastors or faithful, remains in its integrity" (*LG* 22). These are not two organs juxtaposed one against the other and limiting one another. The Pope exercises his supreme power in every moment, even when he acts as head of the college of bishops, whereas the college enjoys this same power only when it acts in union with and under the guidance of its head: the Roman Pontiff.

A) The College of Bishops

"The order of bishops is the successor to the college of the apostles in their role as teachers and pastors, and in it the apostolic college is perpetuated. Together with their head, the Supreme Pontiff, and never apart from him, they have supreme and full authority over the universal Church; but this power cannot be exercised without the agreement of the Roman Pontiff" (*LG* 22).

The college of bishops is composed of those who have received episcopal consecration and are in hierarchical communion with their head and with the other members of the college (c. 336). As a class composed of many members placed under one sole head, it simultaneously expresses the variety, universality and unity of the People of God.

It is logical that the college have a full and supreme power over the whole Church, since the Roman Pontiff, Supreme Pastor of the universal Church, is included in it as its head. Thus the duality Pope–College signifies that the Church is governed by the Roman Pontiff either by himself or together with the other bishops.

The college of bishops, as a communion of pastors guiding the Church, is always in action. However, the actions through which it exercises the supreme power are accomplished only in concrete modalities and occasions in which it is called by the Pope to do so, or else in the cases in which the Supreme Pontiff "at least approves or freely admits the corporate action of the unassembled bishops, so that a truly collegiate act may result" (*LG* 22).

The Ecumenical Council

"The college of bishops exercises power over the universal Church in a solemn manner in an ecumenical council" (c. 337 § 1). Having overcome the old conciliarist views according to which a Council is an institution equal or even superior to the Pope, the Second Vatican Council reiterates that "there never is an ecumenical council which is not confirmed or at least recognized as such by Peter's successor. And it is the prerogative of the Roman Pontiff to convoke such councils, to preside over them and to confirm them" (*LG* 22); and he can also transfer them, suspend them or dissolve them. In fact, if the Pope dies or resigns his office during a council, it remains suspended until his successor decides to continue it or dissolve it (c. 340).

All the members of the college of bishops, and they alone, have the right and duty to participate in a council with a deliberative vote. The Pope can call others to participate in the way in which he holds opportune. The council deals with the matters that have been proposed by the Holy Father as well as the ones that have been proposed by conciliar Fathers and approved by him. After the deliberations and the approval of the conciliar decrees in the aula, it belongs to the Roman Pontiff to confirm them and promulgate them; otherwise, they would not have obligatory force (c. 341).

B) The Roman Pontiff

The bishop of Rome is the successor of Saint Peter in the capital office conferred on him by the Lord—the primacy—in virtue of which he exercises full and supreme power over the entire Church. This supreme office or *munus petrinum* is the basis of the other titles of the Roman Pontiff enumerated in c. 331.

The Pope is, first and foremost and always, the head of the college of bishops, which he presides over and governs, his ministry, as Lombardía stresses, is intracollegial. He is the Vicar of Christ, whom he represents and from whom alone his ministry derives. He is the Pastor of the universal Church, and thus of all the faithful, including the pastors.

His power, according to c. 331 is:

Ordinary and proper. It is exercised directly in virtue of his office, and not by commission or mandate of another. The Pope, even though he is elected by cardinals, is not the representative or delegate of the conclave (that is, of the group of voting cardinals), nor can his election be conditioned.

Supreme. Not subject to any other, his decisions are not liable to objection and "there is neither appeal nor recourse against a decision or decree of the Roman Pontiff" (c. 333 § 3).

Full. In that it is not limited to certain matters, places or persons, nor is it to be exercised in accordance with or under the guidance of any other.

Immediate. In that it is received directly from God and exercised directly over each and every member of the faithful and every community, without need of intermediaries.

Because the ministry of the Pope does not come to the ecclesial communities as from outside, but as something interior to them that forms them and maintains them in the communion of the entire Church.[63]

Universal. In that, on the one hand, it covers all matters having to do with the life and mission of the Church (doctrine, liturgy, pastoral care, government, etc.); and on the other hand, the Pope "by virtue of his office, not only has power in the universal Church but also possesses a primacy of ordinary power over all particular Churches and groupings of Churches" (c. 333 § 1).

The Supreme Pontiff can always freely exercise his power, without limits of time, interruption or other conditions.

This does not mean that the Roman Pontiff exercises an unlimited and despotic power in the Church, or that all other power is excluded. He is subject to what Christ the Founder has established for His Church (divine law), and his ministry is in the service of the unity of the entire Church, in which the bishops also preside "in God's stead over the flock of which they are the shepherds," with proper power (*LG* 20).

In fact, in the accomplishment of their ministry, he is "always united in communion with the other bishops and with the universal Church"; but it belongs to him to determine "the manner, either personal or collegial, of exercising this function" (c. 333 § 2).

The specific modes of exercising the supreme ministry have varied depending on the circumstances of place and time. For example, in relation to the Eastern Catholic Churches, the Pope exercises his power differently than in relation to the Latin Churches.[64]

---

63. CONGR. FOR THE DOCTRINE OF THE FAITH, Letter *Comunionis notio*, on the Church as communion, 28.V.1992: *AAS* [1993] 838–850.

64. See CONGR. FOR THE DOCTRINE OF THE FAITH, Considerazioni su libro «Il Primato del successore di Pietro nel mistero della Chiesa» 31.X.1998.

The rules for the election of the Pope have been laid down in the Ap. Const. *Universi Dominici gregis*, promulgated by John Paul II on February 22, 1996. In it, the procedure of the conclave is regulated in detail, as well as the different types of election that are possible. Normally, he who obtains at least two thirds of the votes plus one is elected. The same Ap. Const. determines the tasks of the College of Cardinals while the Roman See is vacant (cf. c. 335).

The election must be accepted by the person elected, but it requires no confirmation on the part of anyone. However, since the power that the Supreme Pontiff must exercise requires episcopal character, if the person who is elected is not already a bishop, he must be consecrated immediately after his acceptance, and only then does he receive the power of the primacy. Likewise, the resignation of the Pope from his office requires no acceptance on the part of anyone (it is sufficient that it be made freely and be duly manifested; c. 332).

The Roman Pontiff exercises his ministry in a continuous way, making use in various ways of the 7assistance and cooperation of the bishops and of other organisms and persons such as the Synod of Bishops, the Cardinals, the Roman Curia, or pontifical legates.

4. Institutions for the Government of the Universal Church

To carry out his pontificate, the Pope makes use of various bodies and persons. Some have a consultative character, such as the Synod of Bishops or the College of Cardinals, which he asks for opinions on given questions. Others, such as the Curia or the legates, have an executive character and help him in a permanent way in carrying out the duties which he has entrusted to them. We shall present them briefly.

The *Synod of Bishops* is an assembly that unites some bishops, chosen from the entire Catholic world, under the authority of the Pope, to study and give counsel on the questions which he has proposed. It is not a permanent institution nor does it have deliberative power except when the Pope confers it in a given case.

The *Cardinals* of the *Holy Roman Church* also form a college. Its origins can be traced back to the bishops of the neighboring towns or suburbs of Rome and the priests and deacons of Rome, whose advice was used by the Supreme Pontiff. Cardinals are freely nominated by the Pope and those who are not already bishops must receive episcopal ordination. It belongs to this college to elect the Roman Pontiff above all. They can also be convoked by the Pope to offer their view on some important questions. Furthermore, the individual cardinals collaborate in the Roman Curia at the head of the most important dicasteries and as members of some of them, to whom it belongs to resolve more important questions.

The *Roman Curia* is a permanent structure which helps the Holy Father in his daily work in the service of the universal Church and the particular Churches. It is composed of the Secretariat of State, the Congregations, Tribunals, Councils and other organisms; their constitution, the competencies assigned to each dicastery, and the way in which they are to be carried out are established in a special law, which currently is the Ap. Const. *Pastor Bonus* (which, as we have said, is a part of the *Corpus* of canon law).

The Cardinals and many bishops of the entire world collaborate in the Curia as members of the dicasteries, helped by consultors, officials and others who can be clerics, religious or laity.

The Curia has no proper power, but exercises the powers received from the Roman Pontiff in his name and with his authority. Therefore, the dicasteries must act in union of intention with him, following these principal criteria:

- "not to do anything important and extraordinary" without previously having communicated it to the Holy Father;

- to submit to the approval of the Holy Father acts of major importance, unless they have already received the competence to realize them.

Furthermore, the dicasteries cannot issue laws or norms having the force of law or derogate from the prescriptions of universal law, except in individual cases and with the specific approval of the Supreme Pontiff (*Pastor Bonus*, art. 18).

However, the acts of a dicastery are attributed to it and not to the Pope, unless he has made them his own by giving them *specific* approval. Therefore, when speaking of the *Holy See* or of the *Apostolic See*, one intends to refer "not only to the Roman Pontiff but also to the Secretariat of State [...] and other institutions of the Roman Curia, unless the nature of the matter or the context of the words makes the contrary evident" (c. 361). The fact that the acts of the Roman Pontiff are unobjectionable whereas those of the Curia can be contested is a significant distinction. On the other hand, the *supreme authority* of the Church refers only to the Pope and to the college of bishops, to the exclusion of the Curia.[65]

Pontifical legates are the stable representatives of the Roman Pontiff to the particular Churches and state governments of the various nations. Their *principal* function is to make the pastoral solicitude of the Holy Father for all the Churches concrete where they are sent, and to strengthen the ties of unity, charity and cooperation between these and the See of Peter. They principally carry out a work of information for the Holy See, in particular with regard to the conditions of the life of the Church and of candidates for the episcopate; they assist, advice and cooperate with the local bishops and with the conferences of bishops (of which, however, they are not members); they defend the freedom of the Church before

65. F. G. MORRISEY, *Papal and Curial Pronouncements: Their Canonical Significance in Light of the Code of Canon Law,* 2nd ed. revised and updated by Michel Thériault, Saint Paul University, Ottawa, 1995.

the State authority; and finally they realize the functions and mandates entrusted to them by the Holy See.

Some legates *also* have a diplomatic mission of representation with the state governments, to promote and facilitate good relations between the States and the Church, and to resolve with them questions of common interest, also by means of concordats or similar accords. These legates have the title of *nuncio*, and are sent and revoked according to the norms of international law regarding diplomatic agents. Legates who only have a mission with the local ecclesiastical hierarchy, and not with the State, are called *apostolic delegates*, even if they have contacts with the civil authorities and often are recognized to have diplomatic prerogatives (cc. 362–367). Legates who represent the Holy See with regard to international organizations and conferences are also designated.

5. The Particular Churches

The hierarchical constitution of the Church is also expressed on the particular level in the various Christian communities which compose, and which are gathered together in, the one Catholic Church.

This particular level or dimension of the ecclesiastical constitution is also of divine institution in that it goes back to the ministry of the Apostles, who, put at the head of the first communities, "were careful to appoint successors." These are the bishops who, as members of the college of bishops, "with priests and deacons as helpers," have "received the charge of the community, presiding in God's stead over the flock of which they are the shepherds" (*LG* 20), in communion with the head and with the other members of the college.

The unity of the Church appears therefore not only in the unity of the People of God which gathers together all the baptized under the leadership of the Pope and the college of bishops, but also in the communion of a multiplicity of particular Churches, "which are constituted after the model of the universal Church; it is in these and formed out of them that the one and unique Catholic Church exists" (*LG* 23). The Church is also structured as a body of particular Churches—*corpus Ecclesiarum*—in the communion of the universal Church.

The relationship between the particular Church and the universal Church is not only that between the parts and the whole, since the one and only Church of Christ "is truly present and acts" in the particular Church which, in its turn, is what it is in virtue of the operative presence in it of the one, holy, catholic and apostolic Church of Christ (*CD* 11), in whose image it is formed.

Erecting, suppressing or modifying particular Churches solely belongs to the Pope or to the college of bishops (c. 373). The community that forms a particular Church must be defined and distinguished from others. This is usually done by determining the territorial limits of each so as to include in it all the faithful who live there. In turn, the particular Churches are divided into parishes (c. 374 § 1).

But the distinction between particular Churches can also be made according to personal criteria, such as rite,[66] nationality or language of the faithful, such that in the same territory there is more than one particular Church. The personal structures are usually proper statutes, in which the criteria of distinction, adscription, and coordination of competencies with local communities are established.

A) The Diocese

The theological concept of particular Church is equivalent to and is realized in a full way in the canonical concept of *diocese* (c. 368), defined by the Council as "a section of the People of God entrusted to a bishop to be guided by him with the assistance of his clergy so that, loyal to its pastor and formed by him into one community in the Holy Spirit through the

66. For example, in Lebanon, the Churches are personal because of the rite.

Gospel and the Eucharist, it constitutes one particular Church in which the one, holy, catholic and apostolic Church of Christ is truly present and active" (*CD* 11, c. 369).

There are three fundamental elements in the particular Church: a) a pastor, normally a bishop; b) a people, or portion of the People of God; and c) a presbyterium. These elements relate to each other in such a way that they form a community in the image of the universal Church: the bishop who, as pastor, gathers and presides in the name of Christ over the portion of the people of God entrusted to him, with the collaboration of the presbyterium. At the same time, these three components must be incorporated into the communion of faith, of sacraments, and of discipline of the universal Church. We have already seen that the Roman Pontiff is the pastor of all faithful and communities.

B) Other Ecclesiastical Circumscriptions Similar to the Diocese

In addition to the diocese, there are other portions of the people of God, or Christian communities, organized as particular Churches. For this reason, c. 368 says that, unless determined otherwise, "a territorial prelature, a territorial abbacy, an apostolic vicariate, an apostolic prefecture, and an apostolic administration which has been erected on a stable basis" are equivalent to a diocese.

These communities are briefly described in cc. 370 and 371. The elements and typical relationships of the particular Church are found here, even if at times in a partial way. For example, they do not always have a bishop as head, but a priest who "governs it as its proper pastor, in the manner of a diocesan bishop" (this is the case of the territorial prelature and of the territorial abbacy); or their pastor may govern "in the name of the Supreme Pontiff" and thus not as a proper pastor (this is the case of the vicariates, prefectures and apostolic administrations).

Not only can there be personal dioceses (c. 372 § 2), but there also are structures of a personal nature similar to dioceses called to develop a specific pastoral work which is added to or replaces the personal prelatures and the ritual or military ordinariates.[67]

Personal prelatures (cc. 294–297) can serve various goals defined in their statutes, such as a more adequate distribution of clergy, special pastoral work or missionary work, etc.[68] They can be of regional, national or international extent.[69] They are governed by statutes established by the Holy See. A prelature is constituted by a prelate who governs it as a proper Ordinary, by secular clerics incardinated in it who constitute its presbyterium, and (according to the case) also by laity, who can voluntarily tie themselves to the prelature for the purpose of cooperating with its apostolic work in the manner defined in the statutes.[70]

Ritual ordinariates are constituted for the purpose of providing pastoral care for members of the faithful of an Eastern rite who live in areas of Latin rite.

Military ordinariates provide Catholic pastoral care for those who serve in the army of a nation. They are equivalent to the dioceses; at their head, they have a military Ordinary

67. See J. I. ARRIETA, Commentary on c. 372, in ExComCIC II/1 pp. 735-739; ID., "Le circoscrizioni personali," *Fidelium Iura* [1994] 207–243.

68. This depends on whether they are more or less on an equal footing with the diocese.

69. On this subject, see J. HERVADA, Commentary on Title IV: Personal Prelatures, in ExComCIC II/1 pp. 413-419; W. H. STETSON and J. HERVADA, "Personal Prelatures from Vatican II to the New Code: An Hermeneutical Study of Canons 294–297", *The Jurist* [1985] 379–418; P. RODRÍGUEZ, *Particular Churches and Personal Prelatures*, Four Courts Press, Dublin, 1986; E. CAPARROS, "A New Hierarchical Structure for New Pastoral Needs: Personal Prelatures," (1989) XXIV *Philippiniana Sacra* 379–417.

70. This is the case of Opus Dei, erected as a personal prelature in 1982, for the purpose of promoting sanctity in daily life (especially through work) among people of all conditions. See A. DE FUENMAYOR, V. GÓMEZ-IGLESIAS, J. L. ILLANES, *The Canonical Path of Opus Dei*, Scepter–Midwest Theological Forum, Chicago, 1994.

(who normally is a bishop), and it is composed of the military chaplains and the faithful who, for any reason, are under arms (or other security corps) or live in a military zone. They are regulated by the Ap. Const. *Spirituali militum cura*[71] *in general, but every ordinariate also has its own statutes, which are often defined in an accord between the Church and the State.*[72]

From this it can be concluded: a) that there exist different types of ecclesiastical circumscriptions which serve as particular Churches; and b) that the diocese is taken as the paradigm for all circumscriptions and it is the one that is regulated by the canons. What is prescribed for the diocese must be applied, with the necessary adjustments, to the others circumscriptions.

All have in common the fact that they are "major" ecclesiastical circumscriptions, that is, autonomous one from the others and depending directly on the Holy See.

6. Government and Organization of the Diocese

A) The Diocesan Bishop (cc. 381–402)

All bishops, as successors of the Apostles,[73] "are constituted Pastors of the Church," receive with episcopal consecration the office of sanctifying, teaching and governing. These ministries are exercised with regard to the entire Church as members of the college of bishops, always and only when the bishops are in hierarchical communion with the head of the college and with the other members (c. 375).

The members of the college who have the pastoral care of a diocese entrusted to them are called *diocesan* bishops. The

71. Of April 21, 1986, *AAS* 78 [1986] 481–486.

72. See in this regard E. BAURA, *Legislazione sugli Ordinariati castrensi*, Giuffrè, Milan, 1992.

73. See CONGREGATION FOR BISHOPS, *Directory for the Pastoral Ministry of Bishops* "Apostolorum Successores", LEV, Rome, 2004.

usual procedure in the Latin-rite Church is for the Pope to appoint bishops directly (with the help of the Congregation for Bishops). However, in some dioceses the chapter, or others, has the right to elect or present the candidates to the Pope, who can then confirm or install them.

Although here we shall discuss the power of government and other *juridical aspects* involved in the office of the diocesan bishop; we must not forget that his function is *pastoral* and the juridical power is a means for carrying it out.

In the diocese entrusted to him, the bishop—under the authority of the Supreme Pontiff—is "the visible source and foundation of unity" (*LG* 23). In it he "possesses all the ordinary, proper and immediate power which is required for the exercise of his pastoral office" (c. 381 § 1).

This means that the diocesan bishop, in virtue of his episcopal consecration and the function he has received (*missio canonica*), governs his diocese directly, in his own name and with proper power, directly representing Christ. All the matters and questions having to do with the pastoral care of his diocese belong to him, except those which "the law or a decree of the Supreme Pontiff reserves to the supreme authority of the Church or some other ecclesiastical authority" (c. 381 § 1).

Those who govern a particular Church which is equivalent to a diocese (c. 368) are in law equivalent to the diocesan bishop, and thus have the same rights, duties and powers. What is said in the canons for the diocesan bishop also applies to them, "unless it appears otherwise from the nature of the matter or from a prescription of the law" (c. 381 § 2).

Not only the faithful of the diocese are committed to the pastoral charity of the diocesan bishop, but also those others who are found in it: non-Catholic Christians, and the non-baptized. The clergy which collaborate with the bishop depend on him in the exercise of their ministry, and are entrusted to him in a special way. He must promote "the holiness of the

Christian faithful according to each one's own vocation," (c. 387), vocations to the priesthood and to the consecrated and missionary life (c. 385).

As a pastor, the bishop performs the functions proper to the pastor: he is *teacher, priest* and *head* in his particular Church.

As *teacher* of the Gospel, he takes care that "the truths of the faith which are to be believed and applied to moral issues" are presented to all, according to the conditions of each one, by means of preaching, catechism, etc. It is his duty to defend with firmness the integrity and unity of doctrine.

As *priest*, the bishop is the principal dispenser of the divine mysteries. He is promoter and rector of the entire liturgical life and sees to it that the sacraments are duly celebrated and administered. He himself must offer the Sacrifice of the Mass for his people on Sundays and holy days of obligation.

As *head* of his Church, with respect to the universal law, the bishop:

- exercises personally the legislative power: he alone is the legislator in the diocese;
- can judge cases either personally or by means of his judicial vicar and the other judges;
- exercises executive power by himself or by means of the vicar general and his episcopal vicars;
- is the juridical representative of the diocese and administrator of its goods.

As the guardian of the ecclesiastical communion, the bishop is to be watchful that in his diocese the common discipline of the whole Church is respected, that the laws are observed and that abuses are not introduced. He is to foster the legitimate diversity of charisms and forms of apostolate, coordinating them for the common good.

After he has completed 75 years of age, or when on account of illness or for some other serious reason, he becomes less suited to carry out his office, the bishop is invited by c. 401 to present his resignation to the Holy Father.

When for any reason the bishop ceases to occupy his office, the diocesan see is said to be vacant (c. 416); when for reason of captivity, banishment, exile or incapacity, he can no longer communicate with the people of his diocese, the see is said to be impeded (c. 412).

B) Institutions and Offices for the Government of the Diocese

The diocesan bishop counts on the ministerial collaboration of the clerics and on the commitment of all the faithful in carrying out his pastoral office. However, there are various offices and organisms which aid him in his task of government. We shall consider them briefly.

Coadjutor and Auxiliary Bishops (cc. 403–411)

These are bishops placed by the Holy See at the side of the diocesan bishop in order to help him in circumstances of pastoral necessity or difficulty, with various faculties according to the case (extension of the diocese, age, personal motives, etc.). The fact that there are other bishops in the diocese greatly eases the work of the diocesan bishop, above all for what has to do with the *acts proper to the bishop* (pontificals, confirmations, ordinations, etc.), which often are very numerous.

The *coadjutor* bishop enjoys the right of succession, which means that he automatically becomes diocesan bishop when the see is vacant. Therefore, there can only be one coadjutor bishop, and he is appointed vicar general by the diocesan bishop. There can be more than one *auxiliary* bishop and they are nominated as vicars general or episcopal vicars. One of them can receive special faculties from the Apostolic See; he is then named vicar general.

Far from creating division, the presence of these bishops in the diocese makes it function better, although it raises certain questions. The coadjutor and the auxiliary bishops fulfill their office in union with the diocesan bishop, who remains the head of the diocese, but who must consult them with regard to acts of major importance.

The Diocesan Synod (cc. 460–468)

This is a consultative assembly, not permanent but occasional, which the diocesan bishop can convoke when the circumstances suggest, in order to confer on various questions and projects that are to be carried out in the diocese. Some persons belong to the synod by reason of the office they have in the diocese (bishop, vicars, rector of the seminary, etc.), whereas others are elected or designated by the diocesan bishop so that all the ecclesial realities be represented (clerics, laity, consecrated persons, associations).

The synod is put under the guidance of the diocesan bishop who presides over it personally or by means of his vicar; it belongs to him to suspend or dissolve it. All the questions that have been proposed are freely discussed in the synod, and can be put to a vote. However, this vote has only a consultative value because it solely belongs to the diocesan bishop—as the only legislator in the diocese—to decide how the synodal conclusions should be published and to make them operative.

The Diocesan Curia (cc. 469–474)

This is a permanent structure which the bishop uses in carrying out various tasks of his pastoral function of government. It is made up of the vicars, the tribunal, the chancellor, the notaries, employees, etc. A vicar general can be nominated as moderator to coordinate the activities of the curia. Logically, the diocesan curia acts under the authority and in union with the diocesan bishop, in whose administrative and judicial power it participates, and to whom the power of nomination belongs for the various offices of the curia.

The Diocesan Vicars (cc. 475–481)

In every diocese there is at least one vicar *general*; there can be other *episcopal* vicars. All of them enjoy ordinary executive power, but whereas the vicar general has it for the entire diocese and for all administrative matters, the episcopal vicars have it only for a zone of the diocese or over one given type of affair (for example, pastoral activity, consecrated life, catechesis). There is also the *judicial* vicar, who enjoys ordinary judicial power and directs the activity of the tribunal.

All the vicars exercise the competencies of their office in the name and in representation of the diocesan bishop; these are positions of trust whose nomination belongs to the bishop. As we have seen, if there is a coadjutor bishop, he will also be nominated vicar general, and the auxiliary bishops will also be nominated vicars.

Since the vicars have ordinary executive power they are also territorial ordinaries according to the provisions of c. 134. This means that when in the Code or elsewhere a certain act is said to belong to the *Ordinary* or to the *local Ordinary,* both the diocesan bishop and the vicars have the capacity to realize them. An example of this would be dispensation from impediments (cc. 1078 ff.). Instead, when the law makes express mention of the *diocesan bishop*, it should be understood as referring to him and to him alone, and not to his vicars, unless they have received a special mandate (c. 134 § 3). This distinction is important for the correct interpretation of the norms as, for example, in cc. 87 and 88 on the power to dispense from laws.

The Finance Committee (cc. 492 and 493)

The finance committee also forms a part of the diocesan curia. It is composed of at least three financial and legal experts named by the bishop, who presides over the committee in person or by means of a delegate. Its main task is setting the annual budget following the indications of the diocesan bishop, and approving the accounts for year-end income and expenditure. In the most important affairs, the bishop has the obligation to listen to their opinion, and for issues of extraordinary administration, he must obtain their consent, without which the affair will be invalid as, for example, with regard to sales which exceed a certain amount (c. 1277).

The Diocesan Financial Administrator (c. 494)

The financial administrator is nominated by the bishop to administer the goods of the diocese under his authority. It is a technical function for which he must select a truly expert and honest person. His task is the ordinary daily administration of the budget approved by the finance committee; he can also carry out other tasks assigned to him by the bishop. Every year he must present the budget of income and expenditures to the finance committee for approval.

The Council of Priests (cc. 495–501)

In addition to the organs of the diocesan curia, there are four colleges in the diocese which help the bishop by carrying out various tasks. The council of priests is a college of priests which represents the presbyterium of the diocese and constitutes "as it were, the bishop's senate," assisting him in pastoral government. It must have its own statutes, approved by the bishop, that determine the way its members are designated and its mode of procedure.

About half of its members are elected by the priests who carry out an office in the diocese, whether they are diocesan, secular or religious; others are members in virtue of the office that is entrusted to them (for example, the vicars, the rector of the seminary, etc.); others, finally, are freely designated by the diocesan bishop.

It belongs to the bishop to convoke it, to preside over it, to dissolve it, to determine the questions to be examined by it or to accept those which are proposed. In every case the council has only a consultative vote and cannot act without the diocesan bishop. However, he must listen to it in the most important questions in the diocese, and he must obtain their consent in cases expressly indicated by law.

The College of Consultors (c. 502)

Among the members of the council of priests the diocesan bishop selects some—not less than six but not more than 12—who form the college of consultors. Whereas the council of priests meets a few times each year, this college is called to advise the bishop in a more continuous way. The law establishes the cases in which the bishop must ask its opinion and those in which he must obtain its consent (such as, for example, all acts of extraordinary administration of goods, cc. 1277, 1292).

When the see is vacant the college of consultors is not dissolved; on the contrary, it belongs to it to elect the diocesan administrator who governs the diocese until the nomination of a new diocesan bishop. The administrator has a reduced power, and for this reason he needs the consent of the college of consultors for acts of major importance. The conference of bishops can determine that the functions of this college are to be carried out by the cathedral chapter.

The Chapter of Canons (cc. 503–510)

The chapter of canons carries out the most solemn liturgical functions in the cathedral and the other tasks which law or the bishop entrust to them. It is a very ancient institution which first performed the roles which are now carried out by the two previously mentioned colleges (the council of priests and the college of consultors). It has a certain autonomy, even patrimonial, defined in the statutes that must be approved by the bishop. Today it belongs to the bishop to confer the canonry upon priests who have exercised their ministry in a praiseworthy manner. If the president is elected by the canons, he must then obtain the confirmation of the bishop.

One of the canons is the penitentiary who has the faculty of absolving in the sacramental forum from *latæ sententiæ* censures: that is, from those in which one falls automatically once the offence has been committed (cf. Chapter XI).

The Pastoral Council (cc. 511–514)

If he deems it opportune, the diocesan bishop can establish a pastoral council "whose responsibility it is to investigate under the authority of the bishop all those things which pertain to pastoral works, to ponder them and to propose practical conclusions about them" (c. 511). It is composed of faithful of every type, above all laity, who are in full communion with the Church and are distinguished by "proven faith, good morals and outstanding prudence," chosen in a manner determined by the bishop, so that they are like a reflection of the entire diocese.

This council has only a consultative role, which it carries out according to the statutes given by the bishop. It is his responsibility to establish it, convene it, preside over it and publish its conclusions. When the see is vacant, this council ceases to exist.

C) The Parish (cc. 515–552)

As stated above, every particular Church must be divided into parishes. The parish is a community of the faithful constituted in a stable way within the particular Church; its pastoral care is entrusted, under the authority of the diocesan bishop, to a pastor (parish priest) who is its proper shepherd (c. 515 § 1). The parish constitutes the typical and immediate pastoral unity of ecclesiastical organization, in which the faithful normally receive and practice their Christian life. Thus the efficacy and vitality of the parish is of great importance for the entire Church. The parish is a community, open to all and where all are called to collaborate in a concrete way, according to their own vocation and possibilities, in communion with the diocese and with the universal Church.[74]

74. See JOHN PAUL II, *Address* of Oct. 21, 1984 to the Congr. of the Clergy.

The diocesan bishop erects, suppresses, or modifies parishes, after having heard the opinion of the council of priests. Normally the territory determines the parish, but there can be personal parishes determined by rite, language, nationality, etc., of the faithful of whom it is composed. Once it has been established, the parish has a juridical personality by law, and its representative is the pastor. Every parish has its parish church to which the other churches of the territory belong (rectories, churches of religious, etc.).

The pastor, as proper shepherd of the parish community, exercises in it under the authority of the bishop the functions of teaching, sanctifying and governing, together with the help of other priests, deacons, religious or members of the laity. It normally belongs to the diocesan bishop, having determined the suitability of the candidate, to freely appoint the pastors, generally for a fixed period of six years, renewable for other terms. The pastor lapses in his office by reason of the causes established by law. When he turns 75, he is invited to present his resignation.

Normally the pastor is a priest to whom only one parish is entrusted, but in certain circumstances it can happen that he is simultaneously pastor of more than one parish, or that one or more parishes are entrusted to a team of priests (secular or religious). However, in this case, one of them directs the entire pastoral activity as moderator and is responsible before the bishop.

Likewise, if because of scarcity of priests some parish activities must be entrusted to persons who are not priests (deacons, religious communities, etc.), the bishop must name a priest who directs the pastoral care with the power of pastor, exercising those functions which necessarily require priestly character.

As shepherd, the pastor is to ensure above all that the faithful participate abundantly in the means of salvation: the Word of God and the sacraments, prayer and works of charity. Personally and with the help of other priests and members of the laity, he is to promote preaching and catechesis, the liturgical life and prayer, the associations of the faithful, spiritual and material assistance to the sick and suffering, and various forms of apostolate.[75]

Concretely, the law entrusts to him certain *parish functions* which others may not exercise without his authorization: baptisms, assistance at marriages, attention to the dying, funerals, the more solemn celebration of the Eucharist on Sundays and holy days of obligation (which he must offer for the parish community), etc. In addition, he must take adequate care of all the administrative and material aspects of the parish: places and objects of worship, parochial registers, archives, publications, administration of goods, cultural patrimony.[76]

In order to do all of this, the pastor must regularly reside in his own parish and not be absent without informing the local Ordinary so that a substitute can be provided. In addition, he can be helped by one or more *parochial vicars*: priests who cooperate with him under his guidance in the pastoral work, whether in general or in part (taking care, for example, of a zone of the parish or a particular group of faithful, or of a specific ministry or activity).

Regarding financial affairs, there is a *parochial finance committee*, with at least two advisors, and governed by the norms given by the bishop. This committee, in addition to studying the problems and proposing solutions, can help the pastor in a direct way in the administration of goods, realizing certain functions on his mandate, although it is always the pastor who represents the parish.

If the diocesan bishop judges fit, a *pastoral council* is also to be established in the parish. Under the presidency of the

---

75. E. A. SWEENY, *The Obligations and Rights of the Pastor of a Parish*, St. Paul, New York, 2002.

76. In administrative matters it is of great importance to know the State laws regarding ecclesiastical entities.

pastor, this council includes the other clerics who participate in the pastoral work, and other members of the faithful. Its aim is to promote various initiatives and to organize the parochial activities. This council is governed by the norms given by the bishop and has a consultative vote only.

The faithful fulfill their apostolic responsibility with their life of piety and apostolate, collaborating in the activities and in the apostolate of the parish, or participating when they are called in the parochial council. In this way they can at times offer an irreplaceable contribution to the life of the community, enabling the parish to reach all those who live there by means of an efficacious irradiation of Christian life.

D) Vicars Forane (cc. 553–555)

Various neighboring parishes are grouped together in larger districts called a vicariate forane. A vicar forane, also called a dean or archpriest, is placed over it, nominated by the diocesan bishop. His role is above all to coordinate the pastoral activity, making sure that the clerics of the vicariate fulfill their duties and conduct themselves in a dignified way, receiving the necessary spiritual and material help, and watching over the decorum of the liturgy and the proper order of ecclesiastical administration. In order to do this he will have to regularly visit the parishes of the district in the way determined by the bishop.

E) Rectors of Churches (cc. 556–563)

The parochial church is the center of the liturgical and pastoral life of the community, but frequently there are other churches in the territory of the parish which can contribute greatly in enabling the faithful to make use of the means of salvation with more ease and variety. These churches, that are open to public but are not parochial, and which do not have their own chapter of canons (capitular), are called rectorates.

They are entrusted to a rector, usually appointed by the diocesan bishop. If the church belongs to a clerical religious institute of pontifical right, the rector is presented by the superior and appointed by the bishop. The rector is responsible for the liturgy and pastoral care of his church, to be carried out in coordination with that of the parish. For this reason the rector cannot perform the *parochial functions* which, as we have seen, the law entrusts specifically to the pastor (baptisms, marriages, funerals, etc.), except by mandate of the local Ordinary or with the permission or delegation of the pastor.

F) Chaplains (cc. 564–572)

There are communities of the faithful which for various reasons need a specific pastoral attention in addition to what is normally offered to all in the parish: schools, immigrants, religious communities, army barracks, associations, boats, prisons, hospitals...

The priest to whom the pastoral care of one of these communities is entrusted is the *chaplain*. He is normally nominated by the local Ordinary either freely or after presentation or election of those who have the right to it, unless this nomination is attributed to others by law or by the regulations which govern the community itself (as, for example, for some communities of nuns, or for the military).

The chaplain, even if he is not the pastor, must have all the faculties necessary for his office. Concretely, c. 566 directly gives him the faculties of preaching and hearing the confessions of the faithful entrusted to him and, in danger of death, of administering to them the sacrament of confirmation, anointing of the sick, and Viaticum. Also by law the chaplain has the faculty of absolving from censures *latæ sententiæ*. Furthermore, he will have the faculties that are given to him by particular law or by special delegation. If the community has its own church, the chaplain, if possible, will also be its rector.

Military chaplains, as mentioned before, belong to a specific structure of a personal character which is the military ordinariate headed by a bishop. In practice, with regard to military personnel, they have the same responsibilities and faculties as pastors.

7. Organisms Above the Diocesan Level

What has just been said does not mean that the various dioceses of one territory (or their bishops) do not maintain relations among themselves for the purpose of coordinating their pastoral care and collaborating with one another. In fact, there exist structures and organisms above the diocesan level, but in the Latin Church these do not establish a hierarchical dependence between the dioceses nor do they constitute a particular Church above the particular Churches.

A) The Ecclesiastical Province

The ecclesiastical province is a circumscription that unites various neighboring dioceses for the purpose of promoting a common pastoral action. As a rule, all dioceses should belong to a province. They are constituted by the supreme authority of the Church (c. 431) and have juridical personality by the very fact of being constituted (c. 432 § 2).

The organs of government of the province are the provincial council and the metropolitan (c. 432 § 1). The assembly of the bishops of a province also exercises a certain competence in it (cc. 952 § 1 and 1264).

In every province there is an archdiocese with an archbishop who is the metropolitan of the province (c. 435); the other dioceses are called suffragans. The metropolitan does not have functions of direct government in the dioceses of the province, but he must watch over them and inform the Roman Pontiff concerning any abuses that are introduced. He intervenes also in the nomination of the diocesan administrator when a diocese is vacant. In certain cases, other functions can be conferred on the metropolitan by the Holy See (c. 436).

B) The Ecclesiastical Region

If the circumstances dictate, there can also be ecclesiastical regions which group together various neighboring provinces, constituted by the Apostolic See at the proposal of the conference of bishops. The region does not have juridical personality by law, but it can be erected as a person by the Apostolic See (c. 433).

The regional assembly of bishops facilitates a common pastoral action, but it does not have any juridical competencies except those which are conceded in a special way by the Holy See (c. 434).[77]

C) Particular Councils

Particular councils are those which gather the bishops of a given territory. If the territory is that of a conference of bishops, it is called *plenary* (c. 439); if it is that of a province, it is called *provincial* (c. 440).

The plenary council is organized by the conference of bishops with the previous approval of the Apostolic See (c. 441); the provincial council is organized and presided over by the metropolitan (c. 442).

In every council, all the bishops who exercise an office in the territory have a right to participate with a deliberative vote (c. 443 § 1). Other bishops who are found there can also be called, and in this case they also have a deliberative vote (c. 443 § 2).

Diocesan vicars, some superiors of institutes of consecrated life and societies of apostolic life, rectors and deans of universities and seminaries, etc. (c. 443 § 3) are to be called to participate but with a consultative vote only. Other priests and faithful can also be called to participate with a consultative vote (c. 443 § 4). Other persons can be invited as guests (c. 443 § 6).

---

77. This is the case in Italy, where the regional conferences exercise certain competencies that have been attributed to them.

A person who is called to a council is bound to participate if he does not have a legitimate impediment, of which he must inform the president. In this case, those who are absent can be represented by a proxy who, however, only has a consultative vote (c. 444).

The particular council has the general power of government over its territory. Therefore, it can legislate, within the universal law, on all matters that concern the life of the Church (doctrine, discipline, liturgy, catechesis, etc.).

The deliberations of a particular council cannot be promulgated until all the acts are reviewed by the Holy See, after which it belongs to the council to promulgate them (c. 446).

D) The Conferences of Bishops

In contrast with councils, which are sporadic assemblies, the conference of bishops is a permanent organism which gathers together the bishops of an entire nation or territory, for the purpose of exercising together some pastoral functions and promoting a coordinated pastoral action in the service of the Churches entrusted to them (cc. 447 and 448). Born in the 19th century, the conferences have received a great impulse from the Second Vatican Council, which asked that they be constituted in those places where they did not yet exist, and that under certain conditions they could make binding decisions (*CD* 37, 38).

Their relatively recent existence explains some ambiguities that have arisen regarding this concept (relation to Episcopal collegiality, episcopal foundation or pastoral foundation, competencies, power of Magisterium, etc.) that have required reflection. The M.P. *Apostolos suos* constitutes progress in clarifying them.[78]

78. JOHN PAUL II, M.P. *Apostolos suos* (May 21, 1998) on the Theological and Juridical Nature of Episcopal Conferences, in *Origins* 28 [July 30, 1998] 152–158.

It solely belongs to the Holy See to erect, modify or suppress conferences of bishops which, once they are constituted, have a canonical juridical personality (c. 449). Every conference develops its own statutes which must be reviewed by the Apostolic See (c. 451).

All bishops who exercise a function in the territory, and those who by law are likened to a diocesan bishop, are members of the conference of bishops by law. Pontifical legates and bishops who do not have a function in the territory are not members by law (but they can be, according to the norm of the statutes; c. 450).

With regard to voting, however, only diocesan bishops, those equivalent to them by law, and coadjutor bishops always have a deliberative vote. The other bishops (auxiliary and titular) can have a deliberative or consultative vote, according to what has been prescribed in the statutes. For this reason, only those who have a deliberative vote by law can vote in the drawing up or modification of the statutes (c. 454).

The normative competence of the conferences is not general. They can issue norms only in matters expressly prescribed in universal law, or by special mandate of the Holy See (c. 455 § 1). Decisions on other matters do not bind the individual bishops unless they are made unanimously (c. 455 § 4).[79]

Furthermore, for a normative decision to be binding, at least two thirds of the members of the conference who enjoy a deliberative vote must actually vote, and then it must obtain the *"recognitio"* of the Apostolic See, after which it will be promulgated (c. 455 § 2). These limits on the power of the conference of bishops correspond, among other things, to the

79. F. G. MORRISEY, "Decisions of Episcopal Conferences in Implementing the New Law," *Studia canonica* 20 [1986] 105–122. It must be observed, however, that in certain countries, like Italy and Spain, the concordat with the State can also attribute certain competencies to the conference. This occurs, for example, with regard to the teaching of the Catholic religion in the public schools.

need to safeguard the legitimate autonomy of each bishop in his diocese, and to avoid that the conference substitute for the role of the diocesan bishop, who is answerable in his function to the Roman Pontiff alone. The conference of bishops does not constitute an intermediary level between the particular Churches and the Roman See.

As a permanent institute, the conference of bishops has an internal organization (president, secretary, permanent council, various commissions); however, only the plenary assembly can make important decisions.

There also exist organizations that serve to facilitate relations between the conferences of bishops of the same geographical area (for Latin America, Europe, etc.); they have a different juridical configuration according to the case (c. 459).

Chapter VII.

Consecrated Life

In Chapter V we saw that some members of the faithful (clergy and laity) embrace a specific state of life characterized by a special consecration to God "through the profession of the evangelical counsels by means of vows or other sacred bonds recognized and sanctioned by the Church" (c. 207 § 2).

From the beginnings of the Church, some of the faithful felt themselves called to consecrate their life in a particular way to the service of God and their brethren, giving witness before the community to their separation from the world by means of the profession of the evangelical counsels of chastity, poverty and obedience. In this way there arose the orders of virgins, hermits and widows, to which we already find references in the letters of Saint Paul.

After these individual experiences, followed (first in the East and then in the West) those of common fraternal life, determined by the prescriptions of a rule and submission to a superior. Communities that followed the same rule multiplied, giving rise to the religious orders. The oldest rules, which then inspired others, are those of Saint Basil in the East, and Saint Augustine and Saint Benedict in the West.

As the Second Vatican Council says, "[f]rom the God-given seed of the counsels a wonderful and wide-spreading tree has grown up in the field of the Lord, branching out into various forms of religious life lived in solitude or in community. Different religious families have come into existence in which spiritual resources are multiplied for the progress in holiness of their members and for the good of the entire Body of Christ" (*LG* 43). The Church receives the different forms of consecrated life as a manifestation of the richness of the gifts of the Holy Spirit. The ecclesiastical authority interprets the counsels, regulates their practice, and, on their basis, constitutes stable forms of life, which are the institutes of consecrated life.

From the juridical point of view, the consecrated life[80] is the special state of life assumed by the faithful who profess the evangelical counsels. As stated in the Catechism of the Catholic Church: "It is the *profession* of these counsels, within a permanent state of life recognized by the Church, that characterizes the life consecrated to God" (n. 915). Law has a particular relevance for two related aspects of consecrated life: the *state* of the persons who profess the counsels, and the organization and activity of the *institutes* of consecrated life.

The *state* of consecrated life implies a specific form of living the Christian vocation common to all the faithful, marked by:

- a *special consecration* to God. All the faithful are consecrated and called to sanctity and to the spreading of the Kingdom of God in virtue of baptism, but those who choose the consecrated life totally dedicate themselves to God and to the building up of the Church by a new and special title. This consecration does not make them become more Christian than the others, but it commits them to seek the perfection to which all of us are called, in a stable form and by a concrete path;
- this path is precisely the *profession of the evangelical counsels*. In the Gospel, many counsels are found which can

80. See JOHN PAUL II, Apostolic Exhortation *Vita Consecrata*, in *Origins* 25 [April 4, 1996] 681–719. See V. DE PAOLIS, *La vita consacrata nella Chiesa*, EDB, Bologna, 1992.

be summarized in the beatitudes, proposed by Jesus not to only a few, but to all of his disciples (CCC 915). However, the consecrated life carries with it the *profession*, before the Church, of the three counsels of chastity in celibacy (loving God with an undivided heart), poverty (limitation and dependence on others in the use and disposition of earthly goods), and obedience (submission to the will of the superiors);

- the profession of the counsels implies their being taken on by means of *vows* or *other sacred bonds*, through a personal act of the virtue of religion, by which the person consecrates himself to God and embraces the special state of consecrated life. This profession is received by the Church which recognizes the divine gift of consecrated life, supports and promotes it, establishing the rights and duties of the faithful who freely assume it;

- in the forms recognized by the ecclesiastical authority, consecrated life is thus a *stable form of Christian life* that belongs to the life and sanctity of the Church, expressing in a special way the spousal mystery between Christ and the Church. It reveals "the heavenly goods which are already present in this age," and gives witness to the glorious future, "as a sign which can and should effectively inspire" the members of the Church to "unflaggingly fulfill the duties of their Christian calling" (*LG* 44).

Fruits of the action of the Holy Spirit, there continually appear new and varied forms of consecrated life in the Church. It belongs to the diocesan bishops to discern their evangelical authenticity and to help their founders to define them as well as possible so as to be able to ask the Apostolic See for their approval (c. 605).[81]

---

81. See in this regard A. NERI, *Nuove forme di vita consacrata*, Pontificia Università Lateranense, Rome, 1995.

In the Code, the consecrated life is recognized in different forms, both individual and in community. The *individual* recognized forms are:

- the *eremitic* or anchoritic life "by which the Christian faithful devote their life to the praise of God and the salvation of the world through a stricter separation from the world, the silence of solitude and assiduous prayer and penance." The hermit enters into consecrated life "if he or she publicly professes the three evangelical counsels confirmed by a vow or other sacred bond, in the hands of the diocesan bishop and observes his or her own plan of life under his direction" (c. 603);

- the order of virgins who are consecrated to God by the diocesan bishop to dedicate themselves to the service of the Church. The consecrated virgins live in the world and can freely associate to help one another in their commitment (c. 604; CCC 922–924).

The *associated* forms of consecrated life are those lived by the members of *institutes of consecrated life* canonically erected by the ecclesiastical authority.[82]

1. Institutes of Consecrated Life

There are many institutes of consecrated life in the Church, which reflect the diversity of the gifts of the Spirit, and the different paths that can be taken in the following of Christ. The Code groups them in two different types: *religious institutes*

82. According to the official statistics, on December 31, 2004, there were 137,058 religious priests, 55,030 lay men religious (not priests), 767,459 nuns, and 28,942 members of secular institutes in the Church (SECRETARIA STATUS, *Statistical Yearbook of the Church 2004*, LEV, 2006, p. 101).

and *secular institutes*. They represent the two principal forms of the consecrated life as described above.[83]

The institutes of consecrated life arise as associations of those who feel themselves called to live the consecrated life according to the spirit and the rules determined by a founder and approved by the ecclesiastical authority. In the first place there is the initiative of the founder that is then accepted and recognized by the authority, which canonically erects the institute and approves the rules which define its specific features. There are thus two elements: a) the initiative of faithful, who intend to live the consecrated life in a given way; and b) the intervention of the hierarchy of the Church which evaluates, approves and watches over the charism and the law of each institute. Furthermore, all institutes are subject to the supreme authority of the Church, and their individual members have the Roman Pontiff as their highest superior (c. 590).

The diocesan bishop can, with the permission of the Holy See, erect institutes of consecrated life in his diocese: then the institute is of *diocesan right*, and it depends on the bishop. When an institute is erected by the Holy See, it is of *pontifical right*, and it depends exclusively on the Apostolic See by means of the Congregation for the Institutes of Consecrated Life. Erection means the recognition that the institute represents a legitimate and stable form of living the consecrated life, approving its own norms, and conferring juridical personality on it (normally this occurs in a subsequent moment). Since the consecrated life is a publicly recognized form of Christian life, the institutes enjoy public juridical personality.

83. J. HITE, S. HOLLAND, D. WARD (eds.), *A Handbook on Canons 573–746. Religious Institutes, Secular Institutes, Societies of the Apostolic Life*, The Liturgical Press, Collegeville, 1985; M. A. O'REILLY, "The Proper Law of Institutes of Religious Life and of Societies of Apostolic Life", *Unico Ecclesiæ Servitio*, Saint Paul University, Ottawa, 1991, pp. 289–303.

We have seen that both members of the laity and clerics can embrace the consecrated life. Another classification of institutes of consecrated life distinguishes them precisely between *clerical* and *lay*, according to whether or not their purpose or their activities imply the exercise of holy orders (for example, preaching friars must be priests but not those who dedicate themselves to the sick or to schools). In practice, however, what is important is whether the institute has been recognized by the ecclesiastical authority as lay or clerical. Obviously, all feminine institutes are lay.

Every institute is also governed, in addition to the universal laws of canon law pertaining to the institutes of consecrated life, by its own proper regulations which are called constitutions, rules, regulations, statutes, etc., and which, having been approved by the authority, constitute the *particular law* of the institute. In this particular law, the proper charism of each institute is defined, together with its autonomy of organization and government. Although subject to ecclesiastical authority, especially with regard to some of the most important acts and their external activity, the institutes enjoy ample autonomy in their internal daily life: they have their own hierarchy (superiors, chapters), their own divisions (provinces, houses, monasteries), their own apostolic works, their own patrimony, etc.

The members of an institute are subject to its internal hierarchy in virtue of the evangelical counsel of obedience and according to their own constitutions. Therefore, they are bound to their superiors by a tie of an associative nature different from what exists between the faithful and the ecclesiastical hierarchy. The latter is of a sacramental nature originating from baptism (which determines the subjects of the Church) and from holy orders (which determines the members of the hierarchy).

In this regard, there is a difference between lay and clerical institutes, in so far as the latter, being governed by priests (members of the hierarchy), also have the ecclesiastical power of governance in addition to the power deriving from the tie of association (vow of obedience). In fact, the major superiors of clerical religious institutes of pontifical right are the ordinaries for their subjects (c. 134 § 1).

A) Religious Institutes

The religious life is the most traditional form of consecrated life which arose in the first centuries of the Church, and which has been perpetuated by the religious institutes (religious orders and congregations). Religious life is distinguished from other forms of consecrated life by:

- special dedication to the worship of God and to prayer (Holy Mass, liturgy of the hours, fixed times of prayer in common);
- the profession of counsels by means of perpetual or at least definitive *public vows* (the latter are to be renewed when they have lapsed);
- fraternal common life: the religious must live in a legitimately constituted religious house under the authority of the superior;
- the public witness of the beatitudes by means of a certain separation from the world.

All of these aspects are regulated by the particular law of each institute (c. 607; cf. CCC 925–927).

The government of religious institutes is normally organized on three levels: that of every individual community or religious house, the provincial level, and the general level. The government of each of these levels belongs to a superior with the assistance of a council, whose opinion must be heard, or whose consent obtained in the cases indicated by law. The superiors are normally elected or nominated for a certain time.

The provincial and general superiors (called the supreme moderator of the institute by the CIC) are *major superiors*. In addition, there are religious institutes organized so that every house constitutes an autonomous and independent unit (monasteries). In this case, the superiors of these communities are major superiors. As we have seen, these superiors of clerical religious institutes of pontifical right are the proper ordinaries of their subjects.

Chapters are gatherings of members whose function is to protect, in their own area, the spiritual patrimony proper to each institute, to elect the corresponding superiors, to handle affairs of major importance, and to issue norms. They can be general, provincial, and in certain cases, of the local community.

The institute, its provinces, and its houses, are public juridical persons and have a proper patrimony administered in accordance with the common laws of the Church and with those proper to the institute, which must manifest the spirit of poverty typical to the religious life. Every institute, every province, and, if possible, every house, must have a finance officer distinct from the superior, who carries out the administration of goods under the direction of the superior.

The Religious

Those Catholics can embrace the consecrated life who, freely desiring to correspond to their vocation, have the necessary age and other conditions required by the institute.

Religious life begins with admission to the novitiate by the superiors of the institute, after having ascertained that the candidate possesses the necessary conditions.

The *novitiate* is a period of formation during which the novices confirm their vocation to the institute and experience the institute's way of life, and the superiors test their suitability and rectitude of intention. It is normally accomplished in a house designated for this purpose (generally called the novitiate house) and must last at least one year but not more than two. During this time the novices, under the guidance of a novice master, are introduced to the path and demands of religious life and formed in the spirit and life specific to the institute. Since it is a time of probation, the novice can freely leave the institute and the superiors can also dismiss the novice (cc. 646–653).

Once the novitiate is completed, those who have been judged suitable are admitted, according to the rules of the institute, to religious *profession*. Profession marks the entrance of the faithful into consecrated life. It consists in the assumption of the public vows of poverty, chastity and obedience to be lived according to the universal and particular laws, and which must be received by the legitimate superior. It can be *temporary* (for a given period) or *perpetual*. However, when the time provided for the successive temporary professions has elapsed, the religious must make perpetual profession or leave the institute (cc. 654–658).

The religious life (always inspired by the Gospel) is expressed in various forms according to the charism proper to each institute, but it is always marked by an assiduous application to liturgical life, especially the Holy Mass and the liturgy of the hours, by reading and meditation of Holy Scripture, by personal and community prayer. To this there is adjoined common life and, according to the case, the works proper to the institute.

In every religious house there must be *cloister*, which is a manifestation of the separation from the world typical of the religious life; that is why religious must live in houses exclusively reserved to them from which they cannot absent themselves without permission. Cloister will be more or less rigorous according to the character, purpose and rules of each institute. In monasteries of contemplative life it is always more rigorous, and in those of nuns, the so-called *papal cloister* is observed, namely in conformity with the norms given by the Holy See (cc. 665 and 667).[84]

---

84. Contained in the Instruction of the Congr. for the Institutes of sacred life and the Societies of apostolic life *Verbi Sponsa*, 13.V.1999.

Before profession, the religious must also renounce their own goods in the form and measure determined by the rule, whether giving up the administration of them, or also their use of them altogether or in part; or renouncing their own property and the capacity to acquire. After profession, all what the religious acquires from his work (wages, subsidy, pension) belongs to the institute (c. 668).

Religious must also wear the habit of the institute, the sign of their consecration and a testimony of poverty. For these reasons they must not accept functions or offices outside of the institute without permission from the superior. Likewise, they must observe the dispositions concerning clerics with regard to the preservation of the decorum of their state: they must not involve themselves in secular affairs of an economic, political, or union-related type. They must observe the norms of prudence with regard to chastity and they must be constructors of peace and justice (cc. 669, 671 and 672).

Religious have the right to receive from their own institute what is necessary to realize the finality of their own vocation. This includes the means to conduct a dignified life, the necessary formation and spiritual aid, and the other rights and duties established in particular law (c. 670).

When a religious is nominated bishop, he continues to belong to his institute, but he is under the obedience to the Roman Pontiff only and he is not subject to the obligations that limit his economic capacity and others which he holds incompatible with his condition. This norm has the purpose of guaranteeing the freedom and independence of the bishop in carrying out the office with which he has been entrusted (cc. 705–707).

The *separation* of a religious from his own institute can happen:

- by *transfer* to another religious institute, with the consent of the supreme moderator of each institute and of their councils. It is necessary to have the permission of the Holy See to pass from a secular institute to a society of apostolic life (cc. 684–685);

- by *exclaustration* or temporary departure which can be conceded or even imposed for a grave reason. It carries with it the suspension of certain rights and duties but not the loss of state, so that the religious continues to remain dependent on and under the care of his superiors and also of the local Ordinary (cc. 686–687);

- by *expiration* of temporary profession if he decides to abandon the institute or if the institute does not admit him to a subsequent profession for just and grave reasons (cc. 688–690);

- by *indult* to leave the institute definitively, requested by the interested party and conceded by the Holy See (if the institute is of pontifical right) or by the diocesan bishop (if it is of diocesan right; cc. 691–693);

- by *dismissal* in consequence of certain offences or other grave acts committed by the religious. Dismissal is automatic when he has notoriously abandoned the faith or has contracted or attempted to contract marriage. Otherwise, the religious is dismissed only after a trial in which he can defend himself against the accusations. If the religious has not been accused of an offence, after a warning, he can amend his behavior. If the process is concluded with the decree of dismissal, it must express the motives and then be confirmed by the Holy See or by the diocesan bishop, and the person expelled has the right to recourse against the decree.

Both an indult of definitive departure and dismissal carry with them the dispensation from vows and from all obligations and rights deriving from profession. However, if the religious is a cleric, he continues to be one and must find a bishop who wishes to accept him in his diocese (cc. 694–704).

B) Secular Institutes

Secular institutes are institutes that propose to live the consecrated life in the world. Their members are consecrated to God without abandoning secular affairs. Rather, they seek the sanctification of earthly realities operating from within as leaven (CCC 928–929). They do not assume the religious state, but remain in their lay or clerical condition (cc. 710–711).

The members of secular institutes profess the evangelical counsels of chastity in celibacy, poverty and obedience, assuming them by means of vows or other sacred bonds (promises, oaths) in the way defined in each institute. These ties are not public even if they are recognized by the Church (c. 712).

In contrast to religious institutes, common life is not proper to secular institutes, because their members live "according to the norm of the constitutions, in the ordinary conditions of the world, either alone or each in their respective families, or in a group of brothers or sisters" (c. 714). However, the members are united among themselves by a spirit of true fraternity and participate in the life of the institute (c. 716).

They give witness to their consecration in the world by means of fidelity to their commitments, the coherence of their lives in the midst of earthly realities which they seek to animate with the force of the Gospel and also with their collaboration in the service of the ecclesial community, always "according to their particular secular way of life" (c. 713). If they are clerics, they give witness with the work of their ministry, whether in the diocese or in their own institute.

The clerics of secular institutes can be incardinated in the diocese (and then they depend on the diocesan bishop like the other clerics of the diocese), or in the institute itself to dedicate themselves to its government or its specific apostolate (c. 715).

The organization and government of secular institutes must be defined in their own constitutions within the general framework of the institutes of consecrated life and what is specific to secular institutes. Likewise, for what concerns temporal goods and economic relations between the institute and the members, the constitutions will express their own way of living poverty, both individual and communal.

With regard to the incorporation of a member of the faithful to a secular institute there is also a *period of probation* (not of novitiate). After this is completed, one may proceed to the *first incorporation* assuming the three counsels with a temporary sacred bond. After at least five years, one can be admitted to *definitive incorporation* by means of perpetual bonds (or temporary bonds, to be renewed perpetually). *Separation* from the institute occurs in ways similar to those for the religious.

2. Societies of Apostolic Life (cc. 731–746)

Societies of apostolic life are institutes *comparable* to those of consecrated life. Their members, without religious vows, conduct a fraternal life of community and dedicate themselves to an apostolic purpose proper to the society. In some of these societies the members also assume the evangelical counsels with some type of bond defined in the constitutions (CCC 930).

Although they are not institutes of consecrated life in themselves, the dispositions regarding such institutes apply to them (with regard to canonical erection, types of society, their autonomy, etc.), adapted to the nature and characteristics of each of them. Particular importance is held by the societies of clerics who have a missionary apostolate as their purpose.

Chapter VIII.

The Means of Salvation. The Word of God

The Church received from Jesus Christ the mission of evangelizing all peoples, offering to men the salvation wrought by Christ with his life, his word and his grace. Evangelizing means accomplishing the mandate that Jesus himself gave to the Apostles: "Go therefore and make disciples of all nations, baptizing them [...], teaching them to observe all that I have commanded you; and lo, I am with you always, to the close of the age" (Mt 28, 19–20).

The means of salvation are principally the Word of God and the sacraments, through which Christ, sent by the Father through the Holy Spirit, is present in His Church. Through the Church, He makes Himself present in the life of each man and of society. For this reason it is said that the Church herself is a sacrament, because she is the sign and efficacious instrument of the salvation worked by God.

The Word and the sacraments can be distinguished but not separated because each one requires the other. The Word of God prepares for the sacrament and the celebration of the sacrament includes the Word. Evangelization does not only consist in showing men the way that leads to heaven, but also in giving them grace, which is the power by which they can travel along the way until the end. Therefore, the way, the truth and the life are one thing in Christ, and likewise they are one in His Church.

Nevertheless, just as it is said of Christ that He is priest, prophet and king, likewise in the Church one can distinguish these three ministries or functions (*tria munera*) of sanctifying, teaching, and governing, that the Church has received from her Founder, and of which all the faithful are made participants.

1. The Teaching Function

The Church has the mission of teaching the Catholic faith. It is a doctrine that is not her own, but which she has received in trust from Christ the Lord, and which, with the assistance of the Holy Spirit, the Church safeguards, examines more deeply, and faithfully teaches.[85]

Preaching the Gospel to all peoples is a duty and a right proper to the Church, which she realizes with independence from any human power, and without need for any authorization or permission.

This teaching refers to the revealed truth, and to the moral principles that derive from it regarding human behavior, on the personal and social levels. It follows that the Church can give a moral judgment on any human reality, declaring it to be in conformity or not with the Gospel (c. 747).

There are various juridical consequences of the fact that God has entrusted His word to His Church. The most important is that the Church herself is founded and structured by the Word of God, from which she attains the truth about herself. On the other hand, conserving and transmitting the divine Word implies specific rights and duties for each of the faithful according to their condition and situation in the Church.

---

85. On this aspect of the mission of the Church, see C. J. ERRÁZURIZ, *Il "munus docendi Ecclesiae": diritti e doveri dei fedeli,* Giuffrè, Milan, 1991; GRUPPO ITALIANO DOCENTI DI DIRITTO CANONICO, "La funzione di insegnare della Chiesa," in *Quaderni della Mendola* 1, Glossa, Milan, 1994.

Since God "wills all men to be saved and to arrive to the knowledge of the truth" (1 Tim 2, 4), they have the duty before the Lord to seek it and, once it has been found, to observe it. This truth can only be found in its entirety and without error in the Catholic Church. However, since "truth can impose itself on the mind of man only in virtue of its own truth" (*DH* 1), all have the right not to be forced to embrace the faith against their own conscience, and it is never lawful to force others to embrace the faith against their conscience (c. 748).

In this context of religious liberty, the Church accomplishes its function of preaching Jesus Christ and His Gospel, a living and efficacious word destined, by the grace of God, to touch the life of those who hear it. Therefore, the function of teaching is never a simple communication of ideas or of information.

A) The Ecclesiastical Magisterium of the Church

The Magisterium is the office of interpreting and expounding the Word of God authentically, which means with the authority and in the name of Jesus Christ. This ministry was entrusted by Jesus to the Apostles, who transmitted it to their successors: the Roman Pontiff and the bishops in communion with him (cf. *DV* 10, CCC 85 and 100).

The function of the Magisterium is exercised by the Pastors with different degrees of authority and in different ways.

According to its *authority*, the Magisterium is:

- *authentic* when it is exercised in virtue of one's proper office in the Church. It is *private* when it is exercised as a private doctor, and then it does not constitute ecclesiastical Magisterium;
- authentic Magisterium is *infallible* when, by a special assistance of the Holy Spirit, it cannot err in the teaching of a doctrine concerning faith or morals. The infallible Magisterium is exercised by the Pope in the first place when, in the exercise of his primacy, he proclaims by means of a definitive act that a doctrine

is to be held as infallibly defined (c. 749 § 1). The college of bishops is also the subject of infallible Magisterium when it acts either in a solemn mode (gathered in an ecumenical council) or in an ordinary mode (the bishops dispersed through out the world in communion among themselves and with the head of the college), declaring and teaching that a doctrine must be held as definitive;

- no doctrine is understood to be infallibly defined unless it is clearly seen to be such (c. 749 § 2–3);
- the Magisterium that is simply *authentic* is the doctrine concerning faith and morals that is taught in the whole Church by the Pope and the college of bishops, when they do not intend to declare it in a definitive way. Also *authentic* is the particular Magisterium of the bishops in communion with the Roman Pontiff, both as individuals or gathered in the conferences of bishops or in particular councils.

The M.P. *Apostolos suos* has specified the power of Magisterium of the conference of bishops, and states that a doctrinal declaration of the conference "may constitute authentic Magisterium and be published in the name of the Conference itself," when "unanimously approved by the Bishops who are members, or receive the *recognitio* of the Apostolic See if approved in plenary assembly by at least two thirds of the Bishops belonging to the Conference and have a deliberative vote."[86]

According to its *modality*, the Magisterium is:

- *solemn* when a teaching is expressed in a solemn way or with solemn formulas. This is the case of the teaching of ecumenical councils and that of the Roman Pontiff when he teaches *ex cathedra*;

86. JOHN PAUL II, M.P. *Apostolos suos* (May 21, 1998): *AAS* [1998] 641–658, nn. 21 ff. and Complementary Norms, art. 1.

- it is *ordinary* when it is exercised through ordinary means of expression (encyclicals, pastoral letters, etc.).

According to its *extension*, the Magisterium is:

- *universal* if it is a teaching that is proposed to the entire Church by the Roman Pontiff or by the college of bishops;
- it is *particular* if it is proposed to a part of the faithful (nation, diocese, parish) by their Pastors.

Obligations Concerning Catholic Doctrine

The faithful are bound by the authentic Magisterium. By means of their adherence to the teachings of the Pastors, the Christian people give witness to the infallibility of the Church since "the whole body of the faithful [...] cannot err in matters of belief [...], when, 'from the bishops to the last of the faithful' they manifest a universal consent in matters of faith and morals" (*LG* 12).

Adherence to the teachings of the Magisterium of the Church means accepting the doctrine proposed by it and rejecting all what has been rejected or condemned by it.

All the truths which make up Catholic doctrine require the adherence of the faithful. However, the adherence that is required differs according to the authority, solemnity, definitiveness, and infallibility with which the Magisterium of the Church teaches a given doctrine, and according to whether it is contained in or connected to the deposit of Revelation.AQUI

Accordingly, Catholic doctrine is composed of truths of different orders which call for a different degree of adherence. We shall see them briefly.[87]

---

87. The M.P. *Ad tuendam fidem* of May 18, 1998, has introduced modifications in this regard in cc. 750 and 1371 (likewise in cc. 598 and 1436 of the CCEO). There are also important clarifications contained in the CONGR. FOR THE DOCTRINE OF THE FAITH, Doctrinal Note *Inde ab ipsis primordiis* concerning the concluding formula of the *Professio fidei*, June 29, 1998. Both documents in *AAS* [1998] 457–461 and 542–551; English translation: *Origins* 28 [July 16, 1998] 113–119; and in CCLA, under c. 833, pp. 645-650.

a) One must give an *assent of theological faith* to all the truths contained in the Word of God (written or handed down) and which are taught as divinely revealed truths by the universal Magisterium of the Church, whether in a solemn or ordinary mode. This includes all the doctrines that the infallible Magisterium of the Church holds to belong to the deposit of the faith (c. 750 § 1).

The faithful must avoid any doctrine contrary to the revealed truth. Obstinately denying, contradicting or doubting any of these truths of faith constitutes *heresy*, whereas the entire repudiation of them is *apostasy*. *Schism*, on the other hand, is the refusal of submission to the Supreme Pontiff or of communion with the members of the Church who are subject to him (c. 751). These sins against the faith and against ecclesiastical communion, if exteriorly manifested (for example, in the mass media), are also offences which automatically incur excommunication (c. 1364).

b) One must also accept and hold in a full and irrevocable way all the truths concerning faith and morals which the Magisterium proposes definitively for belief. Although they have not been set forth as belonging to the deposit of Revelation, these doctrines have been definitively established and are *connected to the revealed truths in such a way* that they are necessary for the holy keeping and faithful exposition of revealed truth (c. 750 § 2).

A person who rejects any of these truths taught in a definitive way by the Magisterium sets himself against the teaching of the Church. If this rejection is external and obstinate, the offence treated in c. 1371, 1° is incurred.

c) A *religious respect* of intellect and will is to be paid to the doctrines taught by the Supreme Pontiff and by the college of bishops when they exercise an authentic Magisterium, even if they do not intend to propose them as definitive (c. 752).

Anyone who rejects a doctrine proposed in this way sets himself against the authority of the Church, and at the very least puts himself rashly into danger of falling into error. Thus the offence of c. 1371, 1° can also be incurred.

Within their particular area, the faithful must also accept with religious respect the authentic Magisterium of the bishops in communion with the Roman Pontiff and with the other members of the college, both as individuals or united in conferences of bishops or particular councils (c. 753).

Finally, all the faithful must observe the constitutions and decrees of the ecclesiastical authority, especially if issued by the Pope or college of bishops, which expound doctrine or condemn errors (c. 754).

It should also be added that the teaching of the Church is directed not only to the faithful, but also to all men so that all can know with certainty the truths about God and His Church, as well as the moral principles that arise from the very nature of man and society and are thus valid for all.

On certain occasions, the faithful must explicitly manifest their adherence to Catholic doctrine. This can happen when the law requires them to emit a profession of faith, normally when acceding to an office, position, or function. These cases, among others, are listed in c. 833: the participants in a council or synod, those promoted to the cardinalate, episcopate or diaconate, the teachers of ecclesiastical sciences, pastors, superiors of institutes of consecrated life, parish priests, rectors, or professors of an ecclesiastical or Catholic university, etc.

In these cases the *professio fidei* must be made publicly before the authority indicated and according to the formula approved by the Apostolic See. It contains the Creed and three propositions in which the three types of truth that have been examined above are distinctly accepted.

B) Ecumenism

The "ecumenical movement" refers to the activities and initiatives undertaken for the purpose of re-establishing the unity of

Christians, such as encounters of dialogue or prayer, collaboration, etc., with the other Christian communities (*UR* 4).

All the faithful must cooperate for this purpose according to their possibilities. However, promoting, channeling, and directing concrete initiatives belong "to the entire college of bishops and to the Apostolic See" in the first place and, in accordance with what they have established, to individual bishops and conferences of bishops (c. 755) as well.

C) The Ministry of the Divine Word

Preaching the Gospel is the task of the entire Church: "On all Christians, accordingly, rests the noble obligation of working to bring all men throughout the whole world to hear and accept the divine message of salvation" (*AA* 3). In this common responsibility every member of the faithful participates in the manner and with the authority and responsibility—public or private—that corresponds to his situation in the Church.

The *public* ministry of the word falls in the first place on Pastors, who have the responsibility to expound the message of salvation in its entirety and with authority to the people entrusted to them and to all men. The Roman Pontiff and the college of bishops accomplish this with regard to the universal Church. The individual bishops do so in the particular Church entrusted to them (c. 386 § 1). Their collaborators are the priests, especially the parish priests (c. 528 § 1), and the others who have care of souls, and deacons (cc. 756–757).

With the support of the teaching of the Pastors, the other members of the faithful can accomplish the part that belongs to them in the ministry of the word. The consecrated faithful, in virtue of their consecration, make a special testimony to the Gospel which is also expressed by their particular charism. They can be called by the bishop to help in preaching the Gospel (c. 758).

The laity, in virtue of baptism and confirmation, also have the right and the duty to spread the Christian truth by word and example. Above all it belongs to them to make sure that the Gospel message reaches all sectors of life so that temporal realities are illuminated with the light of the Gospel and ordered according to the will of God (c. 759). As the Second Vatican Council exhorts, "[l]et the laity, therefore, diligently apply themselves to a more profound knowledge of revealed truth and earnestly beg of God the gift of wisdom" (*LG* 35).

The means used in the ministry of the word can be quite various. Special importance goes to preaching and catechism, traditionally used means in the Church and specifically regulated by canon law. However, canon law is also concerned with schools and other instruments of social communication, which the Church has the right to possess and to use.

Preaching (cc. 762–772)

Preaching is the authoritative presentation of doctrine to gatherings of the people. Already in the first origins of the Church we find the disciples and others united to listen to the preaching of Saint Peter and the other Apostles on whom the Holy Spirit had descended on the day of Pentecost, filling them with His gifts. In this way there was manifested the divine efficacy of the word, which was received by the listeners not as the word of men, but as what it really is: the Word of God.

This is renewed in the Church when gathered to hear the word of salvation by the sacred ministers who have the duty of proclaiming the Gospel to all. Preaching is a typical function of clerics (c. 762).

The realization of this ministry is regulated by the law. We can distinguish: a) those who *can* preach, and in which conditions; and b) those who *must* preach or organize its realization.

a) All *bishops* have the right to preach everywhere, unless the local bishop has expressly forbidden it in particular cases (c. 763).

Priests and *deacons* have the faculty, but not the right, to preach anywhere. To exercise this faculty they must have the consent of the one who has jurisdiction over the place in which they intend to preach. In addition, this same faculty can be limited or taken away by their own Ordinary or by law. For example, one must have the permission of their superior to preach to religious in their churches or oratories (c. 764–765).

The *laity* can be admitted to preach in concrete cases of necessity or of special utility, according to the prescriptions of the conference of bishops.[88] In these cases, they perform a role of substitution, not a function proper to the laity but collaborate with the hierarchical ministry. The homily, however, since it is a liturgical form of preaching, is reserved to clerics, and can never be given by a member of the laity (c. 766).

b) Pastors (those clerics who have a care of souls: diocesan bishop, parish priest, chaplain, etc.) *must* preach to the people entrusted to them. It also belongs to them to organize the preaching in their area of responsibility, so that all, including those far from the Church, receive the proclamation of the Word in a way adapted to their conditions of life. For this purpose, the diocesan bishop can give norms in his diocese.

The homily, as part of the liturgy, is a pre-eminent form of preaching. It represents a privileged occasion of expounding the Word of God to the people in a complete and systematic way during the course of the liturgical year. For this reason the law commands that a homily be given on Sundays and holy days of obligation, and it recommends that it be given also on other days, especially if there is a particular occasion (a special feast day, Advent, Lent, etc.: c. 767 § 2 and 3).

Other forms of preaching, such as spiritual exercises, retreats, missions, are to be organized according to necessity or usefulness.

---

88. See, for example, Decree number 6 of the CCCB (Official document n. 533): *Studia canonica* 19 [1985] 174–177; and in CCLA, Appendix III, pp. 1661-1662.

With regard to the content, preaching must explain to the faithful what one must believe and do for the glory of God and for the salvation of man, including the teaching of the Magisterium of the Church on the human person, the family, civil society, and social justice.

Catechesis

Catechesis is the systematic teaching of Christian doctrine and life, in order "to develop in men a living, explicit and active faith" (*CD* 14; c. 773). Catechesis of Christian initiation and all catechesis which precedes reception of the sacraments are especially important in the Church. However, the entire life of the faithful should be accompanied by catechesis.

All of the faithful must take an active part in catechesis, each according to his role in the Church and under the guidance of the legitimate authority.

Parents have first of all the right and duty of providing for the Christian education of their children (c. 226 § 2), by means of *catechesis in the family* through word and example, but also through the help of others (school, parish, etc.). This right and duty form a part of the more general right and duty to educate one's children, which belongs to the natural order.[89]

In the diocese, it is the responsibility of the bishop to order catechesis with the appropriate norms regarding both the contents and mode of presentation, as well as the instruments to be used (c. 775 § 1).

The pastor, following the directions of the bishop, must organize the catechetical formation of various groups (children, young people, adults, the handicapped, etc.), as well as preparation for the sacraments. In performing this work, he can ask for the help of members of institutes of consecrated life and of the laity, who are invited to give their contribution according to their condition and possibilities (c. 776).

89. F. G. MORRISEY, "The Rights of Parents in the Education of their Children (Canons 796–806)," *Studia canonica* 23 [1989] 429–444.

The function of catechist is a way to cooperate in the ministry of the Word that is proper to the laity. For this purpose, the faithful must acquire the necessary preparation and exercise it in union with the pastors.

There can be many instruments of catechesis. The catechisms which the Church has always used for teaching the faith have a particular importance and traditional value. They provide an ordered and complete synthesis of Christian doctrine which expounds the truths of the Creed, the commandments, the sacraments and the Our Father (prayer).

It belongs to the Holy See to give prescriptions on catechisms and to publish a catechism for the universal Church, which has been done in the *Catechism of the Catholic Church* (1992); a *Compendium* of it has also been published (2005). The conferences of bishops can put out national catechisms with the approval of the Apostolic See, and also prepare catechetical aids for the dioceses. The diocesan bishop can also publish or adopt a catechism for his diocese.

Besides official catechisms, others can also be prepared privately, which must be approved by the local Ordinary (c. 827 § 1).

Missions

The Church, in order to proclaim the Gospel to all peoples, sends missionaries in regions or groups where the Word of God is not yet known or where the Church has not yet taken root.

All the members of the Church are responsible, according to the vocation and condition of each, for missionary activity tending towards the birth of particular Churches, as well as for helping young Churches to grow until they can rely on their own forces and proper means.

The supreme direction and organization of missionary activity belongs to the Roman Pontiff and to the college of bishops. For this purpose, the Pope principally uses the Congr. for the Evangelization of Peoples (*de propaganda Fide*) (c. 782 § 1).

The organization of new mission Churches has certain features of greater dependence on and help from the Holy See, which mark the steps by a which a nascent Church becomes a fully formed particular Church. They are usually started by erecting a *sui iuris* mission or an Apostolic Vicariate while they promote local vocations; then they are erected as a diocese. Once they have matured and are no longer missionary Churches, they pass to dependence on the Congr. for Bishops or on that of Eastern Churches.

At the diocesan level, it is the responsibility of the bishop to promote, foster and sustain missionary initiatives in his diocese, also as a manifestation of the solicitude for all the Churches which falls in a special way on every member of the episcopal college. The diocesan bishop must therefore promote missionary vocations, as well as prayer and material contributions of the faithful for the missions (c. 782 § 2).

Missionary help to the new Churches is accomplished by means of the sending of *missionaries*. These are members of the faithful of any condition (clerics, consecrated, and lay) who manifest their willingness and are sent by the ecclesiastical authority to accomplish apostolic missionary activity (c. 784). Some institutes of consecrated life and societies of apostolic life have the missions as their specific purpose. Some dioceses also send part of their clergy, and there are associations and movements of the faithful who also prepare missionaries so that they can be sent, at least temporarily, in missionary territories.

Nevertheless, it should be remembered that today, because of the strong de-Christianization that they have undergone, not a few traditionally Catholic territories need a new evangelization, because the missionary effort of the faithful is required in the area where they live.

It belongs to the local bishop to guide missionary activity in missionary territories, also by means of norms obligatory for all, and by means of the corresponding agreements with the institutes dedicated to the missions, so as to clearly establish their relationships and modes of collaboration (c. 790).

D) Catholic Education

Educating is to transmit knowledge and criteria of reasoning and behavior in a manner appropriate to the nature of the person, who is a rational, free, social and transcendent being, called to develop and use his own gifts in the quest for his own happiness and that of others. In this perspective, education is always formation and never mere information.

Catholic education is what proposes a Christian view of reality, integrating the revealed truths and the moral demands which they carry with them into the knowledge that is transmitted. This specific education can be accomplished in many different ways while respecting the essential contents of the faith.

The law of the Church is concerned with Catholic education under various aspects. In the first place, it is concerned with the question of *who* has the right and duty to educate, and secondly, with the organization of the *means* by which the task is accomplished (schools and the teaching of religion).

As it has been said, the right and duty to educate children belong by the law of nature to parents in the first place. For Catholic parents, this task includes the Catholic education of their children. They also have the right and responsibility to select the means and the institutions which they are to use for this purpose, and they cannot allow their children to be educated in a non-Catholic religion (cc. 793 and 1366).

On another level, the Church also has the right and duty to educate, since this forms part of her mission to teach the Christian life to all peoples (c. 794). The Church is free: this freedom includes being able to offer Catholic education to all (first of all to the faithful), by promoting educational centers of any type and at any level (cc. 800 § 1 and 807).

Civil society, which has the goal of providing for the temporal good of all its members, also has rights and duties with regard to education. For this purpose, the State, as promoter of the common good, exercises certain competencies of organization and coordination. However, it is not directly called to educate, but rather to make sure that all can enjoy the right to education. Society and the State must recognize the freedom of choice of the parents and make possible the concrete exercise of that freedom, also with regard to the religious education of their children (cc. 797, 799). This is recognized in international human rights documents.

The Church carries out her educational task in many ways. We shall consider two in particular: the teaching of Catholic religion, and Catholic schools. It is necessary, in fact, to distinguish between the *educational institutions* of the Church, and the Catholic religion as a *subject* of instruction also offered by schools which are not officially Catholic (public or private).

The Teaching of the Catholic Religion

The deposit of the faith has been entrusted by God to His Church with the task of passing it on. Therefore, the teaching of the Catholic religion is subject to ecclesiastical authority, no matter how or where this is done. In fact, it is the responsibility of the ecclesiastical hierarchy to guarantee the authenticity of Catholic religious education (c. 804). Under the guidance of the hierarchy, the faithful find in this field a concrete possibility of collaborating in the teaching function of the Church.

The competencies concerning religious instruction are entrusted by the Code to the episcopal conference and to the diocesan bishop. It belongs to the conference to give general norms to it, and to the bishop to regulate it further and to watch over its realization. These competencies concern the teachers of religion (of religious subjects) as well as the contents.

The Ordinary of the diocese has the right to nominate or to approve the teachers of religion. Criteria of suitability and coherence of Christian life can be established for the teachers, with the possibility to ask for their removal for reasons of infidelity to the faith or moral conduct (c. 805).

With regard to the contents, canon law demands that texts for the study of religious or moral disciplines be approved by the ecclesiastical authority (c. 827 § 2).

In some countries, this area is also the object of a concordat between the Church and the State, so as to guarantee the teaching of the Catholic religion to those who freely choose it in public schools. Those agreements constitute a good instrument for defining the characteristics and methods of this teaching (teachers, programs, texts, content).

Catholic Schools

Catholic schools are those directed by the ecclesiastical authority or by a public ecclesiastical juridical person, and also those recognized as Catholic schools by the ecclesiastical authority by means of a written document (c. 803 § 1). Since they are guaranteed by the Church and, in a certain sense, act in her name, these schools are subject to the corresponding canonical norms and controls of the authority, to which it belongs to concede, deny or revoke the title of *Catholic*.

This does not mean that the only schools that provide Catholic education are these schools linked to the Church. There are others which educate the students according to the Catholic religion, although they are not officially Catholic and therefore do not depend as such on the ecclesiastical hierarchy.

The Church reserves to herself the right to found and direct schools of any type and grade (nursery schools, primary schools, high schools, universities). The faithful should help them (c. 800). In addition to the educational institutions that the hierarchy may establish directly, there are various institutions in the Church, both those of consecrated life and others, which have education as their purpose. This end is also accomplished by means of their own schools, which they can establish with the consent of the diocesan bishop (c. 801).

It is the responsibility of the diocesan bishop to give general norms for all Catholic schools in the diocese, to visit them and make sure that the instruction is based on Catholic doctrine and that the teachers are exemplary persons. He must also make sure that the quality of education is at least equal to that of other schools in the area.

Catholic parents can select for their children a Catholic school or not, but they must always watch over their effective Catholic education. For this reason, where there are no schools which guarantee such instruction, they will have to provide for it by other means.

Catholic Universities and Other Institutes of Higher Learning

Canon law also regulates centers of higher studies (universities and others) promoted and directed by the Church, for the purpose of guaranteeing the authenticity of their operation. They can be promoted by the Holy See, by the conference of bishops, by the diocese or by another canonical public person.

As for the schools, no university or institute can call itself *Catholic* without the consent of the ecclesiastical authority (c. 808), which has the duty of making sure that the principles of Catholic doctrine are respected and that the teachers lead an upright life. Otherwise they can be removed (c. 810). Within these directives, they enjoy scientific autonomy and are governed according to their own statutes approved by the same authority.[90]

Catholic universities are concerned with teaching and research in various subjects, principally *secular*. However, c. 811 requests that there be a center of theological studies for the purpose of promoting dialogue between the various

90. In addition to the Code, Catholic universities must conform to what is established in the Ap. Const. *Ex corde Ecclesiæ* (August 15, 1990), in *AAS* [1990] 1475–1509: *Origins* 20 [October 4, 1990] 265–276. The CCCB has promulgated a Decree and Ordinances on May 31 2005, for the application of the Ap. Const. in Canada, see for the full text http//www.cccb.ca. Other Conferences could have also proceeded in a similar manner.

disciplines so as to manifest the unity of knowledge and the continuity between faith and reason. This dialogue must be opened to non-Catholic universities, seeing to it that they also give some place to the sacred sciences as well.

In addition to the requirements of suitability and competence, theological sciences teachers at the level of higher studies must have a mandate from the competent ecclesiastical authority, since it is a matter of participation in the teaching function of the Church which must be exercised in communion with and under the guidance of the hierarchy (c. 812).

Centers of higher studies are not universities. They deal with some specific disciplines (in departments, institutes, etc.) at the scientific level. Within their area, the same norms apply to them as for the universities.

Ecclesiastical Universities and Faculties

Ecclesiastical universities and faculties are specifically concerned with *sacred sciences* (theology, Sacred Scripture, canon law, pastoral theology, etc.; c. 815) and other sciences which are connected to the sacred sciences.

With regard to these centers of studies, ample competencies are reserved to the Holy See, because the teaching of the sacred disciplines, the conferral of academic degrees with a canonical value and the role that they play in the formation of clerics, members of institutes of consecrated life and the laity, have a considerable impact on the entire Church and on the unity of the faith.

Concretely, the following responsibilities belong to the Apostolic See (cc. 816–817):

- to erect or approve these institutions even if they are promoted by other ecclesial institutions (dioceses, conferences of bishops, institutes of consecrated life, associations of the faithful). Without erection or approval of the Holy See, no university or faculty can validly confer diplomas or degrees with canonical effects;

- to approve their statutes and programs of study;
- to exercise the superior direction of all ecclesiastical universities and faculties, to which the proper authority of each must conform;
- to watch over the doctrinal correctness of the teaching and of the instructors, as well as over their uprightness of life, asking for their removal if these requirements are not fulfilled.

At a distinct level from ecclesiastical universities and faculties, there are *higher institutes for the religious sciences,* in which the theological disciplines and others concerning Christian culture are taught. These institutes must be promoted or at least approved by the conference of bishops or by the diocesan bishop, according to their extension. They confer diplomas for the teaching of sacred sciences in the schools, in accordance with the norms given by these authorities (c. 821).

The right of all the members of the faithful to Catholic formation (c. 217) includes the possibility of enrolling—according to the established conditions—in faculties or institutes of higher studies, of obtaining the corresponding degrees (diploma, licentiate, doctorate), and of being able to become professors of the sacred sciences.

E) Means of Communication and Books

The Church has the right to use the proper means of communication to spread the teaching of the Gospel. In addition, all the faithful, whether pastors or not, according to their possibilities, must endeavor to see that the truths of Catholic faith and morality are faithfully expounded through the means of social communication (c. 822).

On their part, the pastors of the Church, each in their own area, have the right and duty of watching to make sure that the use of the instruments of communication do not damage the formation of the faithful. Among other things,

- they must identify and denounce writings (books or other publications) which are contrary to true doctrine or morals. The faithful, for their part, have the moral duty to adhere to the judgment of the competent authority concerning writings, dramas and films;
- they must demand that the faithful submit their writings concerning faith or morals to the approval of the local Ordinary before publication.

These competencies of vigilance belong to the supreme authority with regard to the whole Church, and to bishops individually or united in particular councils or conferences of bishops, with regard to the faithful entrusted to their pastoral care (c. 823).

Concretely, the Code establishes that:

- the editions of books of Holy Scripture be approved by the Holy See or by the conference of bishops. Translations in the vernacular or ecumenical translations must in addition be supplied with notes and sufficient explanations (c. 825);
- liturgical books must be prepared and published by the Holy See. Translations in the vernacular must be prepared by the conference of bishops and authorized by the Apostolic See. For other editions, total or partial, the Ordinary of the place where it is published must attest that it corresponds with the approved original (cc. 826 and 828);
- books of prayer for public use cannot be published without permission of the local Ordinary;
- catechisms and other books of catechesis must have the approval of the local Ordinary, except those prepared by the Holy See, by the conference of bishops or by the diocesan bishop (c. 775);

- texts for instruction in the schools, which deal with questions of religion or morality, must be approved by the competent ecclesiastical authority (diocesan Ordinary or conference of bishops; c. 827);
- editions of legislative texts or of acts of the ecclesiastic authority require a previous permission of the same authority (c. 828);
- in churches and oratories it is only possible to sell, distribute or display those books published with permission of the authority (c. 827 § 4).

For other texts which deal with religious or moral questions, it is recommended that they be submitted to the judgment of the local Ordinary (c. 827 § 3).

To obtain the permission or approval of a writing, this must be sent to the local Ordinary of the author or place of publication. The Ordinary submits it to the examination of an expert censor who must give his opinion in writing with regard to the doctrinal correctness of the work. On the basis of this response, the Ordinary will give or deny permission for the publication. If the decision is negative, he will communicate to the author the reasons for this (c. 830). Religious must also obtain the permission of their own superior.

The faithful must not contribute without a just cause in newspapers, magazines or other publications which frequently attack religion or proper morality. Clerics and consecrated faithful must in addition have the permission of the local Ordinary in order to contribute.

Chapter IX.

The Means of Salvation. Divine Worship

1. The Sanctifying Office in the Church

The Church is also a worshipping community. By means of the liturgy she renders public cult to God and realizes the sanctification of men (CCC 1066 ff.).

Acts of *public worship* are those which are done in the name of the Church by legitimate ministers and according to the rites approved by the authority (c. 834 § 2). The principal part of this worship is the sacraments, of which the Eucharist is the center. Next to them there are the other acts of public worship.

In this work of sanctification, the Church acts as a Body united to her Head, Jesus Christ, the only Priest and mediator. All the faithful have been made participants in His priesthood, although in ways that are essentially different. All of the baptized have received the *common priesthood*; the members of the hierarchy, according to the grade of the sacrament of orders they have received, participate in the *ministerial priesthood*.

The bishops who have received the fullness of the priesthood are the principal dispensers of the mysteries of God: they are the moderators, promoters and custodians of the liturgy.[91]

91. T. J. GREEN, "The Church's Sanctifying Mission: Some Aspects of the Normative Role of the Diocesan Bishop," *Studia canonica* 25 [1991] 245–276.

Presbyters are also priests, consecrated to celebrate worship and to sanctify the people under the authority of the bishops. The deacons are not priests but ministers of worship, called to serve according to their ministry.

All the faithful, by virtue of the baptism, are called to participate in the function of sanctifying, to offer spiritual sacrifices together with the offering of Christ in the Eucharist, with honest fulfillment of all their works and actively sharing in the liturgy according to the established modalities (c. 835).

The participation and exercise of the priesthood of Christ that is actualized in the liturgy of the Church has various juridical consequences also. In the first place, the sacraments are a structuring element of the Church herself. For example, baptism constructs the People of God, within which holy orders constitutes the hierarchy. Secondly, the sacraments establish certain qualities, functions, rights, and duties of those who receive them or are called to receive and administrate them. Finally, worship, in so far as it is an action of the whole Church, must be ordered and regulated in such a way that it truly becomes an expression of faith and spiritual nourishment.

Regulating the liturgy and watching over its correct realization is the responsibility of the ecclesiastical authority: the Apostolic See for the entire Church, and the diocesan bishop for his diocese. The norms on this matter are contained in the liturgical books published by the Holy See. The translation of them into vernacular languages and their adaptation to the customs of the place belong to the conference of bishops, with the approval of the Holy See. The diocesan bishop, as the moderator of the worship of the Church, may provide other norms within the provisions in the liturgical books (c. 838).

2. The Sacraments

The sacraments are sensible signs realized by Christ through the Church, through which worship is rendered to God and the sanctification of men is realized. They express and confirm the faith and the ecclesiastical communion. The fundamental aspects of the sacraments are of a theological nature (biblical, dogmatic, moral, pastoral, etc.; cf. CCC 1113 ff.), but in order to safeguard this reality, which is a fundamental part of the common good of the Church, their adequate celebration is regulated by law.[92]

For example, Catholic doctrine teaches that three sacraments (baptism, confirmation and orders) imprint an indelible character in the person who receives them, and therefore they cannot be repeated. This is the reason for the norm of c. 845 which prohibits this repetition and establishes the practice to be followed in cases in which there arises a doubt as to whether someone has validly received one of these three sacraments.

The seven sacraments are the same for the entire Church and belong to the deposit of Revelation. Their substance is immutable, and therefore it belongs to the supreme authority only (Roman Pontiff and college of bishops) to determine the requirements for their *validity*. But for what concerns their *licitness* and the *rite* to be followed in their celebration, the conference of bishops and the diocesan bishop are also competent, with respect for the norms given by the Apostolic See (c. 841).

The pastoral action of the Church hinges principally on the sacraments. Therefore, canonical discipline on the sacraments is above all concerned with the relationship which is established in this matter between the pastors and the faithful. It establishes rules for their validity and licit celebration, and for their fruitful reception by the faithful, so that they can receive the abundance of grace that is offered them in the sacraments.

We have seen (Chapter V) that one of the fundamental rights of the faithful is "to receive assistance from the sacred pastors out of the spiritual goods of the Church, especially

92. W. H. WOESTMAN O.M.I., *Sacraments: Initiation, Penance, Anointing of the Sick. Commentary on Canons 840–1007*, 3rd ed., Saint Paul University, Ottawa, 2004.

the Word of God and the sacraments" (c. 213). Regarding this right, c. 843 establishes that the ministers cannot deny the sacraments to those who ask for them at appropriate times, are well disposed and have no impediment. Furthermore, the pastors and other faithful, each according to their own task, must cooperate so that all who are called to receive the sacraments acquire the necessary preparation.

There is a relation among the sacraments. At the center of them all there is the Eucharist. Baptism, confirmation and the Eucharist are the sacraments of Christian initiation, namely, those which incorporate the members of the faithful into the Church; penitence and anointing of the sick are the sacraments of healing; order and marriage "are in the service of the communion and mission of the faithful" (CCC 1210–1212).

In the following pages, we shall see the principal norms regarding the individual sacraments. More space is dedicated to the treatment of the sacrament of marriage, because of the effect that it has on the lives of most of the faithful and of the attentive reflection on it that is offered by the Code.

A) Baptism

Baptism is the sacrament of regeneration to the life of grace which makes us children of God in Jesus Christ, and members of His Body the Church. It is the *gate* to the other sacraments, so that he who has not yet received it cannot validly receive the others (c. 842 § 1; cf. CCC 1213 ff.).

Outside of the Church there is no salvation, and therefore baptism is absolutely necessary. However, it can be received spiritually by means of desire and also by means of martyrdom (CCC 1257–1261). The Code deals with baptism with water celebrated according to the established rite (c. 849). From the *necessity* of baptism there arise the principal rights and duties with regard to this sacrament:

- in cases of emergency it is lawful to suppress all the non-essential rites (the pouring of water and the Trinitarian formula are essential; cf. CCC 1239–1240);

- every person not yet baptized has the right to be baptized if he desires it; and if he is not prepared yet, he has the right to appropriate catechetical instruction;
- the parents have the right and duty to see that their children are baptized in the first weeks, for which reason already before birth they should request baptism for their child and duly prepare themselves. If the child is in danger of death, he must be baptized immediately, even against the will of the parents;
- in case of necessity anyone can baptize, so that it is important that the faithful (especially health care workers) know how to administer baptism correctly (c. 861 § 2);
- abandoned children or foundlings should be baptized if there is no clear proof of their having been baptized. One must also baptize, within the limits of possibility, aborted foetuses (cc. 870 and 871);
- if, after an accurate investigation, there remains doubt concerning the reception of baptism or its validity, it is to be administered under condition (c. 869).[93]

Every person not yet baptized, whether child or adult (here adult refers to a person who is over seven years of age), is a *subject* of baptism.

For the baptism of an adult, it is necessary that there be free consent. Furthermore, he must be instructed in the faith and proven in Christian life, ordinarily following the practice

93. The question may arise on the validity of the baptism received in a given religious confession. The Congr. for the Doctrine of the Faith has resolved some questions of this kind. For example, on June 5, 2001, it said "*Question*: Whether the baptism conferred by the community 'The Church of Jesus Christ of Latter-day Saints,' called 'Mormons' in the vernacular, is valid. *Response*: Negative": *AAS* [2001] 476.

of the catechumenate.[94] However, if there is danger of death, an adult can be baptized if he has manifested his desire in some way, briefly explaining to him the principal truths and commandments (c. 865).

For a child to be licitly baptized, at least one of his parents must consent, and there must be hope that he will be educated in the Catholic religion. Otherwise, it is better that baptism be deferred, explaining the reasons to the parents.

The ordinary *minister* of baptism is any cleric. Normally, baptism belongs to the local parish pastor. In the absence of the ordinary minister, the function of baptizing can be entrusted to others (a missionary, catechist, etc.). Baptism of adults is to be deferred to the diocesan bishop so that, if he deems it opportune, he may personally administer it.

The *sponsors* have the task, together with the parents, of presenting the child to be baptized and of assisting him in Christian initiation, helping him to conduct a coherent life. They are designated by the person receiving baptism or by his parents (or, if these are lacking, by the pastor or minister). They must not be more than two (male and female sponsor) and they must assume responsibility for their role.

These tasks of the sponsors explain the requirements established for their admission, which are (c. 874):

- that they be 16 years old;
- that they be Catholic, having received confirmation and the Eucharist, that they lead a life in conformity with the function that they are assuming, and that they not be bound by any canonical penalty. Baptized non-Catholics can only be admitted as witnesses together with a Catholic sponsor;

94. See for the USA the *National Statutes for the Catechumenate*, issued by the NCCB as Appendix III of the *Rite of Christian Initiation of Adults*, Washington, 1988, pp. 362–375.

- that they be well instructed on the responsibility and tasks of the sponsor;
- that they not be the father or mother of the person receiving baptism.

The *celebration* of baptism must occur according to the approved rite, in a church or oratory (normally in the parish church), ordinarily on Sunday or, if possible, on the Easter Vigil. It must be conferred by means of immersion or by pouring water that has been duly blessed. The person receiving baptism is to be given a name that is not foreign to a Christian mentality. Without a state of necessity or grave cause, baptism is not to be administered in private houses or hospitals.

When an adult is baptized, he is also given the sacraments of confirmation and the Eucharist in the same ceremony. These are the three sacraments of Christian initiation. In the Eastern Churches the same is done with children also.

The baptism must be registered in the parish baptismal book, recording all the data required by law (name, parents, sponsors, minister, etc.). This registration serves as a proof of baptism received, but if it is lacking, the administration of the sacrament can also be proven by witnesses or by the person himself if he received it as an adult (cc. 875–878).

B) Confirmation

Confirmation is a sacrament of Christian initiation that corroborates and increases the grace of baptism in the faithful, enriches them with the seal of the gift of the Holy Spirit, ties them more perfectly to the Church and gives them the strength to give witness and to spread the faith through their life and word (c. 879; cf. CCC 1286 ff.).

It is also called chrismation, since it is conferred by means of an anointing of chrism on the forehead, which is done with imposition of the hands and by means of the words: "Be sealed with the Gift of the Holy Spirit." The sacred chrism must be made of vegetable oil and consecrated by the bishop in the Chrism Mass of Holy Thursday (CCC 1300 and 1297).

The *subject* of confirmation is only a baptized person who has not yet received it. In danger of death, this requirement is sufficient. In fact, this sacrament cannot be repeated because it imprints an indelible character in those who receive it, which is like a spiritual mark that signifies a definitive belonging to God and to His Church (c. 889).

For licitness, the faithful must have reached the use of reason, be adequately prepared, well disposed, and capable of renewing the baptismal promises. This carries with it the duty of the parents and the pastors to provide for the appropriate catechesis. The age for confirmation is the age of discretion (around seven years old), but the conference of bishops can fix another age.[95]

Although it is not a sacrament that is absolutely necessary, it would be temerarious to procrastinate without reason in receiving it. Therefore, the law imposes on the faithful the obligation to receive it promptly, so that one can make use of the power of the sacrament when the struggle to remain faithful to the commitments of baptism becomes more arduous (CCC 1306).

Many steps of the Christian life require the maturity that flows from confirmation: to be a sponsor, to marry, to receive orders or enter into consecrated life, etc.

The ordinary *minister* of confirmation is the bishop. However, a priest can validly give confirmation if he has received the faculty to do so by law or by special concession

95. The NCCB has established that "[c]onfirmation in the Latin Rite shall be conferred between the age of discretion and about sixteen years of age, within the limits determined by the diocesan bishop and with regard for the legitimate exceptions given in canon 891." The CCCB remits "at the age determined in the approved catechetical programmes." The CBC of the Philippines maintains the "seven -7- years, or after the first communion."

from the competent authority. For example, the faculty to administer confirmation is possessed by those who are equivalent in law to the diocesan bishop, by the priest who baptizes an adult, or by any priest when the recipient is in danger of death (c. 883).

However, the chrism consecrated by a bishop must always be used (c. 880 § 2).

There must be a sponsor for confirmation also, preferably the same as for baptism. The requirements for being a sponsor of confirmation are the same as those for baptism (cc. 892, 893).

The conferral of confirmation is to be noted both in the confirmation register, and next to that of baptism (cc. 894–896).

C) The Holy Eucharist

The Eucharist is the source and summit of Christian worship and life (*LG* 11; CCC 1324 ff.) because in it "is contained the whole spiritual good of the Church, namely Christ himself" (*PO* 5). The Eucharistic sacrifice is the same sacrifice of the Cross realized sacramentally. In it, Jesus Christ, together with his Church, and in a non-bloody manner, again offers to the Father his own sacrifice and gives himself as food to his faithful.

The Eucharist builds up the Church in a wonderful way, in that it signifies and accomplishes the communion of all the faithful in the Body of Christ, for the sanctification of the world, in the faith that works through charity. The other sacraments and all the works of apostolate are ordered to the Eucharist and from it they draw their efficacy.

The sacrament of the most holy Eucharist can be contemplated from a threefold point of view: as sacrifice, as communion, and as the adorable Presence of the Lord. In addition to requiring supreme devotion and honor for this most elevated sacrament, canon law establishes the discipline that is to be observed with regard to the three aspects that have been mentioned.

The Holy Sacrifice of the Mass

The Eucharistic celebration is an action of Christ and of the Church.[96] All of the faithful are called to participate in it, according to their proper condition and liturgical role (c. 899).

The *minister* capable of celebrating the Holy Mass is only a validly ordained priest (i.e., a bishop or presbyter).

It is properly in the Eucharist that the fundamental structure of the People of God is realized in an exemplary manner. This consists in the essential distinction and the relationship between the common priesthood of the faithful and the ministerial priesthood. The Lord only commanded the Apostles to "do this in memory of me." Therefore, only those who have received the priesthood through the apostolic succession can offer the sacrifice in the person of Christ, who is always the "Author and principal Subject of this His proper sacrifice."[97] The other members of the faithful, in virtue of their common priesthood, take part in the celebration with the offering of their own spiritual sacrifices and with their active participation (*LG* 10).

This participation is concretely determined by the liturgical norms, which must be observed faithfully. Thus c. 907 states that it is forbidden "for deacons and lay persons to say prayers, in particular the Eucharistic prayer, or perform actions which are proper to the celebrating priest."

In order to licitly celebrate Mass, the priest must not be impeded by a canonical penalty and must observe the laws regarding the Eucharistic celebration, especially those contained in the Code itself (c. 900 § 2).

---

96. See in general for this section: BENEDICT XVI, Post-synodal Apostolic Exhortation *Sacramentum Caritatis*, February, 22, 2007, Vatican City/Ottawa, LEV/CCCB, 2007.

97. JOHN PAUL II, Lett. *Dominicæ Cenæ*, 8, *AAS* 72 [1980] 115–134: *Origins* 9 [March 27, 1980] pp. 653–666; cf. Enc. *Ecclesia de Eucharistia*, 26–29.

Priests can concelebrate unless the welfare of the faithful urges otherwise. In fact, an adequate pastoral attention to the faithful and the scarcity of clergy may require that more Masses be celebrated. Furthermore, every priest has the right to celebrate the Mass individually, but not while there is a concelebration in the same place (c. 902).

Since the Eucharist is the mystery of the faith which requires full ecclesiastical communion, it is forbidden for Catholic priests to concelebrate with priests or ministers of Churches or communities that are not in full communion with the Catholic Church (c. 908). However, Catholic priests of different rites can concelebrate, in the cases specified by law.

The Code strongly recommends priests to celebrate the Eucharist every day. This is their principal task, even when other faithful cannot be present, since every Mass is an action of Christ and of the Church. However, it is not licit to celebrate more than once a day, except in certain instances specified by law or by permission of the local Ordinary. A priest cannot celebrate without the presence of some member of the faithful, except for a just and reasonable cause (cc. 905–906).

The ministers must use the prescribed liturgical vestments and the approved liturgical books in the celebration of the Mass and for the distribution of Communion.

If he is sick or elderly, the priest can celebrate sitting down, observing the liturgical laws. However, he cannot do this before the people (except by permission of the local Ordinary). If he is blind or affected by a similar infirmity, he can always say the same Mass, aided if necessary by a cleric or by a layman.

Before celebrating, the priest must prepare himself well through prayer, and make a thanksgiving after the celebration.

With regard to the *matter*, the holy Sacrifice must be offered with bread made of wheat alone, and with natural wine of the grape, to which he adds a small amount of water. In the tradition of the Latin Church, the bread must be unleavened.

It is never licit to consecrate one matter without the other, since the sacrifice is signified by the double consecration of the Body and the Blood of the Lord. Nor is it licit to consecrate the matter outside of a Eucharistic celebration.

The Eucharist must be celebrated in a sacred *place* (church, oratory or chapel) and on an altar that has been dedicated or blessed. In cases of particular necessity, the Mass can be celebrated in another place that is decorous and then one must use a suitable table, as long as it is covered by a cloth and corporal.

With the express permission of the local Ordinary, one can celebrate the Mass in a non-Catholic Christian temple, if there is no danger of scandal.

The Mass can be celebrated on any day or hour, except those excluded by the liturgical norms.

Eucharistic Communion

The ordinary minister of Holy Communion is only a cleric (bishop, presbyter or deacon, c. 910 §1). In case of necessity or lack of clerics, an acolyte or any member of the faithful can receive the function of distributing Communion as an extraordinary minister (c. 910 §2).[98]

In the Latin Church Communion is given under the form of bread alone, except in the cases specified by the liturgical laws in which one may receive under both kinds. In cases of necessity (for example, illness), Communion may be given under the form of wine alone.

Pastors who have care of souls (parish priests, chaplains) have the duty of bringing Communion in the form of Viaticum to the sick entrusted to their care. In case of necessity, this duty falls on any priest or ordained minister (cc. 921, 922).

98. A response of the Pontifical Council for Legislative Texts (June 1, 1988) establishes, in relation with this canon that if other non-impeded sacred ministers are present in the church, one is not to have recourse to an extraordinary minister for the distribution of the Eucharist (*AAS* [1988] 1373).

Every baptized person can and must be admitted to Holy Communion if law does not forbid this. The law forbids participation in the Eucharist by those who are excommunicated, under interdict, or who obstinately persevere in manifesting grave sin (for example, unmarried couples living together, or those who are only civilly married, etc.). Baptized non-Catholics cannot be admitted to Communion except in the cases established by law.

Furthermore, a person who is in grave sin can neither celebrate nor communicate without previous sacramental confession, unless this is impossible and there is a grave reason for receiving Communion. In this case, he must make an act of perfect contrition which includes the intention of confessing as soon as possible (c. 916; cf. CCC 1385).

Children are not to receive Holy Communion without an adequate catechism which enables them to perceive the mystery according to their capacity, and to receive the Body of Christ with faith and devotion. However, in danger of death, they can receive Communion if they are capable of distinguishing the Body of the Lord from common food and of receiving the sacrament with devotion (cc. 913 and 914).

A person who has already received the Eucharist can receive it again in the same day, only within the celebration of the Mass or as Viaticum in danger of death (c. 917).

No food or drink, except water or medicine, is to be taken for the period of one hour before Communion. The elderly, the sick, and those who care for them, are not bound by this norm. Priests who must celebrate more than one Mass may also take some nourishment between one Mass and another, even if the interval is less than an hour.

The Church recommends the faithful to receive Holy Communion frequently and with devotion. The faithful are bound by precept to receive at least once a year in the Easter season, unless for a just cause this is fulfilled at another time during the year.

The sick must receive holy Viaticum, and can do so several times during their illness. Pastors are to be vigilant so that they can receive the comfort of the Eucharist while they are still in full possession of their faculties. In this regard, the relatives and others who take care of them have a special responsibility.

It is licit for the faithful to participate in the Eucharistic sacrifice and receive Communion in any Catholic rite. However, such participation is not licit in a non-Catholic church or community except in the cases permitted by law (c. 923).

Conservation and Veneration of the Most Holy Eucharist

The Eucharist is also the sacrament of the real presence of Jesus Christ under the forms of bread and wine. This presence remains after the celebration of the Sacrifice. The Church conserves the Eucharist with veneration and renders worship to this permanent Eucharistic presence of the Lord in various ways.

The Eucharist *must* be conserved in cathedral and parish churches, and in the church or oratory connected to the house of religious or of a society of apostolic life.

It *can* also be conserved in the private chapel of a bishop, and, by permission of the local Ordinary, in other churches, oratories or private chapels (c. 934).

Normally, the Eucharist is conserved in only one tabernacle of a church or oratory. It must be situated in a beautifully decorated and prominent place, adapted for prayer. The tabernacle must be immovable, solid, opaque and securely locked so as to avoid the danger of profanation as far as possible. If there is a grave reason, the Holy Eucharist can be transferred, especially during the night, to another more secure place that is also decorous (c. 938).

A special lamp is to burn at all times in front of the tabernacle, indicating and honoring the presence of Christ (c. 940).

Wherever the Eucharist is conserved, there must always be someone who has care of it and diligently safeguards the key of the tabernacle. If it is a church, it must remain open to the faithful for at least some hours every day, so that they can pray before the Most Blessed Sacrament.

In the Latin Church, the Eucharist is conserved under the form of bread only. The consecrated hosts are conserved in a ciborium or other sufficiently noble vessel. It must be renewed frequently, properly consuming the old hosts. For this reason, if possible, Mass should be celebrated there at least twice each month (c. 939).

In the place where the Eucharist is conserved, exposition can be made of the Most Blessed Sacrament, either with the ciborium or with a monstrance, according to the rubrics, although not during the Mass. It is recommended that there be a solemn exposition at least once a year with a prolonged time of adoration (cc. 941–942).

The *minister* of Eucharistic exposition and benediction is the priest or deacon. In special cases the acolyte, the extraordinary minister of Holy Communion or another person designated by the local Ordinary, observing the prescriptions of the diocesan bishop, can perform the exposition without benediction (c. 943).

It is also recommended, if the diocesan bishop judges that it is possible, to have a public procession on the solemnity of the Body and Blood of the Lord, in a way to be determined by the bishop (c. 944).

Offerings for the Celebration of the Mass (cc. 945–958)
The priest has the faculty to apply the Mass that he is celebrating for anyone, living or dead. It is a legitimate and ancient usage of the Church that the faithful give the celebrant an offering so that he may apply the Mass according to their intention. In this way the faithful help in the support of worship and the clergy.

The rules of canon law on this matter aim above all that this tradition be lived with clarity and that abuses or confusion be avoided. They can be summarized as follows:

- the amount of the offering that is to be made for the celebration is to be established by the bishops of the province or by custom. The faithful can give more. On the other hand, the priests must be open to celebrate for the intentions of those who cannot give an offering;

- the priest must apply a Mass for each offering received, except in exceptional cases in which the law permits him to accumulate in one sole Mass the intentions of various donors who consent to this[99];
- priests who accept offerings for Masses have the obligation of applying them, within the year, for the intentions of those who make the offerings, or to have them applied by another to whom he transmits the offering that has been received. This makes it necessary on the part of priests, as well as in places of worship, that there be an accurate registration of the commitments that have been assumed, satisfied, and are to be satisfied.

D) The Sacrament of Penance

Penance is the sacrament of the remission of sins committed after baptism (see CCC 1422 ff.). It is obtained by means of the contrite confession of sins together with the purpose of amendment, and the absolution given by the confessor (c. 959).

The *minister* of the sacrament of confession is the priest only. In fact, only a person who has received the ministerial priesthood can act in the person of Christ, Shepherd and Judge, as occurs in confession.

However, for the priest to be able to *validly* give absolution, it is furthermore necessary that he has the *faculty* to absolve the penitents who have recourse to him. It can be

99. These so-called pluri-intentional Masses are regulated by a Decree of the Congr. of the Clergy of February 22, 1991: *Origins* 20 [April 4, 1991] 705–706.

said that even if every priest has the capacity or power to absolve sins, he still needs the authorization or license to be able to exercise this power over concrete penitents who come to him.

This faculty of absolving is acquired by law or by concession of the competent authority. By law it is held by the Pope, Cardinals and bishops in the entire world; others pastors who have care of souls (parish priests, chaplains) hold it for their subjects or for their territory. Other priests receive the faculty by concession of the authority (cc. 966–975).

In order to facilitate confession of the faithful, the law regulates the faculty of confessors in the following way:

- a priest who has received the faculty to hear confessions from the Ordinary of his place of incardination or domicile, can hear confessions anywhere unless, in a particular case, the local Ordinary denies it (c. 967 § 2);
- any penitent in danger of death can be absolved by any priest of any sin or censure (c. 976; CCC 1463);
- in the case of error or reasonable doubt, the Church supplies and therefore absolution is to be held to be valid (c. 144).

The confessor must exercise his ministry according to truth, justice and mercy. Therefore, he must question penitents with prudence, judge and advise them according to the doctrine of the Church, and absolve those who are found to be well disposed, after having given an appropriate penance.

Furthermore he is bound to keep the secret, which cannot be violated for any cause. Anyone of the faithful who has acquired knowledge of sins from the confessional, in any way, is bound to maintain the secret in the same way as the confessor (cc. 978–983).

Pastors must make it easy for their faithful to go to individual confession, establishing convenient days and hours. Any confessor is obliged to hear the confessions of the faithful who reasonably ask him for it,[100] and in danger of death any priest is so obliged (c. 986).

Every member of the faithful who has committed sin after baptism is a *subject* of the sacrament of Penance.

For the validity of the confession, the penitent must convert himself to God, which means repudiating the sins committed and having a purpose of amendment (c. 987).

Besides these interior dispositions, he is bound to confess, according to their kind and number, all the grave sins committed after baptism which have not yet been confessed, which he remembers of after a diligent examination of conscience; a generic confession or a confession limited to some sins is not sufficient.[101] It is recommended that venial sins be confessed also (c. 988).

Every member of the faithful has the obligation of confessing grave sins at least once a year (c. 989).

The faithful have the right to choose their own confessor among those that are approved, even of another Catholic rite (c. 991). However, a confessor cannot validly absolve his own accomplice in a sin against the sixth commandment, except in danger of death (c. 977).

The proper place for confession is a church or oratory. There must always be confessionals with a fixed grate between the confessor and the penitent. In fact, the penitent is not bound to reveal his identity to the confessor. For this reason, the faithful always have the right to be able to confess through the grate, which also serves to protect the dignity of the sacrament, encourage sincerity and remove the danger of scandal; for that reason the confessor may also decide to use it.[102] In addition, the conference of bishops can determine that there also be other types of confessionals without a grate (c. 964).

---

100. This is provided in M.P. *Misericordia Dei*, April, 7, 2002, nn. 1 and 2: *AAS* [2002] 452–459.
101. Ibid., n. 3.
102. Ibid., n. 9b; Answer from the PCLT, of July, 7 1998: *AAS* [1998] 711.

Collective Absolution (cc. 961–963)

Personal and complete confession of grave sins, followed by absolution, is the only ordinary way to obtain reconciliation with God and with the Church. For this reason, only in case of a physical or moral impossibility can pardon be obtained in other ways (c. 960).

Recently, some abuses concerning collective absolution have occurred, when the priest gives absolution to several penitents together without previous individual confession of sins.[103] The legislator has willed to determine with precision the cases and conditions in which such an absolution is valid. There are two cases:

a) The first is that there be an immanent danger of death and not enough priests to hear the confessions of each of the individual penitents.

b) The second is that there be a grave necessity. This occurs:

- when there is a scarcity of confessors and of time, which does not permit the individual penitents to be heard;
- when, as a consequence, the penitents would remain long deprived of grace or of Holy Communion without any fault of their own[104];
- a large influx of penitents, that can occur on great feasts and pilgrimages for instance, is not considered to constitute a grave necessity;
- it belongs to the diocesan bishop, not to the confessor, to judge and determine when there are circumstances of grave necessity.

Normally these cases are present in mission territories, but also in places of holiday resorts, or similar places, when it is impossible to have enough priests. However, it is an

103. Clearly distinct from these are the communitarian celebrations of Penance, in which, after a common preparation, each of the faithful individually confesses his own sins to the confessor and receives absolution.

104. The M.P. *Misericordia Dei* (4d) interprets "long time" as more than one month.

extraordinary recourse imposed by the circumstances, and never voluntarily provoked.

In order to validly receive absolution in this way, the penitent must have the required dispositions (contrition, purpose of amendment) and also have the intention of confessing individually, as soon as there is an opportunity to do so, the sins which he cannot confess then and there. Penitents must be informed of these requirements before the collective absolution (CCC 1483–1484).

Indulgences (cc. 992–997)

After the remission of sins by absolution, there still remains the temporal punishment connected with them. An indulgence is the total or partial remission of this temporal punishment by concession of the Church, which is the dispenser of the treasure of the satisfactions of Christ and the saints.

It therefore belongs to the competent ecclesiastical authority to give indulgences, which are normally conceded by connecting them to the completion of certain works in the way and time prescribed.

Every member of the faithful can gain indulgences for themselves or apply them for the dead, as long as they are not excommunicated, and are in a state of grace and have the intention of acquiring them.

The works and conditions according to which indulgences can be obtained (plenary or partial) are found in the *Enchiridion indulgentiarum* promulgated by Paul VI.[105]

E) The Anointing of the Sick

This sacrament is conferred on members of the faithful who are gravely ill, by means of anointing with oil and with the prescribed words, so that the Lord, by the ministry of the Church, may raise them up and save them (*LG* 11, c. 998, CCC 1499 ff.).

105. The *Enchiridion* is published by the Apostolic Penitentiary; last edition: 1999.

The *minister* of the anointing of the sick is the priest only. The right and duty of administering the sacrament belong to pastors with respect to the members of the faithful entrusted to their pastoral care. However, any priest can confer it if there is a reasonable cause. In fact, every priest is authorized to carry with him blessed oil for administering the sacrament of the anointing of the sick in case of necessity (c. 1003).

The *subject* of this sacrament is a member of the faithful who, having reached the use of reason, finds himself in danger of death for reasons of sickness or old age. In case of doubt as to whether the subject has reached the use of reason, or whether he is gravely sick or whether he is dead, the sacrament is to be conferred (cc. 1004–1008).

As for any sacrament received by an adult, it is also necessary to have his consent. However, since this is an aid that can decisively help in attaining salvation, anointing of the sick is to be conferred on those who, when in possession of their mental faculties, at least implicitly requested it (c. 1006).

On the other hand, the sacrament is not to be given to those who obstinately persist in manifest grave sin (c. 1007).

The oil for the sick must be blessed. This blessing can be given by:

- every bishop;
- all those who are equivalent in law to the diocesan bishop;
- in case of necessity, any priest, but only in the celebration of the sacrament (c. 999).

Anointing must be accomplished together with the words established in the liturgical books. However, in case of necessity, it is sufficient to have one single anointing on the forehead, or in another part of the body, pronouncing the complete formula (c. 1000).

F) The Sacrament of Orders

Holy orders are the sacrament of the apostolic ministry, "through which the mission entrusted by Christ to his apostles continues to be exercised in the Church" (CCC 1536). Those who receive it are consecrated as sacred ministers, so that through their configuration with Christ the Head, they receive the capacity to fulfill in His person the functions of teaching, sanctifying and governing, each according to the grade that they have received (c. 1008).

It is a sacrament of service to the community which marks those who receive it with an indelible character, and which therefore cannot be repeated.

There are many important ecclesial and juridical implications of holy orders, including the fact that it is the sacrament through which subsists in time the apostolic hierarchy in the Church, as constituted by Jesus Christ (cf. Chapter V).

A specific characteristic of this sacrament is that it can be given in different grades or orders. These are: the episcopate, the presbyterate, and the diaconate. They are conferred by means of the imposition of hands and the prescribed consecratory prayer (c. 1009; CCC 1554 ff.).

The episcopate confers the fullness of the priesthood on the consecrated man and makes him a member of the college of bishops, successor of the Apostles. The presbyterate constitutes those who receive it into collaborators of the bishops in the exercise of the priesthood. The diaconate is a non-priestly ministry of service.

The *minister* of holy ordination is the bishop. As successor of the Apostles in the fullness of the priesthood, he has the power to confer on others the three grades of orders (c. 1012).

The choice of those who will receive the episcopate, and thus will enter into the college of bishops, belongs to the Roman Pontiff at the end. He exercises this competence either by appointing him directly or by appointing one who has been presented or by approving the election of a candidate. For this reason, it is not licit for any bishop to consecrate another bishop without a pontifical mandate. The infraction of this prohibition is an offence that carries with it an automatic excommunication (*ipso facto*), both of the one who consecrates and of the one who is consecrated (cc. 1013 and 1382).

The choice, on the other hand, of those who are to be promoted to the presbyterate or the diaconate belongs to the authority of the institution where the candidate will be incardinated (diocese or personal prelature, religious institute or society of apostolic life, etc.). Therefore, no bishop is to ordain someone who is not his subject without the written request (dimissorial letter) of the above-mentioned authority, according to the norm of law (cc. 1015 and 1383).

The *subject* of ordination can only be a baptized person of the male sex (c. 1024). By uninterrupted tradition, on the basis of the will of the Lord when He chose His Apostles, women cannot receive this sacrament.[106]

However, this does not imply any discrimination. First, because no one has the right to be ordained in the Church, since holy orders are for the service of the Church. Therefore, in the last analysis, it is always up to the authority of the Church to decide who is to be ordained. Secondly, this is because holy orders is not the culmination of Christian life, nor are the members of the hierarchy called to a more elevated sanctity. No one is precluded from the fullness of Christian life by the fact that they are not admitted to holy orders (CCC 1577–1578).

Since it is a sacrament that permanently—and generally exclusively—destines a person to the service of ecclesial

106. On this subject, JOHN PAUL II, in the Apostolic Letter *Ordinatio sacerdotalis* (May 22, 1994), has explained the reasons for this constant practice of the Church, and has declared in a definitive way "that the Church has no authority whatsoever to confer priestly ordination on women" (n. 4). English translation in *Origins* 24 [June 9, 1994] 49–52.

society, with a strong impact on the personal *status* of the subject, the Church establishes requirements of various types in order to be able to receive it licitly (cc. 1025–1052):

- there must be a *period of trial and formation* which is accomplished in seminaries for the secular clergy, or in the institute of consecrated life for those who are consecrated. During this period, the prescribed steps must be completed: admission, ministries of lector and acolyte, petition for admission to holy orders and the commitment to accomplish it, assumption of celibacy, etc.;

- the *studies and experience* necessary to be able to adequately fulfill the sacred ministry must have been completed. For candidates for the presbyterate, this includes two years of philosophy and four of theology, according to the program of studies and formation prepared by the Holy See and adapted to the circumstances of the place by the conference of bishops[107];

- *age*: the candidate must be 23 years old for the diaconate, 25 for the presbyterate, and 35 for the episcopate. For the permanent diaconate, the candidate must be 25 years old if not married, and 35 if married, in addition to having the consent of his wife. One must have exercised the preceding one in order to pass to a higher order;

- *freedom*: it is illicit for anyone to be coerced into orders, or to be held back from them if he is suitable;

- there must be a favorable judgment of the bishop or the competent superior concerning *suitability*, taking into account the gifts, preparation and virtues of the candidate. The bishop or superior must evaluate the utility of the ordination in view of service to the Church;

107. For the formation of clerics in the seminary, see cc. 232–264 (Chapter V, 3, a).

- he must have received *confirmation*, and the *orders* preceding what he intends to receive;
- there must *not* be an *impediment*, which is something which by law excludes one from orders.

Perpetual impediments or *irregularities* include psychological illnesses which make one incapable of carrying out the ministry; having committed certain offences such as heresy, apostasy or schism, homicide, mutilations or abortion; having attempted marriage when there was an impediment due to an existing bond, a vow or holy orders, etc. Simple *impediments* are temporary, such as being married (except for the permanent diaconate), exercising civil functions incompatible with the ministry while one is in office, being a neophyte, until the Ordinary holds the candidate to have been sufficiently proven. The faithful have the obligation to reveal to the authorities the impediments which come to their knowledge. All impediments can be dispensed from by the Holy See, and some by the Ordinary also.

It is recommended that ordination be done on a holyday in the cathedral church, but for a just cause, it can be celebrated in another church or on another day (cc. 1010–1011).

Before ordination one must present the necessary documents and certificates to demonstrate the relevant prerequisites (studies, baptism and confirmation, etc.). After ordination, it must be entered in a special register of the place of ordination, and the ordaining bishop is to give each of those ordained a certificate of the ordination received, which is to be also communicated to the pastor of the place of baptism.

3. Marriage

As a human reality, marriage is the covenant between a man and a woman which establishes between them a community of life and love naturally ordained to the good of the spouses and to the procreation and education of children. Unity and indissolubility are essential characteristics of every marriage as God instituted it in the beginning when he created man, male and female (*GS* 48, CCC 1603 ff.).

It is precisely this human reality which, among the baptized, has been elevated by Christ the Lord to the dignity of a sacrament. Therefore, the sacrament of marriage has characteristics which are unique. In fact, it is the baptism of the spouses which makes their matrimonial bond a sacrament, a reality which at the same time is both natural and supernatural, a sign of the union of Christ with His Church (c. 1055 § 1).

The marriage of two *baptized persons* is in itself a sacrament. The sacrament is not an external addition or adjunct to marriage, but it is the marriage itself between two baptized persons which becomes the sign and source of salvation. For this reason, there cannot exist a valid marriage between baptized persons which is not for that very reason a sacrament (c. 1055 § 2).

From this derives the juridical competence of the Church over marriages of *Catholics*. Every marriage is of interest to the Church in so far as marriage is an institution of great personal and social importance. However, in the case of Catholics, this interest becomes juridical competence on account of the sacramental reality contained in it, by which it becomes a special vocation within the Church: the specific path of sanctification of the majority of the faithful.[108]

Therefore, while recognizing the competence of the State over the specifically civil aspects of marriage, the Church claims for herself the right to regulate the marriage of Catholics with regard to its validity and efficacy, as well as the power to pass judgment over these in concrete cases. This regulation, however, is not arbitrary but seeks to correspond

---

108. On marriage as a vocation, see J. ESCRIVA, "Marriage: A Christian Vocation," in *Christ is Passing by*, nn. 22–30, Sinag Tala Publishers, Manila, 2000.

as perfectly as possible with what marriage is, as instituted by God (c. 1059).[109]

As for the other sacraments, canon law only deals with one aspect of marriage. It has a human, theological and ecclesial richness which goes well beyond juridical norms; it would be a mistake to reduce the Church's teaching on marriage to the canons referring to it.[110]

However, one must not forget that marriage is a juridical reality, a covenant, a stable bond between a man and a woman, and canonical matrimonial law has precisely the role of protecting this reality within the bosom of the Church, and, in consequence, within civil society also.

Since marriage is a community of life and of love between a man and a woman, love plays a decisive role. It is love which leads two persons to marry. Marriage is the natural channel where love flows, making this an exclusive and permanent commitment. In this way, whereas two persons who are engaged say to each other: "I want to marry you because I love you"; the two spouses will say: "I love you because I have married you." In marriage, love becomes a bond, a community of life, a duty.

This fully corresponds to human nature, to the intimate and profound aspiration of men and women to love and be loved, to the fact that they find their realization in the gift of themselves. This reflects the image and likeness of God which is in man (cf. *GS* 24). Every person who is in love swears that his love is eternal, unique, total; it is natural that the union that arises from this love be exclusive and indissoluble, and that only in marriage would the giving of one's body make sense.

---

109. Among the many works on canonical marriage, see: J. McAreavey, *The Canon Law of Marriage and the Family*, Four Courts Press, Dublin, 1997; W. Onclin (ed.), *Canon law and Marriage*, Peeters, Leuven, 1995; I. Gramunt, J. Hervada, L. A. Wauck, *Canons and Commentaries on Marriage*, The Liturgical Press, Collegeville, 1987.

110. See: P. J. Viladrich, *The Agony of Legal Marriage: An Introduction to the Basic Conceptual Elements of Matrimony*, University of Navarra, Pamplona, 1992; J. Carreras, *Marriage: Sex, Celebration, and Law*, Four Courts Press, Dublin, 2004.

The Church's teaching on marriage in general—and matrimonial canon law in particular—must be understood in this perspective. Sometimes, however, marriage is spoken of as a kind of indefinitely prolonged engagement, so that if love were to die out, the marriage would also cease to exist. Those who think this way fail to understand that although it is true that it is love that leads to the reciprocal donation of the spouses in marriage, once this donation has occurred it no longer depends on the presence of love.

Marriage is not a continual and revocable donation which depends on the actual love between the spouses, but the realization in life of a donation that has definitively occurred, made for the sake of love. The so-called love without a commitment is a contradiction in terms, a falsity; it does not reflect a person's dignity.

This is the truth and the law of a truly human love which the canonical norms seek to grasp and protect as much as possible. Certainly no human law can bring back to life love that has been extinguished; divine aid and the good will of the persons are necessary for this. Law can only say what is just in a certain situation, keeping in mind that marriage does not only involve the couple but also the children and the entire society, of which the family is the foundation (CCC 1643–1654).

For these reasons, canon law is especially interested in what concerns the validity of marriage. Other aspects are more directly concerned with moral and pastoral theology, etc., although all of these aspects remain strictly connected with one another.

A) General Concepts

There are three points on which the valid celebration of marriage rests: a) consent; b) impediments; and c) the form. As specified by c. 1057 § 1, the act which constitutes marriage is the consent of the parties, legitimately manifested (in the proper form) between persons who are capable according to law (without impediments). We shall see each of them below, but first it is necessary to state some general principles and concepts that are important to know in order to understand the canonical matrimonial system.

First, there is the right to contract marriage (*ius conubii*), by which all can marry unless forbidden by law. This is a natural right; the obstacles established by law precisely tend to protect the correct exercise of this right (they are not arbitrary, and no one can add others to them).

Secondly, it should be noted that marriage, being an institution of great personal and social importance, enjoys the favor of the law. As a result, one must apply the principle that when there is doubt, a marriage celebrated is to be held valid until the contrary is proven (c. 1060). In fact, in matrimonial cases before a tribunal, the question is whether or not the *nullity* of the marriage in question can be established for the reasons adduced, and not whether the marriage is valid. Moreover the public good of the marriage requires that the defender of the bond intervene in all matrimonial causes.[111]

Canonical marriage is that celebrated by a Catholic according to the laws of the Church, even if the other spouse is not Catholic.

Valid marriage *between baptized persons* (which is a sacrament) that is not yet consummated is called *merely ratified* (or also ratified and non-consummated). When it is consummated, the marriage is called *ratified and consummated*. Therefore, not every canonical marriage is ratified (when one of the spouses is not baptized).

The *consummation* of the marriage occurs when the spouses have realized between themselves, *in a human way*, the act which in itself is suitable to the generation of offspring, to which marriage is ordered, and by which the spouses

111. For the same reason, in civil matters pertaining to marriage and family, the attorney general intervenes.

become one flesh. The fact that it must occur in a human way signifies that the conjugal act be freely accepted by the two spouses and realized according to nature. It is not necessary, however, that generation actually occur; it is sufficient that the act be in itself suitable for generation (c. 1061 § 1–2).

The consummation adds a particular firmness to sacramental marriage. Whereas a marriage that is *not* consummated can be dissolved by the Roman Pontiff in certain cases, this is not true of a marriage that is ratified and consummated. The consummation is presumed if the spouses have lived together after the wedding.

Putative marriage is an invalid marriage celebrated in good faith by at least one of the parties, until both become aware of the nullity. Thus it is a marriage that is null in reality but is believed in good faith to be valid by at least one of the parties; for that reason it has some effects (see c. 1137).

B) Matrimonial Consent

Canonical marriage is governed by the principle of consent. Only the free consent of the parties can constitute marriage. No human power can substitute for this consent nor can anyone bind another by his own authority (CCC 1625–1629). In a marriage by proxy, for example, the proxy does no more than *manifest* the consent given in writing by the absent party (c. 1057 § 1).

This consent must be *matrimonial*. This means it must consist in the specific act of the will by which the man and the woman, through an irrevocable covenant, mutually give and accept one another in marriage (c. 1057 § 2).

This definition contains in synthesis the requirements and the conditions for consent to be sufficient to generate marriage: capacity, knowledge, freedom, content, mutual donation and acceptance in marriage. Positive law seeks to identify the cases in which the lack of one of these elements vitiates the consent, establishing objective norms which judges must apply in concrete cases.[112]

The psychological process whereby a man and a woman come to the decision to marry is complex and involves practically all the aspects of the person (affection, intellect, imagination, will, passions...). It is in this process that one can individuate possible defects of consent, but it should not be forgotten that falling in love is a natural phenomenon with a particular logic.

It is necessary, however, to distinguish matrimonial consent from the reasons why a person marries another. Whereas the motives can be quite various (love, goodness, beauty, wealth, health), matrimonial consent is always that defined above: a specific act of the will. The motives contribute to lead one to the decision to marry another person, but this decision, once it has been realized in matrimonial consent, remains generally independent of the reasons that led to it. The motives usually concern qualities, while consent refers to the person of another.

We shall see now the defects of consent which are capable of making marriage null.

Incapacity

Since marriage is a type of union to which man tends by nature, the capacity to celebrate marriage is acquired with the normal development of the person, and that is why it is presumed to exist in everyone after a certain age. However, there are psychological disturbances keeping the individual from being capable of giving a valid consent.[113]

112. C. BURKE, "Canon 1057 and the Object of Matrimonial Consent," *Forum* [1992] 29–43.

113. See M. SABLE (coordinator), *Incapacity for Marriage: Jurisprudence and Interpretation.* Acts of the III Gregorian Colloquium, 1–6 September 1986, St. John's Provincial Seminary, Plymouth, Pontificia Universitas Gregoriana, Rome, 1987.

C. 1095 considers to be incapable of contracting marriage those who:

a) "lack the sufficient use of reason"; namely, those who because of insufficient age or of an illness or a temporary disorder (drugs, inebriation, hypnosis), are not capable of understanding and willing the marriage when it is celebrated. We have already seen that the use of reason is presumed to be reached at age seven (c. 97 § 2), but here it is a matter of the use of reason sufficient for an act with significant consequences, which requires a higher conscience than that for an ordinary act. This use of reason is usually acquired with puberty.

b) "suffer from grave lack of discretion of judgment concerning essential matrimonial rights and duties which are to be mutually given and accepted." Here it is not a matter of the use of reason in general, but of that self-control and exercise of the mental faculties, which is provided to the interpersonal commitment of marriage; that is, the ability to understand, choose, and responsibly accept the essential aspects of the marital union.[114]

A serious lack of discretion may be due to immaturity or to another psychological anomaly notably affecting the free exercise of reason or will.

c) "are not capable of assuming the essential obligations of matrimony due to causes of a psychological nature." This, in a certain sense, is the prolongation of the previous case, which especially takes into consideration the incapacity to fulfill the essential matrimonial duties, even if the capacity to intend and will them exists. This is a cause of incapacity which arises from certain psycho-sexual disorders (homosexuality, nymphomania, satyriasis), but it may be owing to other personality disorders, especially behavioral disorders

---

114. See R. L. BURKE, *Lack of Discretion of Judgment Because of Schizophrenia*, Pontificia Universitas Gregoriana, Roma, 1986.

(violence, erratic behavior, dependence, asociality) that, when grave, certainly prevent the subject from behaving as a spouse (and as a mother or father).

It can be seen that it is not an easy matter to apply these rules to concrete cases. It is necessary to determine what are the essential rights and duties of marriage, and to ascertain (sometimes after many years) the grave presence of the defect at the moment of the wedding, even if the more evident manifestations of them occurred afterwards. This ascertainment normally requires the advice of a medical expert.[115] Logically, an incapacity arising after the celebration of the marriage does not make it invalid.

Ignorance

Consenting to something necessarily implies sufficient knowledge of that to which one is giving consent. To be able to give valid matrimonial consent, it is necessary that the contracting parties not be ignorant that marriage is the permanent community between a man and a woman, ordered to the procreation of offspring by means of some sexual cooperation (c. 1096).

However, it is not required that there be a deeper and well-reasoned knowledge, or still less an experience. What is required is the knowledge which normally occurs with the natural development of the person. Therefore, after the age of puberty, it is presumed that the subject has sufficient knowledge to marry, unless the contrary can be demonstrated.

115. In his annual speeches to the Roman Rota, the Pope often tackled these problems, for example, warning that *maturity* or *normalcy* for marrying does not mean an absolute absence of defects or weaknesses, which we all possess; that we should not confuse *difficulty* with *incapacity* for consent, only the alter makes it invalid; that only a *substantial* disorder of the faculties makes the subject incapable. See T. G. DORAN, "Some thoughts on experts," *Quaderni Studio Rotale* IV, 1989, pp. 59–74.

Error of Law

Precisely because the minimal knowledge required with regard to marriage does not imply an exact knowledge of all its characteristics and properties, error concerning the *essential properties* of marriage (indissolubility, unity and sacramentality) in itself does not render the consent invalid. Only if the error has determined the will of the subject does it vitiate consent (c. 1099). It is not the same to marry *thinking* that marriage is dissoluble, as to marry *willing* that the concrete marriage that is being celebrated be dissoluble. Only in the latter case is one subtracting an essential content from matrimonial consent. One can have many mistaken ideas on marriage in general, but then, when one loves a person, one desires to *truly* marry that person.

In fact, one can even be certain or suppose that a marriage will be null (for example, if one holds that there is an impediment), and nevertheless will to marry. For this reason the knowledge of or the opinion on the nullity of a marriage does not necessarily exclude true matrimonial consent (c. 1100). Even if a marriage is null because of an impediment or a defect of form, the consent which was given is presumed to continue unless its revocation has been proven (c. 1107).

Error of Fact

On the other hand, matrimonial consent cannot be generic ("I want to marry"), but must be between two concrete persons ("I want to marry you"). For this reason, *error concerning the person* makes the marriage invalid (c. 1097 § 1).

However, it is the persons who marry, and not their qualities. As a result, *error concerning a quality* of the other is not in itself a cause of nullity, even if the supposed quality of the other was the reason for marrying him or her.

For example, if someone marries another because he or she is held to be rich, and then it turns out that he is poor, this does not cause nullity of the marriage. Everyone, in fact, would like to find good qualities in the other (goodness, health, wealth...), and they will even be convinced that they have them; and thus when the marriage fails, all sincerely say: "I was wrong. If I had known that he was like this, I wouldn't have married him." However, this is insufficient to prove that she did not want to marry him.

This type of discourse would be valid before marriage during the period of engagement, but it cannot be transferred to the case of a marriage that has already been celebrated. One marries the person, with all his good points and bad points, even if they are not known or are insufficiently evaluated. The validity of the marriage cannot depend on the satisfaction of the expectations that were formed with regard to the spouse.

However, there are two cases in which error concerning the quality of the spouse renders the marriage null (c. 1097 § 2):

- when the quality is of such a nature as to identify the person as such. The example is usually given of someone who does not know the other person, but only knows that he is the firstborn of such a family. In this case, error about primogeniture is equivalent to error regarding the person. Today it is a very rare case;
- when the error concerns a quality "directly and principally intended" (obviously before marriage). In this case, in fact, the quality is not only a reason for the sake of which consent is given, but becomes the *object* of the matrimonial consent itself. It is like a condition, in the sense that the person who directly and principally intends a quality of the other would not consent except in so far as such a quality exists.

In practice it is not easy to distinguish if a quality is desired in general—in the sense that every spouse expects and presupposes the existence of such quality—or if it is desired directly and principally. This difficulty is present, for example, with regard to fertility. Certainly every spouse hopes for, expects and desires that the other spouse can generate, but by no means can it be affirmed that this quality has always been directly and principally intended.

Deceit (c. 1098)

A particular type of error is that provoked by deceit (i.e. bad faith) perpetrated in order to obtain consent. In this case, if the deception concerns a quality of the other party which by its nature is capable of gravely perturbing the conjugal partnership, the marriage is invalid. In fact, an error provoked by fraud diminishes the knowledge and thus the free choice of the person who has been deceived. In any case, it is necessary that the deception have effectively occurred, that it be plotted by fraud and with the precise purpose of obtaining consent. On the other hand, it is not required that the author of the fraud be the other spouse (it can also be a third party). Sterility would be an example of a quality with a grave effect on the marital partnership, if it is hidden through deceit. Sometimes it is hard to discern whether one was deceived or deceived oneself; it is more common to call it deceit after disappointment.

Simulation (c. 1101)

This is the discordance between what one says to desire, and what one desires in reality. Marriage cannot arise without true consent, for which reason the Church counts on the real consent of the parties, beyond the formalities of the celebration. However, the fact remains that such intentions frequently remain in the soul of the spouses.

First, one presumes that the words or gestures used in the celebration are in conformity with the internal acts of the soul. In fact, in a matter as important as marriage, people do not normally sham.

However, if in reality one or both of the parties exclude marriage itself or an essential property of it with a positive act of the will, the marriage is invalid. The intention to exclude must be *positive*; it is not sufficient, for example, to think, prefer, or wish for the marriage to be dissoluble, but rather marrying excluding the perpetuity of the concrete marriage celebrated.

The exclusion of marriage itself is called *total simulation*: in this case the simulator in reality does not want to marry, even though the wedding is celebrated and he says yes, there is no consent.

The exclusion of some element or essential property is called *partial simulation*. Fidelity, indissolubility, sacramentality, and offspring are essential elements (not optional). In this case the person desires to marry while positively refusing to accept a part of the specific and necessary content of marriage. Thus there is a *non-matrimonial* consent, in that what is desired in reality is another type of union.[116]

The procedural evidence of simulation requires above all the demonstration of the positive intention to exclude; this, as we said, may be difficult if this intention was hidden. Then it is necessary to resort to circumstantial evidence: for example, the fact that there were reasons to simulate that were stronger than the reasons to marry.

Conditions (c. 1102)

Matrimonial consent is given under condition when it depends on any fact or circumstance (for ex.: "I marry you if you are a virgin"). The condition may concern a fact that is past, present, or future.[117]

The law does not permit marriages based on a condition concerning the future because marriage cannot be left in suspense nor considered as a trial. It either is or is not. For this reason, a future condition makes the consent invalid. Therefore, one cannot contract marriage with the condition "if we have children," or "if you stop taking drugs."

---

116. See C. BURKE, "Matrimonial Consent and the *bonum prolis*," *Monitor Ecclesiasticus* [1989] 397–404; ID, "The Content of the *bonum fidei*," *The Jurist* [1991] 138–154.

117. It is understood that we are not speaking of the condition in its proper sense, which only refers to a future, uncertain act.

If, on the other hand, the matrimonial consent is given under a condition concerning the past or the present, it is valid or invalid insofar as the condition is realized or not. If one were to say "I marry you if you truly are pregnant," the marriage would be valid if in fact the pregnancy existed; otherwise it would not be valid.

It is obvious that it is dangerous to pose conditions to consent. One reason for this, among others, is that it is not licit to begin living together until one knows if the condition is realized, which determines whether the marriage truly exists or not. For this reason, it is not licit to pose present or past conditions without the written permission of the Ordinary.

Furthermore, it is necessary to distinguish whether the condition refers to the decision to marry or to the matrimonial consent itself. In the normal process of dialogue, the future spouses frequently express desires or requests ("we will live with my parents," "I will work at home," "we will have children") which then do not enter into the matrimonial consent as true and proper conditions.

Violence and Fear

Consent must be free. Therefore, those who feel constrained to marry by reason of violence or grave fear that is provoked externally, even if not intentionally, are in reality not truly free and their consent is vitiated (c. 1103).

Violence is a physical coercion, which quite evidently makes marriage invalid. The case is different with regard to fear which, being of a psychological nature, admits various intensities of reaction in those who undergo it.

In order for fear to make the consent invalid, it must be: a) *grave*, which means that it causes a serious commotion in the person who experiences it; b) *external*, which means that it is not the fruit of the fantasy of the subject; and c) *efficacious*, which means that the spouse has truly been constrained to choose marriage as a way out (even if this is not the intent of the other party). The pressure of the parents or the fear of causing displeasure are not sufficient in themselves to coerce someone into marriage. Sufficient causes would be the threat of suicide from the other party, grave threats from the parents of the woman, blackmail, etc.

Finally, it should be said that for matrimonial consent to be valid, it must be given by both parties, simultaneously present in person or by means of a proxy, and given with words or signs expressing the present indicative ("I marry you," not "I will marry you," nor "I would like to marry you").

C) Impediments

Impediments are facts or circumstances which impede marriage by making the person incapable of validly celebrating it (c. 1073). For example, if one of the parties is already married, there is the impediment of the bond. The impediments have the purpose of protecting the dignity of marriage itself, the rights or duties of the persons concerned, and the common good in general. Since they are exceptions to the natural right to contract marriage, the impediments must be expressly defined by the law and are to be interpreted in the strict sense.[118]

Only the supreme authority can establish impediments. No custom can establish or abolish impediments. In particular cases, the local Ordinary can establish a temporary prohibition for a serious reason, but its violation does not make the marriage invalid, but only illicit (cc. 1075–1077).

An impediment is held to be *public* if it can be proven in the external forum (witnesses, documents, etc.); otherwise, it is *occult* (c. 1074), but sometimes something not divulged is also called occult.

---

118. Remember what was said about invalidating and incapacitating laws. (Chap. II, 3).

Impediments can be of *divine law* or of *ecclesiastical law.* Those of divine law cannot be dispensed. Therefore, dispensation from impediments always refers to those of ecclesiastical law. It belongs solely to the supreme authority of the Church to declare when an impediment is of divine law.

Dispensation from impediments depends on various circumstances (cc. 1078–1082).

a) In normal *circumstances* dispensations can be given by:

- the Holy See with regard to all impediments. However, no dispensation is ever given from consanguinity in the direct line or in the second degree of the collateral line (between brother and sister);

- the local Ordinary with regard to his subjects and those who dwell in his territory, with respect to all impediments except those of holy orders, public perpetual vows of chastity given in a religious institute of pontifical right, and crime, whose dispensation is reserved to the Holy See.

b) If one discovers that there is an impediment *when everything is ready for the wedding* and it is not possible to wait for the arrival of the dispensation without grave damage, a dispensation from all impediments except that of holy orders can be given by:

- the local Ordinary;

- the parish priest and the sacred minister who assists at the marriage, if it is not possible to have recourse even to the local Ordinary and the case is occult;

- the confessor in the internal forum, if the case is occult.

c) In cases of *urgent danger of death*, all impediments except that of holy orders with regard to the presbyterate (thus including that of the diaconate also) can be dispensed by:

- the local Ordinary;

- the parish priest and the sacred minister who assists at the marriage, if it is not possible to have recourse even to the local Ordinary;
- the confessor in the internal forum, only when the impediments are occult.

The Impediments in Particular

Age. A woman under 14 and a man under 16 cannot validly marry. The conference of bishops can fix an older age, but only with regard to licitness. The episcopal conference may set an older age, but only for lawfulness; often it is done by adapting it to the age required by state law (c. 1083).

The purpose of this impediment is to objectively fix the minimum of biological and psychological maturity for marriage. However, it is a limit imposed by ecclesiastical law and not by nature, since some naturally mature earlier than others. Therefore, this impediment can receive a dispensation if that maturity is reached before the legal age (a typical reason is if the woman is pregnant).

Impotence. Since the conjugal act is essential to marriage itself, copulative impotence—which means the impossibility to accomplish the conjugal act (because of an organic or psychological anomaly)—makes the marriage null if it is antecedent and perpetual. This is an impediment of natural (divine) law which cannot be dispensed from. It does not matter if the impotence is of the man or of the woman, absolute (impossibility to accomplish the conjugal act with anyone) or relative (impossibility to accomplish it with the spouse).

Impotence which begins after marriage or which can be cured with licit and proportionate means, does not impede the marriage. Impotence is different from sterility, which does not in itself invalidate the marriage (c. 1084).

Bond (c. 1085). A person who is already bound in marriage, even if not consummated, cannot contract marriage. This impediment is required by the exclusivity and indissolubility of the bond. As such it is an impediment which cannot be dispensed from.

Even if the first marriage is null or dissolved, it is not *licit* to celebrate another marriage until the nullity or the dissolution has been established with certainty.

Disparity of cult. A Catholic cannot validly marry a non-baptized person without the requisite dispensation (c. 1086).

Mixed marriages normally present dangers and difficulties for the faith of the Catholic party and for the well-being of the marriage itself, which is the reason for the prohibition. Nevertheless, this impediment can be dispensed from if the Catholic party can provide guarantees that he will be able to avoid the danger of falling away from the faith and will do everything possible to baptize and educate the children in the Church; the non-Catholic party must be informed of this (see cc. 1125–1126 and CCC 1633–1637).

In any event, both parties must acknowledge and not exclude the essential characteristics of marriage (fidelity, perpetuity, etc.).

The Church considers the marriage between a non-Catholic and a Catholic, who has separated from the Church by means of a formal act, to be valid, since in this case the aforementioned dangers are not applicable.

If a doubt concerning the baptism of one of the parties arises after marriage, the marriage is held to be valid until the certainty of the absence of baptism has been proven.

Holy orders. Those who have received the sacrament of orders in any grade (deacon, priest or bishop) cannot validly marry.

In the Church, holy orders carry with them the commitment to celibacy. Thus the law has established this impediment, which also binds permanent deacons, who cannot marry *after* ordination. The dispensation from this impediment is normally reserved to the Holy See and carries with it the prohibition from exercising orders (c. 1087).

Vow. Those who have made a perpetual public vow of chastity in a religious institute cannot validly marry (c. 1088).

This impediment has the purpose of protecting the commitments of religious profession. It does not apply, however, to the assumption of the evangelical counsel of chastity in a secular institute, to temporary vows, or to other sacred bonds different from a vow (promise, oath, etc.). Dispensation from this impediment in the case of an institute of pontifical right is reserved to the Holy See, except in danger of death.

Abduction. If a man abducts or at least detains a woman for the purpose of marrying her, there arises the impediment of abduction. On this account there cannot be a valid marriage between them until the woman—separated from her abductor and established in a place that is free and safe—chooses the marriage of her own accord (c. 1089).

The purpose of this cause of invalidity is to protect the freedom of the woman and to avoid doubts concerning the validity of her consent. Logically, this impediment cannot be dispensed from, but the marriage contracted while it existed may be validated.

Crime. This impediment arises between two specific persons, one of whose spouse has been killed. This includes two different cases: a) those who, *for the purpose* of entering into marriage with another person, bring about the death of their own spouse or the spouse of the person they intend to marry, invalidly attempt such marriage; b) when two persons have cooperated in the killing of one of their spouses, *even if not for the purpose* of entering into marriage, they cannot validly marry.

It is a matter of protecting the life of persons, the stability and dignity of the family, and of dissuading potential criminals. Because of the gravity of the matter, dispensation is regularly reserved to the Holy See (cc. 1090 and 1078 § 2, 2°).

Consanguinity (c. 1091). Marriage is invalid between persons related by consanguinity in any degree in the direct line (between ancestors and descendants), and up to and including the fourth degree in the collateral line (brothers and sisters, aunts/uncles and nieces/nephews, cousins).

The impediments which arise between relatives have the purpose of impeding that the normal relations within a family be made unnatural, and to avoid endogamy. Consanguinity in the direct line or in the second degree of the collateral line (brothers and sisters) is never dispensed from, and in cases of doubt in this regard, marriage is never to be permitted.

Affinity (c. 1092). This is the tie of relationship that arises between a spouse and the blood relations of the other spouse (acquired relatives). Marriage is rendered null only in the direct line (father- or mother-in-law with their son- or daughter-in-law).

Public propriety. This is the relationship that arises from the fact that two persons actually live together (putative marriage or concubinage). The impediment prohibits marriage between the man and the blood relatives of the woman in the first grade of the direct line (mother or daughter), and vice versa (c. 1093).

Legal relationship (c. 1094). This arises through adoption. The impediment invalidates marriage in the direct line (between the person who adopts and the one who is adopted), and in the second grade of the collateral line (brothers and sisters).

D) The Form of Marriage

The social relevance of marriage requires that it be celebrated publicly, in order to protect the freedom of the spouses, and to make evident and certain the existence of the bond between them.

Even though the consent of the parties constitutes the marriage, the Church requires that this consent be manifested in a legitimate form for the marriage to be *valid*. This means that the couple must wed in the presence of the local Ordinary or pastor (or a priest or deacon delegated by them), and in the presence of two witnesses. The sacred minister *assists* at the marriage when he personally asks those who are contracting marriage to manifest their consent, and receives this manifestation in the name of the Church (c. 1108).

The sacred minister *assists* at marriage as a *qualified witness*, not as the minister of the sacrament. In the Latin Church, the ministers of the sacrament are the spouses themselves. Therefore, even a lay person, in certain cases, can receive the delegation to assist at marriage as a qualified witness (c. 1112).

Because the validity of marriage is at stake, the law establishes precise norms on the canonical form of marriage (competence and its delegation, exemption and the dispensation from the form, mixed marriages, etc.).

The canonical form must be observed for the validity of the marriage (invalidating law) when at least one of the parties is a Catholic who has not left the Church by a formal act.

It is necessary to distinguish between the *juridical* or canonical form (what is required by law: assisting minister and two witnesses), and the *liturgical* form, which is the rite within which the juridical formalities are normally realized, but which is not necessary for validity.

Besides the ordinary juridical form (assisting minister and two witnesses), there exists the form which is called *extraordinary*, which consists in celebrating the marriage in the presence of the two witnesses only.

This extraordinary form is validly used when one cannot obtain the presence of or go to the competent assisting minister without grave inconvenience. In addition, there must be:

- danger of death; or
- although there is no danger of death, it is foreseen that the difficulties regarding the presence of the competent assisting minister will last for at least a month.

The purpose of this is to facilitate the exercise of the right to marry when the observance of the ordinary form is impossible or overly burdensome (due to distance, war, persecution, etc.).

For a just cause, the obligation of the canonical form can be also dispensed from in concrete cases, for example, a mixed marriage in which the non-Catholic party does not want to marry in the Church. In these cases some public form of celebration, such as the civil form, must be observed in order for the marriage to be valid. The marriage is canonical in any case, and also a sacrament if both parties are baptized.

Once the marriage has been celebrated in any form (ordinary or extraordinary canonical form, or civil form), it must be entered in the marriage register and in the baptismal register of the spouses, to show their married state (cc. 1121–1123).

The marriage can be also celebrated in secret if there are grave reasons for it, and with the permission of the local Ordinary (for example, two persons who have lived together—and who are held to be married by all—want then to celebrate the marriage). This means that the pre-matrimonial investigation is to be made secretly, that all who are present are bound to the secret (the spouses, the local Ordinary, the assisting minister, the witnesses), and that the annotation of the marriage be accomplished in a special register of the diocesan curia (cc. 1131–1133).

E) Effects of Marriage

Once the marriage has been validly celebrated, there arises a perpetual and exclusive bond between the spouses. The sacrament then gives to the Christian spouses the grace to live the married state in harmony with their Christian vocation, despite the difficulties that can arise in the conjugal partnership (c. 1134).

Each of the spouses has equal rights and duties in the conjugal community, especially with regard to the education of the children (c. 1135).

Legitimate children are those who are conceived or born in a valid or putative marriage (a marriage which is null, but in good faith for at least one of the spouses). One presumes that the father of the children born of a married woman is the husband of the mother, unless the contrary is proven. Children born outside of wedlock are legitimized by the subsequent marriage of the parents and they are equivalent in everything to legitimate children, except when the law expressly states otherwise (cc. 1137–1140).

F) Dissolution of the Marriage Bond

Every marriage is perpetual and indissoluble in itself. Ratified and consummated marriage cannot be dissolved by any human power or by any cause other than death (c. 1141).

Besides death, there are two cases in which a marriage can be dissolved by the authority: a) when it has not been consummated; and b) when it is not *ratified* or sacramental. Let us consider them.

Dispensation of Non-Consummated Marriage (c. 1142)
Marriage that has not been consummated, between baptized persons or between one who has been baptized and another not baptized, can be dissolved by the Roman Pontiff if there is a just cause and if at least one of the parties asks for it (even if the other is opposed). It is a *dispensation* from the law of indissolubility. The indissolubility was not "consolidated" because of the lack of consummation.

The request for dissolution implies the opening of a particular procedure intended to prove that there are extreme reasons for the concession of the dispensation. It begins in the diocese and then passes to the Congr. for the Sacraments (see Chapter XII, 7).

We have seen that the consummation is presumed if the spouses have lived together after the celebration of the marriage (c. 1061 § 2). In this case, the lack of consummation can nevertheless be demonstrated with various arguments in the process mentioned above.

Dissolution in Favor of the Faith (cc. 1143–1150)

This case of two *not baptized* persons who marry, and then one of the spouses converts and is baptized.[119] If the non-baptized party does not want to live with the baptized party peacefully and without offending the Creator, the marriage can be dissolved in favor of the faith of the baptized party.

As a basis for this dissolution, the passage from Saint Paul in 1 Cor 7, 12–15 is invoked; hence it is called the Pauline privilege.

The dissolution occurs precisely in the moment when the baptized party celebrates a new marriage, but in order to do so validly, it is necessary:

- that after baptism no just cause for separation was given by the baptized party to the non-baptized party;
- that the non-baptized party be interrogated on whether he or she also wishes to receive baptism or whether he or she at least wishes to cohabit in peace with the baptized party without insult to the Creator. This interrogation can be omitted if it is impossible to perform it or if it is evident that it would be useless (for example, if the spouses were separated for a long time or even divorced).

If the answer is negative (in words or in facts), then the party who has converted can celebrate a new marriage.

Another case of dissolution in favor of the faith is when baptism is received by someone who simultaneously has more than one wife or husband, and either he cannot, or it is difficult, to remain with the first spouse he married. In this case he can choose to canonically marry one of them, leaving the others.

119. In practice, this form of dissolution is applied to all marriages which are not *ratified*, that is, non-sacramental.

The same applies to the case of a person who receives baptism and who cannot restore cohabitation with a non-baptized spouse because of prison or persecution. In this case he can marry another person. An example of this would be someone who has been separated from his family and deported, and who then converts and receives baptism but cannot return to his spouse.

G) Separation of the Spouses

Separation refers to the rupture of the common life of the spouses, while the bond remains. Conjugal living together is a right and a duty for the spouses, but it can be interrupted for legitimate causes (c. 1151). These can be:

- adultery: the innocent spouse has the right to permanently interrupt conjugal life, except when he or she has consented to the adultery, or given cause for it, or likewise committed adultery. Nevertheless, the innocent spouse is earnestly recommended to pardon for the good of the family (c. 1152);
- if the moral or physical health of the spouse or children has been put in grave danger or if the common life has in any case been made too difficult (torture, dangerous illness, deviations, etc.). This is a cause of separation as long as this state of affairs lasts (c. 1153).

Separation, even if it is undertaken on one's own initiative, must then be deferred to the Church authority so that it can be examined whether it is well-founded and if there is the possibility of re-establishing cohabitation.

Once cohabitation has been removed, the duties that arise from the bond still remain: fidelity, support, education of the children, etc.

H) Convalidation of the Marriage

The convalidation of a marriage occurs when a marriage, which one knows or suspects to be null, becomes certainly valid. Nullity, as we have seen, may come from a defect of consent, from an impediment, or from an irregularity in the form.

Consent cannot be substituted by any human power. Therefore the convalidation of a marriage in which the consent of one party was defective can only come about when that party gives that consent. On the other hand, one presumes that valid consent remains, unless the contrary is proven, even if the marriage is null for other reasons (impediment, form).

There can be both a simple convalidation and a retroactive validation (radical sanation).

Simple Convalidation (cc. 1156–1160)

Simple convalidation consists in the renewal of the consent by at least one of the parties as long as the other perseveres in the consent given at the moment of celebration. The possibilities are:

a) When the marriage is null due to an *impediment*. Once the impediment has ceased or the dispensation has been obtained:

- if the impediment is *occult* (i.e. if it cannot be proven in the external forum), the private and secret consent of the party who is aware of it is sufficient, as long as the other party perseveres in his consent. If it is known by both, both must renew their consent, privately and in secret;
- if, on the other hand, the impediment is *public*, the consent must always be renewed by both parties and according to the canonical form. More than a convalidation, what is done is remarrying, albeit in secret.

b) When the nullity comes from a *defect of consent*, the marriage is convalidated if the party whose consent had been defective gives that consent, provided the consent of the other still exists (cf. c. 1107):

- if the defect cannot be proven, it suffices that the consent be given privately and in secret;
- if, on the other hand, the defect can be proven, the consent must be given with the canonical form.

c) When the nullity comes from a *defect of form*, the marriage must be contracted anew according to the canonical form.

Retroactive Validation (Radical Sanation, cc. 1161–1165)

Retroactive validation consists in the convalidation which occurs *without* renewal of the consent and by *concession* of the competent authority. This concession implies dispensation from the impediment, if there was any, and from the canonical form, if it was not observed. It is obvious that a marriage which is null because of the defect of consent cannot be remedied, because consent cannot be dispensed from.

Retroactive validation serves therefore to convalidate a marriage which was null because of an impediment or by a defect in the form, even if not known by the parties or by one of them, as long as they both persevere in their consent (which, as we saw, is presumed until proven otherwise, c. 1107). The parish priest, the confessor, or the party discovering the nullity of the marriage may request it.

Logically, if it is an impediment of divine law, the validation cannot occur before the impediment ceases, because dispensation is not allowed (it would be the case of an impediment of the bond).

Retroactive validation can be conceded by the Holy See, and also by the diocesan bishop for the impediments that he can dispense from and for the form.

I) Pastoral Care and Preparation for Marriage (cc. 1063–1072)

Pastoral care before and after the celebration of the marriage must be put in close connection with the strictly juridical aspects of marriage which we have seen up until now. In reality, it is a matter that concerns law only partially, although it is of great importance for the life of the Church. Therefore, after having mentioned the obligation of the pastors to give the faithful an adequate pastoral care in the path of matrimony, the canons center their attention on the aspects which are connected with the valid and licit celebration of marriage, namely, the previous investigation which must be realized for this purpose.

This non-contentious pre-matrimonial process includes the examination of the spouses, the marriage banns, the acquisition of the documents and other means to prove that there are no impediments, that the parties are aware of the commitments of marriage, and are marrying freely.

It is up to the conference of bishops to determine with greater precision the way to conduct the pre-matrimonial investigation.

Furthermore, there are various circumstances which are not true and proper impediments but which, nevertheless, represent a certain difficulty to admit the parties to the sacrament. For this reason the law commands that in the presence of any of them, one must first obtain the *permission* of the local Ordinary. These circumstances are:

- the marriage of transients, because of the difficulty of proving their unmarried state;

- a marriage which cannot be recognized or celebrated in accord with the state law, for which reason it could constitute an illicit civil marriage and the spouses would appear unmarried in the eyes of the State;

- a marriage of a person who is bound by natural obligations towards another party or toward children, arising from a previous union (*de facto* or of a solely civil nature), and wishes to marry another person in the Church. In this case the subject is free to contract canonical marriage, but he or she cannot ignore the preceding bonds, even though they do not constitute or derive from true marriage;

- marriage by means of a proxy; in order to secure the validity of the mandate, on which that of the marriage also depends;
- marriage of a person who is bound by a censure (excommunication or interdict) or of someone who has notoriously abandoned the Catholic faith, to secure their rectitude of intention and acceptance of the (also sacramental) commitments of marriage, and to avoid possible scandal among the faithful;
- marriage of a minor child when his parents are unaware of it or reasonably opposed to it.

In these cases, however, even if the marriage is celebrated without the permission of the local Ordinary, it is still valid.

4. Other Acts of Divine Worship

In addition to the sacraments which constitute the nucleus of the liturgy of the Church, there are other acts of worship regulated by canon law in order to secure their valid and correct celebration, and thus the juridical effects deriving from them. These are sacramentals, funeral rites, liturgy of the hours, vows, and oaths. Like the sacraments, they also are public means of sanctification and are therefore included in the sanctifying office of the Church.

A) Sacramentals (cc. 1166–1172)

Sacramentals are sacred signs which, though not sacraments, imitate them in a certain way, since by means of sacramentals, through the prayer of the Church, spiritual effects are signified and obtained (*SC* 60; CCC 1677–1673). They are principally benedictions (of persons, of objects), but also the imposition of hands, anointing, prayers, etc.

Many sacramentals form part of the rites which accompany the sacraments (anointing in baptism, the prayer of the

Our Father, the final blessing, etc.). Here, however, we are interested in those sacramentals which are celebrated as acts of worship in themselves and for their own sake.

The rites for the celebration of the sacramentals are found in the liturgical books, principally in the *Rite of Benedictions*; we only find the principal norms pertaining to them in the Code.

Only the Apostolic See can institute sacramentals, as well as interpret, abolish or modify any of them. Here an essential difference appears with respect to the sacraments. The sacraments have been instituted by Christ, and the Church cannot suppress any of them or add to them, nor modify their substance which is of divine law (matter, form, effects). The sacramentals, on the other hand, are of ecclesiastical law (human law).

The ordinary ministers of the sacramentals are clerics, each according to the grade of the sacrament of orders received, as follows:

- *consecrations* (of persons, for example, virgins; or of things, for example, the holy chrism for confirmation) and *dedications* (of churches and altars) are specifically reserved to bishops, but they can also be validly realized by a priest authorized by law or by a legitimate concession;
- *blessings*, of persons and of things, can be imparted by any priest, except those reserved to the Roman Pontiff (for example, the *Urbi et orbi* blessing) and bishops (for example, the oil for confirmation);
- deacons can only give those blessings which are expressly permitted to them by law.

Lay persons who have the appropriate qualities can administer the sacramentals which the local Ordinary judges fit (parents may bless their children, the blessing of the families may be entrusted to a lay person, religious or a catechist…).

The *subjects* of blessings are Catholics, but also catechumens, and even non-Catholics unless there is a prohibition by the Church. This is another difference with respect to the sacraments, which can only be received by the baptized.

Those things which are destined for divine worship (churches, vestments, chalices...) are also to be dedicated or blessed. This constitutes them as *sacred things* that must be treated with reverence and not used for profane or improper purposes, even if they belong to private individuals.

Exorcisms are a special type of sacramental, in which a priest asks the Lord to remove the devil from a person, animal or thing. Since these are difficult cases, the law establishes that exorcisms be realized only by those who have a special and express permission of the local Ordinary, who in turn will grant this permission only to priests who are learned, pious, prudent and of exemplary life (c. 1172).

B) The Liturgy of the Hours (cc. 1173–1175)

The liturgy of the hours has been an important part of the public worship of the Church for a long time. Its purpose is to consecrate the hours of the day to God, fulfilling the exhortation of the Lord "to pray always" (Lk 18, 1). All the faithful are invited to take part in this uninterrupted public prayer with which the Church praises her Lord. However, clerics and members of institutes of consecrated life must perform this ministry every day in the name of the Church, according to law[120] and according to the approved books (CCC 1174–1178).

C) Church Funerals (cc. 1176–1185)

Funerals are acts of worship with which the Church prays for spiritual aid for the faithful departed, honors their bodies, and brings solace of hope to the living. They must be celebrated

120. For example, according to c. 276 § 2–3, the conference of bishops establishes the times when permanent deacons must pray each day.

according to the liturgical norms, which establish various ways of performing them (CCC 1689 ff.).

It is a duty of pastors to give the funeral rites to the faithful departed, except in cases in which the law establishes that they are to be denied. Catechumens are also to be given funeral rites.

The local Ordinary may allow Church funeral rites for children who died before baptism and whose parents had intended to baptize them, and also for non-Catholic baptized persons, if not evidently contrary to their will and provided that they cannot have their own minister.

Unless they have given some signs of repentance before death, the following persons must be deprived of Church funeral rites:

- heretics, apostates or notorious schismatics;
- those who choose to have their body cremated for reasons contrary to the faith;
- other manifest sinners to whom Church funeral rites cannot be given without scandal of the faithful.

However, if there is some doubt, the competent local Ordinary is to be consulted. The privation of Church funeral rites includes that of any funeral Mass.

Normally, funeral rites are to be celebrated in the parish of the faithful departed or in the parish in which the death occurred, unless the deceased or those responsible have not selected another church for the funeral. The funeral rites of a diocesan bishop (also emeritus) are celebrated in the cathedral, unless another church has been chosen.

The funeral rites of religious and members of a society of apostolic life are celebrated in their church or oratory by the superior or by the chaplain.

The interment is to occur in the cemetery of the parish if it has one, but everyone is free to choose a cemetery for burial, unless there is a prohibition by law (it is no longer permitted for anyone who is not a bishop to be buried in a church). The interment is to be entered in the death registry.

The Church earnestly counsels the faithful to follow the tradition of *burying* the bodies of the faithful departed, as a sign of hope in the resurrection. Nevertheless, cremation is not forbidden, unless it has been chosen for reasons contrary to the faith.

D) Veneration of the Saints, of Sacred Images and of Relics (c. 1186–1190)

Different from worship of God, although in strict relationship with it, is the cult with which the Church venerates the saints, especially the Blessed Mary ever Virgin, the Mother of God. The saints are for us a living sign of the salvific power of the Lord, an example of Christian life, and a support for us through their intercession.

The veneration of saints is regulated by the liturgical norms. The Code only says that it is licit to venerate with public cult solely those servants of God whom the Church has included in the catalogue of the saints or of the blessed (c. 1187).

Devotion to sacred images is an ancient practice in the Church and is to be always conserved, even against doctrines and persecution that have attempted to remove them. Their veneration is not idolatry, it is directed to what they represent. Their purpose is to support the piety of the faithful. That is why they are to be displayed in churches with harmony, so that they do not give opportunity for surprise or deviations from honest devotion (c. 1188).

Precious images, which are those outstanding for antiquity, art or the devotion that they attract, are to be conserved with care and are not to be restored without the written permission of the Ordinary, who must consult with experts before granting it (c. 1189).

The Church also renders cult to sacred relics, which has a long tradition in the Church, which early in her history became accustomed to using the sepulchres of the martyrs as altars. To avoid abuses in this matter, the Church examines the authenticity of relics and prohibits their sale (c. 1190).

Sacred images and relics which are honored with great veneration by the people cannot be validly alienated or perpetually transferred without the permission of the Holy See, to avoid disputes that may hurt the feelings of the faithful (cc. 1292 § 2 and 1377).

E) Vows and Oaths (cc. 1191–1204)

Vows and oaths are acts of the virtue of religion which constitute acts of worship when they are recognized by the Church. In addition, they are bonds which have juridical consequences; this is the reason why the law regulates their principal elements.

A *vow* is a promise freely made to God of a possible and better good (for the person who makes it). Thus it must be realized through the virtue of religion. A vow can be made by anyone who has use of reason and is not prohibited from doing so by law. A vow made by reason of grave or unjust fear or through deception is null. The vow binds only the person who makes it, and not others (cc. 1191–1193).

A vow is *public* if it is accepted in the name of the Church by the legitimate superior (for example, religious vows); otherwise it is *private*. It is *personal* if it consists in an action of the person who makes it (for example, a pilgrimage). It is *real* if the object of the promise is a thing (for example, the giving of alms, candles). It can also be *mixed* (for example, painting a work of art for a church; c. 1192).

The vow ceases for various reasons (c. 1194):

- after the time fixed for its fulfillment, for example, a temporary vow; or a promise to do something within a given period of time, after which the vow ceases, whether or not it was observed;

- when there is a substantial change in the matter promised; in this case the object of the vow can become less upright, harmful or impossible (for example, if someone promises to fast but falls ill and therefore must eat);
- the condition attached to the vow is not realized;
- the purpose for which the vow was made no longer exists; for example, someone vows to make an offering for the construction of a church which then the authority decides not to build.

Also, if a third party has power over the matter of the vow, he can *suspend* the obligation as long as its realization would cause him harm (for example, if the fulfillment of a vow would upset the plans of the entire family). Also vows made before religious profession are suspended as long as the person remains in the institute (c. 1195).

A vow also ceases through *dispensation*. Besides the Roman Pontiff, the following persons can dispense from *private* vows if there is a just cause and no harm is given to the right of another:[121]

- the local Ordinary and the parish priest with regard to their own subjects and also to travelers;
- the superior of a religious institute or society of apostolic life if they are clerical and of pontifical right, with regard to their members, novices and those who dwell in a house of the institute (staff, students, etc.);
- persons to whom the power of dispensation has been delegated by the Apostolic See or by the local Ordinary (c. 1196).

A person who has made a vow can commute its object into a better one.

121. Regarding the dispensation of public vows, see Chapter VII, 1 a).

An *oath* is the invocation of the name of God as a witness to the truth of what is affirmed or of what one promises to do. It is called *assertive* when one swears to tell the truth; it is called *promissory* when one swears to do something. An oath freely made gives rise to a special obligation of religion, which is added to the natural obligation to always tell the truth (cc. 1199–1200 § 1).

In certain cases, law requires corroboration of what is stated or promised with an oath, for example, in a legal proceeding (cc. 1532, 1562 § 2), when taking an office (c. 380), or in certain institutes of consecrated life in which the evangelical counsel is assumed with an oath.

In order to be an act of worship of God, an oath must be made with *truth* (sincerely), with *justice* (one cannot swear something unjust), and with *prudence* (namely, for a proportionate reason and according to one's own possibilities). Furthermore, in order to be valid, the oath must be *free*. In consequence, any oath extorted by violence, fraud or by reasons of grave fear, is null (c. 1200 § 2).

A promissory oath is not valid if what is promised directly threatens harm to a third party, to the public good, or to one's own salvation (c. 1201 § 2).

A promissory oath ceases, is suspended, or can be dispensed from for the same reasons and under the same conditions as a vow. It can also be condoned by the person for whose benefit it was taken.

5. Sacred Places and Times

In the organization of the liturgy, there are norms regarding places for the worship of God, and times of festivity and penance.

A) Sacred Places

Sacred places are those which have been designated for divine worship or for the burial of the faithful by means of a dedication or a blessing prescribed in the liturgical books (churches, oratories, altars, cemeteries, tombs). The sacred character of a place demands that it be only used for acts of worship, piety or religion. Exceptionally, the Ordinary can permit some act which is not of religion if it is not contrary to the holiness of the place.

The *profanation* of a sacred place occurs if injurious and scandalous actions take place that are grave to the extent that in the judgment of the local Ordinary, it is no longer licit to celebrate worship until the injury is repaired by means of the prescribed penitential rite (cc. 1121 and 1376).

Loss of dedication (*execration*) of a place consists in the loss of the sacred character that it had acquired with the dedication or blessing. It occurs if the place is destroyed in large part or if it is permanently destined to profane uses (by decree of the Ordinary or *de facto*, c. 1212). For example, if a church cannot be returned to worship, the diocesan bishop can reduce it to a fitting profane use (diocesan museum, etc.).

The Church authority has the right to freely exercise his power and functions (of worship, jurisdiction and Magisterium) in sacred places. Even if they are not ecclesiastical property, the *use* of sacred places falls under the power of the Church (c. 1213). Normally, state laws guarantee the inviolability of sacred places.[122]

Various Sacred Places

There are various types of sacred places: churches, oratories, private chapels, cemeteries, shrines. Law is concerned with each of them.

The *church* is the sacred building where the faithful have the right to enter to participate in public worship. Entrance during sacred functions must be free and gratuitous (cc. 1214 and 1221).

---

122. As, for example, in the Accord between the Holy See and the Republic of Italy of 1984, art. 5.

The construction of a church must be authorized by the diocesan bishop, who must first hear the council of priests and the rectors of the neighboring churches (c. 1215). The building or restoration of a church must be in accordance with the principles of the liturgy and of sacred art (c. 1216).

Churches must be dedicated with the prescribed rite. The dedication is reserved to the bishop of the diocese, but he can delegate it to another priest (c. 1217). There must be a written document attesting to the dedication (c. 1208).

Every church is to have its title (namely, the name in honor of which it is dedicated: Holy Trinity, Our Lady, Saint Francis, etc.), which cannot be changed after the dedication (c. 1218).

All acts of worship can be performed in a church, with due regard for parochial rights. The functions which belong to the pastor require his permission to be done in another church (cc. 1219 and 530).

An *oratory* is a place which, by permission of the Ordinary, is destined for divine worship for the benefit of some *community* or *group* of the faithful. Other members of the faithful may also have access to it with the consent of the competent superior (c. 1223).

Before giving permission, the Ordinary must make sure that the oratory is furnished in a suitable way. It is recommended that oratories be blessed with the prescribed rite. In any case it is to be used for acts of religion only and cannot be converted to profane uses without permission of the same Ordinary (c. 1224).

All ceremonies can be performed in oratories, except for those excluded by law, by the liturgical norms or by the local Ordinary (c. 1225).

The *private chapel* is the place destined for worship, by permission of the local Ordinary, for the benefit of one or more physical persons (for example, a family). It is necessary to have permission from the local Ordinary to celebrate Mass or other functions in a chapel. Bishops, however, have the right to construct their own private chapel where the same functions can be carried out as in an oratory. It is also fitting that the chapel be liturgically blessed (cc. 1226–1229).

A *shrine* is a sacred place of worship in which, for a particular reason of devotion, the faithful make pilgrimages with the approval of the local Ordinary (c. 1230).

Shrines can be diocesan, national, and international. Each of them must have its own statutes approved by the local Ordinary, by the conference of bishops or by the Holy See according to the category of the shrine (cc. 1231, 1232).[123]

Shrines are above all privileged places with regard to liturgical and penitential pastoral care. For this reason they can enjoy some concessions or privileges for the benefit of the pilgrims (absolutions from censures, indulgences, etc., c. 1233).

The *altar* is a table on which the Eucharist is celebrated. It can be *fixed* or *movable* according to whether it is joined to the floor or whether it can be transferred (c. 1235).

It is fitting that a fixed altar be constructed of natural stone, the table being of one piece, if possible. The conference of bishops can authorize other appropriate materials. It must be dedicated with the liturgical rite, preserving the tradition of placing the relics of saints (normally martyrs) under the altar.

A movable altar can be constructed in any worthy material and must be dedicated or blessed (c. 1236).

As sacred places, altars are to be used for worship only. No corpse may be buried under the altar (although relics may be); otherwise it is illicit to celebrate the Mass on it.

---

123. See for the United States the *Norms of the NCCB regarding the Designation of Shrines as National Shrines*, National Conference of Catholic Bishops, Washington, 1992.

A *cemetery* is a sacred place designated for the burial of the faithful departed.

The Church desires to have her own cemeteries or at least an area in public cemeteries. Both are to be liturgically blessed. If this is not possible, the individual graves are to be properly blessed on each occasion (cc. 1240–1241).

According to canon law, every parish and religious institute can have their own cemetery. Other juridical persons and families can have their own cemetery or burial place (c. 1241).

The faithful departed cannot be buried in churches, except for the Pope, cardinals and diocesan bishops, who can be buried in their own proper church.

B) Sacred Times

Sacred times are holy days of obligation and days of penance. Their purpose is to bring to mind in a special way the memory of various religious events, especially the mysteries of the Lord.

It belongs to the supreme ecclesiastical authority to establish or abolish feast days or days of penance for the entire Church.

The diocesan bishop can establish particular feast days or days of penance for his diocese. He can also dispense from universal feast days or days of penance. The pastor, for a just cause and following the prescriptions of the diocesan bishop, can also dispense from the observance of a feast day or a day of penance or commute it into another pious work (cc. 1244, 1245).

The foremost *feast day* in the entire Church is Sunday on which, since apostolic times, the paschal mystery is celebrated.[124] Other holy days of obligation are Christmas,

124. See JOHN PAUL II, Apostolic Letter *Dies Domini* May 31, 1998, Observing and Celebrating the Day of the Lord, in *Origins* 28 [July 30, 1998]. 133–151.

Epiphany, the Ascension, *Corpus Domini*, the divine Maternity of Mary (January 1), the Immaculate Conception, the Assumption, Saint Joseph, the Apostles Saints Peter and Paul, and All Saints Day. However, the conference of bishops can abolish or transfer to Sunday some holy days of obligation, with the approval of the Apostolic See (c. 1246).[125]

The observance of the precept of sanctifying feast days consists in participating in holy Mass and in resting from work or daily affairs, more intensely dedicating oneself to prayer and acts of charity. If there is a serious difficulty, the obligation ceases (for example, sickness, lack of a civil holiday from work, work at home). The precept of the Mass can also be accomplished in the evening of the preceding day (cc. 1247–1248).

Days and *times of penance* common to the entire Church are all Fridays of the year and the season of Lent. During these days, the faithful are to more intensely dedicate themselves to prayer, works of charity, and acts of sacrifice. On certain days one must also observe abstinence from meat (all Fridays of the year), and abstinence together with fasting (Ash Wednesday and Good Friday). If a Friday coincides with a liturgical solemnity, abstinence does not have to be observed (cc. 1249–1251).

Abstinence is binding on those who are 14 years old or older. Fasting is binding on adults until the beginning of their 60th year of age (c. 1252).

---

125. The NCCB has established as holy days of obligation: January 1, the Solemnity of Mary, Mother of God; the Solemnity of the Ascension; August 15, the Solemnity of the Assumption; November 1, the Solemnity of All Saints; December 8, the Solemnity of the Immaculate Conception; December 25, the Solemnity of the Nativity of Our Lord Jesus Christ. Whenever January 1, August 15 or November 1 falls on a Saturday or on a Monday, the precept to attend Mass is abrogated (Decree of December 13, 1991). CCCB transfers or eliminates all the feast days except Christmas Day and the Feast of Mary, Mother of God (Decr. N. 7).

In addition the conference of bishops can (c. 1253):

- determine that abstinence concerns food other than meat;
- further specify the observance of fasting and abstinence;
- substitute them entirely or in part with other forms of penance. Many conferences, in fact, have permitted that on Fridays outside of Lent, abstinence can be substituted by a time of prayer, works of charity, or other sacrifices (visiting the sick, not smoking, not drinking alcoholic beverages, etc.).

Chapter X.

The Temporal Goods of the Church. Patrimonial Canon Law

Like all institutions, the Church also needs to use material means "as often as her mission requires it" (*GS* 76). In consequence the Church has the right, which is proper and independent from any other power, to own, manage, and alienate temporal goods to accomplish her ends.

These ends are principally the support of worship and of the clergy, works of apostolate, and works of charity (the spiritual and material works of mercy), which are part of her religious mission in the world (c. 1254). It is a duty of the faithful to contribute to these purposes (c. 222), which also implies the right, before the state authorities, to give temporal goods to the Church (c. 1261).

The Church organizes her economic resources autonomously. The canonical discipline on the acquisition, ownership, administration, etc., of the goods of the Church, constitutes canonical patrimonial law.[126]

126. See A. J. MAIDA, N. P. CAFARDI, *Church Property, Church Finances, and Church-Related Corporations*, The Catholic Health Association of the United States, St. Louis, 1984. In this matter, the particular law of each nation, diocese and institute has a special importance.

1. Goods

The goods which serve in the functioning of the Church are not grouped in one single patrimony in the name, so to speak, of the entire Catholic Church. They are found spread out in the patrimonies of the ecclesiastical juridical persons to which they belong (the Apostolic See, the dioceses, parishes, associations, institutes of consecrated life, etc.). Nevertheless, among all these goods there is a certain unity since, in one way or in another, all serve the needs of the Church under the supreme authority of the Roman Pontiff.

In other words, in the Church, goods are the property of the specific juridical person who acquires them, but they must also always serve for ecclesial purposes and be under the supreme authority of the Pope, who regulates the exercise of the property of the Church (c. 1256).

Among goods used for ecclesial activities, there is a category of special importance: ecclesiastical goods. These are those which belong to public juridical persons in the Church. Goods belonging to private juridical persons are not ecclesiastical.

In fact, we have seen that a characteristic that defines public juridical persons is that they are constituted by the authority and accomplish their activity in the name of the Church (c. 116 § 1), thus involving her in their operation (cf. Chapter III, 2, b, and Chapter V, 4). Since the subject is public, it is logical that their goods be also considered as public or ecclesiastical goods.

The difference between the goods of public institutions (ecclesiastical goods) and those of private institutions lies in the different juridical regime to which they are subject according to c. 1257. Ecclesiastical goods, in so far as they are public goods, are governed by the canons of Book V of the Code, as well as by the statutes of the juridical person who is the proprietor. The goods of private juridical persons, on the contrary, are principally governed according to their own statutes.[127]

This implies two things: a) ecclesiastical goods, precisely because they belong to a public canonical corporate body, are also of the Church. In patrimonial law, when one speaks of the Church (goods of the Church, property of the Church, rights of the Church, etc.), one normally intends to refer to any public canonical juridical person and not those which are private; b) the Code principally deals with these goods, which will be the case for this book as well; and c) canonical patrimonial law mainly concerns the life of ecclesiastical entities, and rarely the individual faithful.

This does not mean that one cannot also say that the goods of private juridical persons are of the Church. They are in the sense that they belong to an ecclesiastical corporate body whose ends and activities enter into the ends and activities of the Church. However, they are not ecclesiastical goods since these corporate bodies do not act in the name of the Church. In this sense, their patrimony and economic activity are private; they remain in the area of their own autonomy and responsibility.

In summary, it is necessary to distinguish three types of goods or patrimonies according to the proprietor: a) ecclesiastical goods, which are those of public ecclesiastical institutes and are governed by what is prescribed in the Code as well as in the statutes of the titular entity; b) the goods of private canonical institutions, which are not ecclesiastical and follow the statutes of the corporate body which is the proprietor; and c) the goods of individual members of the faithful, which in themselves have no relationship with canon law.

Among ecclesiastical goods, there is a special category which is that of precious things. Precious goods or things are

---

127. This is true for the Latin Church. In the Eastern Code, the possibility of private juridic persons is not provided for: all institutions with personality are public and thus all their goods are ecclesiastical.

those which have a special artistic, historical, cultural or devotional value (for example, a church, a highly venerated image, an archive, a chalice, an ex-voto). For this reason, there are special norms to safeguard the proper finality, integrity and conservation of these goods of the Church.

There is a second category of goods which have a specific relevance for canon law: sacred things. These are, as we know (Chapter IX, 4 and 5), those which are permanently designated by the ecclesiastical authority for divine worship (churches, images, relics, vestments, etc.). This dignity implies that, whoever their proprietor is, these things must be treated or used in the way and according to the acts established by the canonical norms. In these aspects they are subject to Church authority, to which the discipline of worship belongs, even if they belong to private or state corporate bodies, and thus are not ecclesiastical goods.

2. The Acquisition of Goods

This section concerns two different questions. The first regards the ways in which the Church can acquire goods; here it suffices to say that it can do so in all the ways that are just, in the same manner as anyone else: purchase or donation, inheritance, bequest, revenue or income, etc. (c. 1259).

The second issue is the ways or sources of the financing of the Church. Substantially they are the contributions of the faithful, but also one can consider the revenue of its patrimony and possible State support.

The Church has for herself the right to request from the faithful the necessary means for her activities and ends (c. 1260). The faithful have the duty and right to contribute (c. 222). Ecclesiastical communion also includes a certain communication in material goods, which in the first Christian communities was quite intense and generous, as witnessed by the Acts of the Apostles and the Letters of Saint Paul.

The contributions of the faithful to the Church can take various forms. Normally voluntary offerings are preferred.

One counts on their responsible response in the face of various needs. The Church, however, can also require obligatory contributions which in some places, for historical reasons, constitute the largest source of support (Germany, Austria, Switzerland).

Offerings can be of various types, but they are always donations or alms, made by the faithful to the Church. Normally, they are not generic, but have a concrete recipient (the diocese, the seminary, the parish, a convent...), and frequently particular purposes also. In patrimonial law, the principle of respect for the will of the donor is in force; this is why "the offerings given by the faithful for a definite purpose can be applied only for that same purpose" (c. 1267 § 3).

Among different types of voluntary offerings, the collections of money requested by the authority (they are called *subventiones rogatæ* by the Code) are especially important: the faithful are asked to contribute to a given necessity or initiative (the missions, the parish, "Caritas"). This is normally done in feast-day Masses, but also in other ways (on the street, by mail, in newspapers). The conference of bishops is to issue norms in this regard.[128] The local Ordinary can call for special collections to be made in churches and oratories open to the public. Logically, the proceedings must go to the purpose that has been proposed. In order to make a collection for the benefit of an ecclesiastical end or institution, private persons (physical or juridical) must obtain permission from their own Ordinary and that of the place in which the collection is made (cc. 1262–1266).

Other voluntary offerings are spontaneous alms given by the faithful on their own initiative. With regard to these donations, there are some points of interest from the juridical perspective:

a) The offerings given to a physical person who in any way represents a public or private juridical person are under-

128. Both USCB and CCCB authorize each diocesan bishop to provide norms in his jurisdiction.

stood to be given to the juridical person unless the contrary is stated. For example, the offerings given to the pastor are understood to be intended for the parish and not for him.

b) In principle, donations must be accepted. In order to refuse them, there must be a just cause, and, in a matter of importance, the permission of the Ordinary also. However, there are cases in which the donor attaches conditions, obligations or modes of realization to the offering, and thus acceptance of the offering also means a commitment to fulfill the requests of the donor (offering certain Masses, building a hospital, etc.). Therefore, a judgment must be made as to whether it is appropriate to accept the offering or not; in any case, it is necessary to have the permission of the Ordinary to whom the beneficiary juridical corporate body is subject (c. 1267).

Another type of contribution is the offerings the faithful are asked for on the occasion of pastoral services (marriage, baptism, funerals, etc.). Although there exists in these cases a certain duty to make these offerings, they are not a "payment" of the sacraments or sacramentals. To avoid abuses or scandals, the law establishes that the bishops of the province determine how much should be asked of the faithful in each case. They can also give more if they desire, and pastoral services cannot be denied to those who are unable to give the offering.

Obligatory contributions are fees and taxes. Fees (*taxæ*) are expenses that the faithful must pay for administrative acts requested by them (certificates, dispensations, processes, documents). They are of two types: administrative and judicial. Administrative fees must be fixed by the bishops of the province and those who cannot pay them are to be exonerated (c. 1264).

Taxes (*tributi* and *exactiones*) are monetary burdens imposed by the authority on subjects for the general or specific necessities of the Church. As a means of income they normally have an exceptional character since it is preferable to appeal to the responsibility and generosity of the faithful rather than to obligatory exactions. However, the Church has the right to impose them and the Code provides for this possibility, concerning which it always belongs to the diocesan bishop to decide to impose them or not (cc. 1263, 264). Taxes are always of a general, diocesan character and must be moderate and proportionate to the economic income of the passive subject.

- ordinary taxes (*tributi*) are a general and fixed contribution that the diocesan bishop, after having heard the opinion of the finance committee and the council of priests, can impose on public juridical persons subject to him for the necessities of the diocese;

- the diocesan bishop can impose extraordinary taxes (*exactiones*) on other physical and (private) juridical persons subject to him, but only in the case of grave necessity, and thus in an occasional manner;

- the bishop can impose a seminary tax on all juridical persons which have an establishment in the diocese, for the benefit of the seminary (c. 264).

Besides these paths of acquisition of goods, in some countries the State offers some financial support to the Church as, for example, for the maintenance of the clergy, for the building of churches, exemptions from taxes, etc., to be realized in different ways. In Italy today, the State helps the Church (and other confessions) with 0.8% of the personal income tax of the physical persons who have requested this devolution in their declaration, and also with the possibility to deduct the donations made to the Central Institute for the Support of the Clergy (ICSC), up to 2,000,000 lire, from their income subject to taxation.[129]

129. See Legge [Bill] n. 222 of May 20, 1985, art. 46 and 47. A similar system is in force in Spain, but the deductible contributions can be made to any ecclesiastical entity.

3. Administration of Ecclesiastical Goods

Administration refers to the collection of acts and measures undertaken to conserve and increase a patrimony and to make it serve the aims for which it has been designated. It is a complex activity with various aspects guided by juridical and financial criteria; here we shall principally be concerned with the juridical aspects.

In the past the economic organization of the Church was based on the institution of the benefice, which in synthesis consisted in a mass of goods (generally land), through whose income the necessities of certain ecclesiastical institutions were supported (above all of clerics, who were charged with administering them).

For historical reasons (especially State confiscation) as well as functional reasons, this system of immovable capital as the sole source of income for the various necessities became obsolete. The Second Vatican Council provided for the progressive abandonment of the system of benefices (c. 1272).

Today the economic units are juridical persons, mainly the dioceses (the particular Churches) which, though not exclusively, concentrate in themselves all the activity of the Church, and therefore also all her needs (worship, clergy, apostolate, charity). The accounting system in use tends to be that of the balance sheet: the budgeting of annual income and expenditures.

In the Code, a general and optional scheme of financial diocesan organization is delineated which provides for the following:

- an institute for the support of the clergy which serves the diocese as an autonomous corporate body with specific income and expense. Gradually the endowments of benefices which become extinct will be bestowed on this institute. In Italy, through the Church–State accords, the Central Institute and the diocesan Institutes have been constituted for the support of the clergy[130];

- an institute for the social welfare of the clergy, which can be connected on the national level with those of other dioceses according to the norms of the conference of bishops;
- a common diocesan fund for other necessities, especially for the payment of other persons who serve the diocese, which can be connected with that of other dioceses.

Systems of interdiocesan cooperation can be realized on various levels and in various forms, retaining the principle that the goods coming from various dioceses must be administered according to norms agreed to by the concerned bishops (c. 1275).

Apart from the particular Churches, every juridical person must have its economic scheme which provides for a board of directors of at least three persons (the administrator and two advisors). Universal law earnestly recommends that a budget be made every year; particular law can impose this obligation.

From the functional point of view, the administration of ecclesiastical goods is regulated by the following principles:

- the Roman Pontiff, in virtue of his power of government over the entire Church, is the supreme administrator and financial officer of all ecclesiastical goods. Therefore, it belongs to him to regulate the ownership and administration of goods, to require that certain acts be subject to given requirements, etc. (cc. 1256 and 1273);
- the immediate administration of goods belongs to the organs of representation of the person who holds the title to them, according to the norms of universal and

130. See M. MARCHESI, *Diritto canonico complementare italiano*, EDB, Bologna, 1992.

particular law as well as their own proper statutes. We have already seen that every person must have its own economic organs: the administrator and a finance committee (c. 1280);

- this administration is subject to the vigilance and control of the Ordinary to whom the juridical person is subject. It belongs to him to give instructions, to intervene in case of negligence, to appoint administrators for juridical persons who do not have them, to approve acts of extraordinary administration, etc. (cc. 1276–1279).

On this basis the Code establishes the rules that administrators must observe in the fulfillment of the office which, since it regards ecclesiastical goods, is always carried out in the name of the Church (cc. 1282–1289).

There are ordinary and extraordinary acts of administration. The former are those which concern the normal patrimonial activities of the corporate body, according to what is established in the statutes and in the budget, and which can be realized by the administrators in the name of the person. The acts of extraordinary administration, on the other hand, are those which have greater importance and which can affect the economic stability of the juridical person. To validly realize these acts the administrators must first obtain the written permission of the Ordinary to whom the person is subject. In a diocese, the bishop must obtain the consent of the diocesan finance committee and of the college of consultors (c. 1277).[131]

With regard to dioceses, it belongs to the conference of bishops to determine which acts are of extraordinary administration, whereas for other persons, this must be specified in the statutes and in the powers granted to the administrators.

---

131. F. G. MORRISEY, "Ordinary and Extraordinary Administration: Canon 1277," *The Jurist* [1988] 709–726.

4. Alienation of Ecclesiastical Goods

In contracts, the Church conforms to the state laws in force in the territory (so-called canonization), unless there is something in them contrary to divine law, or unless canon law determines otherwise (c. 1290).

Concretely, to validly alienate goods that constitute the stable patrimony of a public corporate body, canon law provides that, above a certain amount, it is necessary to obtain the written permission of the competent authority or even of the Holy See. Public juridical persons, therefore, are not free to autonomously dispose of a significant part of their patrimony.

The conference of bishops of every country must fix two amounts for alienations: a minimum amount, above which one must have the permission of the diocesan bishop (for persons subject to him: parishes, seminary), or of another authority designated by the statutes; and a maximum amount, above which it is also necessary to obtain the permission of the Holy See.[132]

The diocesan bishop must obtain the consent of both the diocesan finance committee and of the college of consultors when he must give his permission for alienations, as well as when he himself wishes to alienate goods of the diocese over and above the minimum amount fixed by the conference.

Furthermore, permission of the Apostolic See is always necessary to validly alienate ex-votos and precious goods. In the Roman Curia, this matter normally is the competence of the Congregation for the Clergy.

---

132. In the United States, the minimum amount is fixed by the NCCB at $500,000 and the maximum amount, which also requires the intervention of the Holy See, is set for $3,000,000. In Canada, the updated (2006) CCCB Decree no. 10 fixes those amounts at Can$448,097 and $4,480,970. In Kenya those amounts are $2,000 and $20,000. F. G. MORRISEY, "The Alienation of Temporal Goods in Contemporary Practice," *Studia canonica* 29 [1995] 293–316.

Alienating ecclesiastical goods without the required permissions constitutes an offence (c. 1377), in addition to creating financial responsibilities due to the invalidity of the act (c. 1296).

The same rules which apply to alienations must also be applied to any transaction which can affect the patrimony of a juridical person and worsen its condition, including leasing (cc. 1295 and 1297).

As it can be seen, the stability of patrimonies is the rule in canon law, since the goods must serve for lasting purposes, a principle typical of juridical persons.

5. Pious Dispositions and Pious Foundations

Pious dispositions are acts through which the faithful dispose of their goods in favor of the Church, destining them to specific ends of worship or charity. The ecclesiastical subject who receives the goods assumes the obligation to accomplish the will of the donor or founder.

Since it is a matter of goods which must serve the ends of the Church, the ecclesiastical authority is concerned with the efficient realization of the will of the donor, and thus with the adequate administration of the goods. Therefore c. 1301 entrusts to the Ordinary the tasks of vigilance and control over the execution of all pious dispositions within his jurisdiction, whoever the subject beneficiary who is charged of carrying it out.

When a pious disposition consists in a capital whose income is used to carry out the desires of the donor, it is referred to as a pious foundation. If the goods themselves are constituted into a juridical person, the foundation is autonomous, having its own statutes and organs of management. If, on the other hand, the foundation is entrusted to an existing juridical person which assumes the management and realization of the ends, the foundation is said to be non-autonomous (cc. 1303 and 115).

In order to be able to constitute a foundation, the authority must verify that the end proposed by the founder is in harmony with the mission of the Church, that the means are sufficient, and that the beneficiary is capable of realizing the end (c. 1304).

Chapter XI.
Penal Canon Law

The People of God is constituted as a society founded on the communion of faith, of the sacraments, and of discipline. The Church, therefore, has the right to react also with penal sanctions with regard to grave offences committed against ecclesial communion, in order to defend and re-establish that communion (c. 1311).[133]

1. Offences

An offence is the external and gravely culpable transgression of a law or precept, for the violation of which the competent authority has threatened a penalty.

Within their area, those who enjoy legislative power can issue penal laws (cc. 1315–1318). Likewise, those who can issue precepts through executive power "can also threaten determinate penalties through a precept" (cc. 1319–1320).

An offence is referred to as completed when the acts of the delinquent in fact were efficacious to produce the delict.

133. See in this regard W. H. WOESTMAN, *Ecclesiastical Sanctions and the Penal Process. A Commentary on the Code of Canon Law*, 2nd ed., St. Paul University, Ottawa, 2003; E. GARCÍA, *Sanctions in the Church, According to the 1983 Code of Canon Law*, University of Santo Tomás Press, Manila, 1985; J. SANCHIS, *La legge penale e il precetto penale*, Giuffrè, Milan, 1993.

If, on the other hand, the delict is not produced (for example, the delinquent desists), we are faced with an attempted delict, which in certain cases can also be punished, but always with a lesser penalty than that established for the completed offence (c. 1328). There are also offences which consist precisely in attempting certain acts, as when a cleric or religious attempts marriage (c. 1394).

2. The Offender

Persons who accomplish an offence intentionally (that is, with malice), or at least with culpable imprudence, are subject to penal sanctions. Someone who acts through inculpable ignorance, inadvertence, error, or simply without use of reason, does not commit an offence (cc. 1321, 1322).

Other circumstances exempt from penalties as, for example, when the person is under 16 years of age, or when the act occurred through an unforeseen accident, in legitimate self-defense, through violence or fear, or in case of necessity (c. 1323).

Attenuating circumstances imply the mitigation of the penalty or its substitution with a penance. C. 1324 lists the most important of these: imperfect use of reason, being under 18 years of age, inculpable ignorance that the fact constituted an offence, unjust provocation on the part of the victim. The judge can also take into account other circumstances that are not listed here.

On the other hand, other circumstances allow the judge to aggravate the penalty, such as obstinate ill-will and the abuse of authority (c. 1326).

Various persons can collaborate to commit one single offence, whether as co-authors of it (participating equally in the criminal act), or as accomplices (physically or morally aiding in an offence against another). They are considered equally delinquent and can be punished with the same penalty if the offence would not have been committed without their assistance (c. 1329).

3. Ecclesiastical Penalties

A penalty is a privation of a spiritual or temporal good as punishment for an offence. In the Church, penalties concern the goods and rights that are possessed in the Church, not those of civil society. Ecclesiastical penalties are of two types: medicinal penalties or censures, and expiatory penalties (c. 1312 § 1).

A) Censures

Censures are the gravest penalties and have the medicinal purpose of making the delinquent change his conduct. Therefore, they last until the guilty party has given clear signs of repentance; only then does he have the right to be absolved from the censure.

There are three censures: excommunication, interdict, and suspension. Excommunication is the gravest because it means, to a certain extent, the expulsion of the guilty party from the ecclesiastical body. He cannot participate as a minister in any act of public worship, administer or receive the sacraments, exercise any office, function, ministry or position in the Church (c. 1331).

Interdict is equal to excommunication in that it forbids the celebration of acts of worship and the reception of the sacraments, but not the exercise of other ecclesiastical functions (c. 1332).

Suspension is a penalty which can be inflicted on clerics only, forbidding them to realize all or some acts of the power of orders (acts of worship, preaching, sacraments), or of the power of governance, as well as the exercise of all or some of the rights or functions of an office, all this according to the norm or decision according to which the penalty was inflicted (cc. 1333, 1334).

B) Expiatory Penalties

Expiatory penalties above all aim at punishing the delinquent, perpetually or temporarily depriving him of certain goods, rights or faculties. The most important are (c. 1336):

- the prohibition or injunction to dwell in a certain territory (for clerics and religious);
- the privation of power, office, rights, functions, privileges, favors, titles, dignities or faculties, or of their exercise or use, everywhere or in a certain territory;
- the penal transfer to another office;
- the dismissal from the clerical state. This penalty cannot be established by a particular law (c. 1317).

The law can threaten other expiatory penalties that are in harmony with the supernatural end of the Church (for example, the expulsion from an association or institute, c. 1312 § 2).

C) Penal Remedies and Penances

In addition to penalties, there are punishments which have the purpose of preventing offences (penal remedies), or of substituting or aggravating the penalties due to them (penances).

Penal remedies include admonition and rebuke. A person can be admonished when he is in the proximate occasion of committing an offence, or when he is suspected of having already done so. A rebuke is to be made to someone whose behavior has caused scandal or disorder (c. 1339).

Penances—consisting in works of piety, charity or religion—are imposed together with the penalty or in lieu of it, for example, a retreat, fast or pilgrimage (c. 1340).

4. The Application of Penalties

Penalties are normally vinflicted by a judgment or decree of condemnation only, after a sanction proceeding.[134]

Before imposing a penalty, the Church attempts to make sure that all other pastoral paths have been tried to obtain the amendment of the guilty party and the restoration of justice. Furthermore, it leaves an ample discretionary space to the judge to assess the circumstances that could advise a mitigation or suspension of the penalty, its deferral or substitution with an appropriate penance, always taking into account the demands of justice and the need to avoid or make reparation for scandal.

The penalty to be inflicted for a certain offence can be determined by law as:

- obligatory or optional. In the former case, the offence must necessarily be punished (normally the law says: "is to be punished"); in the second case the judge is given the power to apply the penalty or not (when the law says: "may be punished");
- determined or undetermined. In the former case the law indicates, in some way, one or more penalties to inflict on the guilty party, and then the judge must choose between them (for example, c. 1372). If, on the other hand, the penalty is undetermined, it belongs to the judge to choose a just penalty (for example, c. 1377). It is undetermined when the penal law does not indicate what penalty should be imposed, but simply says that the criminal should or may be punished with a just penalty; then the judge must or may impose whatever penalty he deems appropriate (see, for example, c. 1377).

134. See P. M. DUGAN (ed.), *The Penal Process and the Protection of Rights in Canon Law*, Gratianus Series, Wilson & Lafleur, Montréal, 2005.

However, there are some penalties, which are called *latæ sententiæ*, which one automatically incurs for the very fact of having committed the offence or directly cooperated in it (c. 1314). The penalty applies to the offender with no need for a previous process, sentence or decree. The decree or the declaration could be promulgated afterwards to determine if the behavior of the accused merited the penalty.

Currently, one incurs excommunication ipso facto for the following offences:

- heresy, apostasy or schism (c. 1364);
- profanation of the consecrated species (c. 1367);
- using physical violence against the Roman Pontiff (c. 1370);
- absolving one's own accomplice in a sin against the sixth commandment, except in danger of death (c. 1378);
- consecrating a bishop without a pontifical mandate (c. 1382);
- direct violation of the seal of confession (c. 1388);
- actually procured abortion (c. 1398).

However, it must be kept in mind that one does not fall under the *latæ sententiæ* penalty when there is any attenuating circumstance (c. 1324 § 3).

5. Cessation of Penalties

After their application, the penalties cease when the condemnation is fulfilled or when the competent authority concedes their remission.

Normally, the following can remit a penalty: the authority who has determined the crime, the Ordinary who has inflicted it (by a judgment or decree of condemnation), and the Ordinary of the place in which the delinquent is found (and also their delegates: for example, the penitentiary). Nevertheless, there are penalties whose remission is reserved to the Holy See (for example, cc. 1367, 1370 § 1, 1382).

Since censures are medicinal penalties aiming at the conversion of the guilty party, until the delinquent has reformed, they cannot be remitted. However once he has given signs of sincere repentance, he has a right to their remission. Censures only cease by their absolution and not by the fulfilment of the condemnation. Hence, it could be considered that censures are standing delicts, but we have already seen that isolated delicts can provoke an automatic excommunication.

Excommunication and interdict forbid receiving the sacraments, including absolution of sins. Besides, it is possible to automatically incur these censures (*latæ sententiæ*) at the moment the offence is committed. Thus it sometimes happens that people go to confession and find out that they are excommunicated or under interdict without there having been any trial or process in their regard. What can the confessor do? He can remit the penalty and then absolve the penitent, if it is difficult for the latter to remain in a state of sin, imposing an appropriate penance. In granting the remission, the confessor is to impose upon the penitent the obligation to have recourse within one month to the competent authority or his delegate and to abide by his instructions. (The recourse, however, may be made even through the confessor, who will not mention the name of the penitent. The latter is to return to the confessor for instructions from the competent authority. Cf. c. 1357.)

Finally, it should be kept in mind that any penitent in danger of death can be absolved from any sin and censure by any priest: the salvation of souls is the supreme law of the Church.

6. Specific Offences

The Code specifies the acts which constitute offences in the entire Church and their corresponding penalties. Particular laws or precepts can establish other offences and penalties in their area. In any case, the legal description of an offence must be precise and clear. For there to be a crime, the offender must have accomplished the acts as described in the law; we already saw that penal laws are strictly interpreted (cc. 18 and 36).

The particular offences specified in the Code are grouped according to matter:

- offences against religion and the unity of the Church (cc. 1364–1369). These include heresy, apostasy and schism; baptizing or educating one's children in a non-Catholic religion; perjury; profaning the Eucharist, blasphemy, slander or incitement to hate or disdain of religion in the media;
- offences against ecclesiastical authorities and the freedom of the Church (cc. 1370–1377). These include physical violence against the Pope, bishops, clerics and religious; the promotion of, direction of, or participation in an association which plots against the Church; the alienation of ecclesiastical goods without due permission from the authority;
- usurpation of ecclesiastical offices and offences committed in their exercise (cc. 1378–1389). These include the simulated celebration of the sacraments or their celebration through simony; consecrating a bishop without a mandate from the Apostolic See; the violation of the seal of confession; abuse or culpable negligence in the exercise of ecclesiastical power;
- crimes of falsehood (cc. 1390–1391). These include various types of calumny, and the falsification, alteration, and/or destruction of documents;
- offences against special obligations (cc. 1392–1396). These include some particularly grave sins against chastity committed by clergy or religious;
- offences against human life and freedom (cc. 1397–1398). These include homicide, abortion, physical violence and kidnapping.

Besides these transgressions, c. 1399 indicates that any other violation of the law can be punished with a penalty, when the gravity of the violation demands it. This norm is debated. It should be understood in the sense that once the subject has receive the warning, maintain his illicit conduct.

Many offences concern clerics and religious: their personal status has a special relevance in the life of the Church. Many others concern any member of the faithful. However, also in these cases, the penalty can be more serious if the guilty party is a cleric or religious: he can even be dismissed from his state.

Chapter XII.
Procedural Law

The existence of rights (and their corresponding duties) in the Church implies the possibility of having those rights prevail in cases in which a person holds that they are being unjustly violated or threatened. This occurs by means of a process. In a process, the rights, duties, and facts connected to them are defined, clarified or established by the authority. Whereas laws determine what is just in a plurality of similar cases, trials determine what is just (*unicuique suum*—what belongs to each one) in a concrete case. The last book of the Code determines the ways and means to effectively protect rights when a controversy arises in their regard: processes.[135]

Therefore every right carries with it the possibility of being claimed in a process before the authority. This possibility is called procedural action or petition.

The Church (in that it is an organized society independent of any other) has the right to judge cases which concern spiritual matters, and those connected with the spiritual, as

135. On this matter, see J. ARROBA, *Diritto processuale canonico*, Ediurcla, 2nd ed., Rome, 1994; P. MONETA, *La giustizia nella Chiesa*, Il Mulino, Bologna, 1993, P. VITO PINTO, *I processi nel Codice di Diritto Canonico*, LEV, Vatican City, 1993; J. LLOBELL, "Processo canonico ordinario," in *Digesto Italiano*, Turin, 1996.

well as the violation of laws of the Church in regard to the imposition of ecclesiastical penalties (c. 1401).[136]

1. Judicial Organization

The power to judge controversies that arise within the Church belongs (as that of legislation and administrative governance) to the ecclesiastical authority. This power resides in the Roman Pontiff for the entire Church, and for each diocese in the diocesan bishop, who normally exercises it by means of judges and tribunals, which act with vicarious or delegated power.

In virtue of his primacy of governance, the Pope is the supreme judge in the Church: he cannot be judged by anyone and he can call any case to his own judgment. Acts or instruments confirmed by the Roman Pontiff in a specific way cannot be judged, unless he himself has given a judge mandate to do so. In fact, the Pope reserves to himself the right to judge (in matters that concern the competence of the Church) heads of State, cardinals, legates, and penal cases against bishops (cc. 1404–1405).

Furthermore, every member of the faithful has the right to have recourse to the judgment of the Holy See in any type of case and at any moment. If, however, a judge has already begun to try a case, he can continue unless the Holy See communicates to him that it has reserved the case to itself (c. 1417).

Thus there are diocesan judges and tribunals, and judges and tribunals of the Apostolic See. The latter are governed by special norms. All the other tribunals of the Church are governed by the norms of the Code. According to c. 87,

136. The causes of canonization of saints have the purpose of verifying the virtues, the miracles, or the martyrdom of *servants of God* and are regulated by a special law, the Ap. Const. *Divinus Perfectionis Magister*, promulgated on the same date as the Code (January 25, 1983, c. 1403); see J. L. GUTIÉRREZ, *Studi sulle cause di canonizzazione*, Giuffrè, Milano, 2005.

procedural laws cannot be dispensed from by the diocesan bishop. Religious institutes can also have their own tribunals to decide controversies that have arisen within the institute (c. 1427).

The ordinary courts of the Apostolic See are the Tribunal of the Roman Rota and the Supreme Tribunal of the Apostolic Signatura, by means of which the Roman Pontiff ordinarily judges the cases referred to him.[137]

The Supreme Pontiff receives the appeals of the faithful via the Roman Rota. To it are also reserved contentious (non-penal) cases against bishops, and cases regarding persons (physical or juridical) who have no superior below the Roman Pontiff (dioceses, institutes of consecrated life of pontifical right, prelates, etc.). It also tries cases which the Pope has reserved to himself and entrusted to the Rota (cc. 1405 § 3 and 1444).

The Apostolic Signatura, the Supreme Tribunal of the Church, receives recourses against decisions of the Rota, adjudicates some cases against the Rota auditors, and decides administrative controversies and conflicts of competence between tribunals which are not subject to the same appeals court. The Signatura also carries out certain functions of supervision and control over lower tribunals.

In every diocese, the bishop is the judge for all cases not reserved to the Holy See. He can judge personally or by means of others. In fact, the diocesan bishop must nominate a judicial vicar who constitutes one tribunal with his bishop. He can also name associate judicial vicars who help the judicial vicar. All of these must be priests, of good reputation, and with at least a licentiate in canon law (cc. 1420–1422).

---

137. Among Apostolic tribunals, there is also the Apostolic Penitentiary for what concerns the internal forum: absolution of censures, certain dispensations, validations.

Furthermore, since there are cases which must be adjudicated by a college of three or five judges (c. 1425), the diocesan bishop must name a sufficient number of diocesan judges to the tribunal. These can be clerics or lay faithful, but in a collegiate tribunal only one of the members can be lay; the others must be ordained. Whenever possible, marriage cases must be judged by a college of three judges.

Adjudication belongs to a judge only, but a judge (or the presiding judge in a collegiate tribunal) can designate an auditor to instruct a case, selecting him among the persons approved by the bishop for this function. The auditor gathers proofs and submits them to the judge (c. 1428). When a case is judged by a single judge, he can select two assessors to serve as consultors. The auditors and the assessors can be clerics or lay persons of upright conduct (c. 1424).

When a collegiate tribunal is adjudicating, it is presided over, if possible, by the judicial vicar or by an associate judicial vicar. The college decides by absolute majority vote. The presiding judge of the collegiate tribunal must designate among its members a *ponens* or *relator* who puts the judgment into writing.

The tribunal must also have a promoter of justice who is bound to intervene in every case in which the public good could be at stake, and in penal cases (c. 1430). He performs a role similar to the public prosecutor in state tribunals.

For cases concerning the nullity of sacred ordination, or the nullity or dissolution of marriage, a defender of the bond is to be appointed. His task is to propose all reasonable arguments against the nullity or dissolution (c. 1432).

Both the promoter of justice and the defender of the bond are parties in the case, with their corresponding rights and duties. They can be clerics or lay persons and are nominated by the diocesan bishop, either for all cases or for individual ones.

A notary must be present in every procedure. His task is to write and sign the acts; otherwise the acts are null (c. 1437).

For every tribunal which judges cases in the first instance, there must be a tribunal of second instance, to which the decisions of the first can be appealed. The rule is that an appeal against a decision of the diocesan tribunal is made to that of the Metropolitan (i.e., of the archdiocese); an appeal against a decision of the tribunal of the archdiocese, when it judges in the first instance, is made in second instance to that court which has been permanently designated by the Metropolitan, with the approval of the Apostolic See (c. 1438).

In lieu of diocesan tribunals, several bishops can agree to set up, with the approval of the Holy See, a single tribunal for their dioceses (c. 1423). In Italy, for example, marriage cases are decided by regional tribunals. The conference of bishops can constitute one or more tribunals of second instance, in its territory and with the approval of the Holy See.

2. The Process

When a person contends that another has failed to recognize or has violated his rights, the instrument or path by means of which he can vindicate these rights is a process or trial. This consists in a successive series of acts posed by the opposing parties before a judge or tribunal, with the purpose of obtaining a binding decision which establishes what is just. It is a dispute ordered by law and directed by the judicial authority, with the purpose of establishing the truth of the facts and the juridical consequences which derive from them.

The acts or steps which comprise the trial are ordered among themselves in such a way that each one must be realized in the moment and phase that has been determined, after which the subsequent phase can be opened. The schematic phases of a trial are: introduction, instruction, discussion, and decision.

There are different types of trial according to the way in which they are carried out or according to their subject: ordinary or special, written or oral, matrimonial, penal, administrative, etc. The Code regulates the phases of the ordinary written trial, making reference to the specific features of the others. Among special trials, the most relevant are marriage nullity trials, to which we shall make some more detailed references.[138]

A) The Parties

By definition, there must be at least two opposing parties in every trial: one who seeks the intervention of justice because he holds himself to be the victim of an unjust situation (the petitioner), and another against which the petitioner takes action (the respondent). This duality of the opposing parties expresses what is called the contradictory or contentious principle. Without two parties there cannot be a true and proper process. The parties can be one or more physical or juridical persons, and can at times receive other names according to the type of case (claimant, resisting party, guilty party, accused, appellant, defendant).

Another fundamental principle of procedural law is that of balance between the parties. Each one must be given equal opportunity to adduce proofs and arguments or to advance requests, in order to defend their position. Otherwise their right of defense would be injured.

To be admitted as a party in a process, the subject, in addition to being capable of rights and duties, and of acting (by himself or by means of a representative), must have a title which legitimizes him to act in a concrete process as an active or passive party. In other words, he must demonstrate that he has a legitimate interest worthy of protection in the object of the case. This requirement is called legitimization. For example, it is not legitimate for anyone whomsoever to claim

138. Matrimonial cases form the great majority of trials which occupy ecclesiastical tribunals. The PCLT has given the Instr. *Dignitas connubii*, January, 25 2005, to be observed by diocesan and interdiocesan tribunals in handling causes of nullity of marriage, Vatican City, LEV, 2005.

the rights of a third party, but only for his representative. Likewise, a person cannot ask that any marriage be declared null, except his own. The promoter of justice and defender of the bond are parties in the cases in which they intervene for the sake of the protection of the public good.

The parties have the possibility, or the necessity, according to the case, of being represented and defended in the process by their procurators and advocates, who with their technical expertise can better exercise the rights of the party they represent. The advocates and procurators, besides the necessary professional qualifications, must be approved by the diocesan bishop and thus inscribed in the list of the tribunal. In order to be able to act in someone's name, they must have received the corresponding mandate and present it to the tribunal. The tribunal itself can have some permanent advocates who can represent and defend those who wish to make use of their services (cc. 1481–1490).

B) The Competence of the Tribunal

In order for a judge or a tribunal to be able to examine and decide a case, it is not sufficient that they have been legally constituted by the authority. They must also be competent, which means that they have to have a legal title which allows them to judge the concrete case which is before them. Likewise, a person who wishes to initiate a case must go to the competent tribunal.

Competence, or the possession of a title, is attributed to different tribunals by the law, according to various criteria: the matter, place, domicile of the parties, grade of the process (first, second or further instance). In fact, we have seen that certain cases are reserved to the Pope and others to tribunals of the Holy See. In Italy, only the regional tribunals are competent for matrimonial cases.

It can be said that provision has already been made for one or more tribunals that are competent to treat every possible litigation. In fact, quite frequently the person who wishes to initiate a process has the possibility of selecting one from among various competent tribunals. As a general rule, the tribunal of the domicile or quasi-domicile of the respondent is always competent, according to c. 1408. In matrimonial cases, the tribunal of the place in which the marriage was celebrated is also competent (c. 1673).

It is evident, therefore, that one of the first things that a judge or tribunal must do when they receive a request, is to examine whether they are competent. If they determine that they are competent, they have the duty of trying the case (and they cannot refuse). If they determine that they are incompetent, they must not try the case (and they must refuse to do so). Otherwise they can be punished (c. 1457).

3. The Carrying Out of the Process

We have said that the process is a linked and ordered series of acts which follow according to precise rules prescribing their steps and phases. They are governed by the principle referred to as preclusion, according to which a subsequent phase can begin only when the preceding phase has been concluded, without the possibility of turning back.

Therefore, the parties must realize their "moves" in the opportune moment, within established limits. Otherwise they may be refused, or they may have to be refused, by the judge. There are limits which are referred to as peremptory (also called fatal), precisely because since they are fixed by law, they cannot be postponed. Other limits are called judicial or conventional. They can be extended for a just reason by the judge, but only before they expire (c. 1465).

It should also be said that the process, in certain respects, is in the hands of the parties, who can freely do or abstain from doing what is permitted or required of them in each moment. In other words, they have initiative. Frequently, the law also asks the judge to act *ex officio*, on his own initiative, either to protect the public good or to avoid that through absence or lack of initiative of the parties, the case be unduly prolonged or arrive at a seriously unjust judgment. At any event, the direction of the process is in the hands of the judge (c. 1452).

A) The Introductory Stage (cc. 1501–1525)

The first moment of the trial has the purpose of clearly establishing the terms: the parties, tribunal, and object of the litigation. It begins with an introductory *libellus* in which the interested party or the promoter of justice presents his petition to the judge. In the *libellus*, or plea, the petitioner must clearly indicate: the judge or tribunal to which the case is being introduced, what is being petitioned (the object of the litigation), for what reasons, and from whom (the respondent). It must in addition indicate in general terms the reasons of law and of fact on which the petition is based (c. 1504).

Once the *libellus* has been received, it belongs to the judge to decide to admit it or to reject it. He will do this by verifying, first of all, as mentioned above, if the case belongs to his competence and if the petitioner has the legitimate capacity to appear in court. Then he must also examine whether the *libellus* is correctly written and if the petition contained in it appears at least to have a minimum foundation (if it does, as it is said, *fumus boni iuris*). If one of these requisites is lacking, the judge is to reject the *libellus* or have it corrected by the petitioner. Inasmuch as the rejection of the *libellus* is equivalent to a denial of his claim, the petitioner can have recourse against it (c. 1505).

If he decides to accept the *libellus*, the judge will cite the other parties for the joinder of the issue, that is, to establish the terms of the controversy together with the parties: what is being claimed and for what concrete reasons. Having heard the petitions and the responses of the parties, the judge establishes by decree the doubt or doubts to which a response is to be given in the judgment. For example, in a case of matrimonial nullity, the question will be whether the nullity of the marriage is evident for this or that reason.

Once the terms of the controversy have been established, they cannot be changed, unless the judge, for a serious reason and at the instance of one of the parties, consents to work out the terms again. This is for the sake of clarity and for the security of all who intervene in the process: they must know what is being contended and for what reasons, to be able to defend their interests.

B) The Evidentiary or Probatory Stage: Proofs (cc. 1526–1586)

Once the issue has been joined by means of the decree of the judge fixing the terms, the prosecution of the suit is opened; it normally must last up until the pronouncement of the definitive judgment. The phase is thus opened in which the proofs of the juridical acts and facts, related to the thing in dispute and on which the parties base their claims, are gathered. The judge must fix an appropriate period of time for the parties to present and complete their proofs.[139]

With regard to the proofs, the principle should be observed that the duty to furnish the proof belongs to the person who makes an allegation: the burden of the proof falls on the one who affirms. However, there is no need to prove what can be presumed from the law itself, or the facts admitted by the contending parties, unless the law or the judge demand it anyway (since in addition to the private interests of the parties, the public good may also be at stake) (c. 1526).

The parties can propose any type of proof that is licit and seems useful for deciding the case (c. 1527). The most common types of proof are:

a) The declarations of the parties (cc. 1530–1538). The judge interrogates the parties if he considers it appropriate;

139. However, it can happen that in the meantime, one of the parties dies or loses his title on account of which he had been called in cause; or that the petitioner renounces his claim or the respondent consents to what is asked of him; or that none of the parties act for six months; in which cases the process ceases.

he must do this at the request of a party or if it is useful for the public interest. He can ask the interrogated party to take an oath. The parties have the duty to answer and to tell the whole truth. In his interrogation, the judge will also keep in mind the questions proposed by other parties.

The admission of a fact surrendered by a party against himself before the judge is called judicial confession. What has been confessed need not be proved by the other party, unless the public good is at stake.

b) The witnesses (cc. 1547–1573). The parties can request that those who know facts regarding the case be called to testify. The judge can also *ex officio* call a witness not proposed by the parties. The Code establishes who can be called to testify and who is excluded or exempt from the duty of doing so (as in the case of clerics and doctors who are bound by professional secrecy, etc.).

Only the judge can interrogate the witnesses. However, the party who calls the witness must make known the matters on which he asks that the witness be questioned. The other parties can also suggest questions to be posed. As a rule, the witnesses are not to know the questions before being examined.

Both the parties and witnesses that have been legitimately cited must present themselves to the tribunal and respond truthfully to the judge. If they refuse or have some impediment, he can command that their deposition be collected in another legitimate way (for example, through the tribunal where they reside, by a parish priest or other delegate, by a notary).

The questions directed to the witnesses are to be brief and simple, accommodated to their capacity, not complicated, captious, sly or suggestive of a response. They are to pertain to the case and not offer offence. Their oral deposition must be immediately recorded in writing by the notary, also by means of a tape recorder. The minutes of the cross-examination is to be read to the witness, giving him the possibility to add, suppress, correct or vary what he deems appropriate, and then it is to be signed by the witness as well as by the judge and the notary.

The testimonies are to be evaluated by the judge taking account of: the condition and honesty of the witness; whether he is speaking by direct knowledge or by hearsay or on the basis of his own opinions; whether he has been coherent and constant in his affirmations or doubtful and fluctuating.

c) Proof by documents (cc. 1540–1546). In every case documents can be presented by the parties or requested by the judge as proofs. Normally they are in writing, but they can also be photographs, tape recordings, and other objects.

The documents can be public or private. Public documents are those released by a public official (state or ecclesiastical) in the exercise of his function and with the prescribed formalities. The others are private. The difference is considerable since what is directly recorded in a public document is presumed to be certain.

The documents are to be exhibited in the original or in an authentic copy, and consigned to the tribunal to be examined by the judge and by the other parties.

d) The proof by experts (cc. 1574–1581). There are facts or things whose demonstration requires the examination and the opinion of someone who has the knowledge and experience necessary to determine their true nature: an expert.

Recourse is to be made to experts whenever the law or the judge holds it necessary to prove certain facts or to truly know their nature. This is the case, for example, when the nullity of a marriage is requested by reason of impotence or mental illness of a spouse, according to c. 1680.

Experts are nominated by the judge, after listening to the parties or on their proposal. The intervention of private experts designated by the parties can also be admitted, as well as the reports made by experts outside of the process.

The acts of the case and all the elements necessary for him to complete his task must be furnished to the expert. The judge is to specify the questions on which the expert is to express his professional opinion.[140]

Each expert is to draw up his report separately from the others. The report must indicate the means and method used in the examination of the persons or things, and above all, the arguments on which he bases his conclusions.

The judge must attentively evaluate the expert opinions, expounding in the judgment the reasons for which he has accepted or rejected their conclusions.

e) Judicial recognizance (cc. 1582–1583). If he considers it opportune for the purpose of having a better knowledge of the facts, the judge can have access to a place or inspect something. A record of the inspection is prepared.

f) Presumptions (cc. 1584–1586). Presumption can be defined as "the probable deduction of something uncertain on the basis of a certain fact." They can be very useful in cases in which other certain proofs are lacking, above all because there are things which are very difficult to prove directly (especially negative facts, for example, the fact that someone was not baptized may be presumed if there is no proof in the records of the parishes where he has lived). A presumption is referred to as of the law (*iuris*) if established by the law itself, or human (*hominis*) if formulated by the judge.

Presumption has the effect of inverting the burden of the proof. In fact, a person who has a presumption of the law on his side is not bound to prove the fact that is presumed. For example, c. 1061 § 2 establishes that if the spouses have lived together after marriage, consummation is presumed. Therefore, a person who denies this in a concrete case will have to demonstrate the lack of consummation.

140. The above quoted Inst. *Dignitas connubii*, art. 209 suggest some concrete questions to be raised by the judge in cases of incapacity; but the judge is free to formulate those and others questions in any terms he deems appropriate.

C) The Publication of the Acts, the Conclusion of the Case, and the Pleadings (cc. 1598–1606)

Once the proofs have been gathered, before concluding the probatory phase, the judge must, under pain of nullity, proceed to the publication of the acts or allow the parties to inspect the acts of the trial. The parties can then present new proofs, which in turn will be published.

When the parties declare that they have no other proofs to produce, or in any case if they do not do so in the prescribed time or if the judge holds that the case has been sufficiently instructed, the judge decrees the conclusion of the case. After this it is no longer permissible to admit new proofs except for serious reasons or with the consent of the parties.

The case then passes to the stage of pleadings in which the parties are called, within an established period of time, to present their defense briefs and observations. Normally the defense briefs are in writing, and are made known to the other parties so that they can respond and present rejoinders. The judge can also convoke the parties for an oral debate.

D) The Judicial Decision (cc. 1607–1618)

Once the discussion is finished, it is the responsibility of the judge (or panel of judges) to pronounce the judgment. The judgment is called definitive if it decides the principal case, and interlocutory if it resolves an incidental question that arises in the course of the process.

In order to issue a judgment, the judge (or judges) must have reached moral certitude regarding the matter to be settled. He must base his decision solely on what is in the acts, evaluating the proofs conscientiously in the tenor of the law. If he does not reach moral certitude, he must pronounce that the right of the petitioner is not established.

The moral certitude that the judge must reach is what is based on the whole of the data of law and of facts that emerge in the process. This must exclude any reasonable doubt, although not requiring physical certitude. The judge must be morally sure of his decision.

If the tribunal is collegiate, the presiding judge is to convoke it to meet for the decision. The individual judges must bring their written conclusions, stating their reasons. On the basis of the individual conclusions, the judges discuss to arrive at a concordant decision. The decision, as mentioned above, is made by absolute majority of votes (c. 1426 § 1).

The judge (or the *ponens* of the collegiate tribunal) must write out the judgment within a month after the decision. The judgment must be definitive and congruent, which means that it must give a response to each of the doubts formulated in the joinder of the issue, determining the obligations which result for the parties and the way in which they must fulfilled. It must set forth the reasons, giving the reasons of law and of fact on which the decision is based. In addition, it must apportion the expenses of the suit.

In order to have force, the judgment must be published and made known to the parties with an indication of the ways in which it can be challenged.

4. Challenging the Judgment

The parties have various possibilities of challenging a judgment which they hold to be unjust, according to the reasons for which they deem it unjust. These recourses are: appeal, complaint of nullity, and total reinstatement (*restitutio in integrum*).

A) Appeal (cc. 1628–1640)

Appeal is the ordinary recourse, in second instance, to the tribunal which is superior with respect to the one which has issued the judgment. The party who considers himself to be injured has the right to file an appeal (also orally) before the same judge who pronounced the challenged judgment, within the period of 15 canonical days from the publication. There are some decisions which cannot be appealed (for example, those of the Roman Pontiff or of the Apostolic Signature). During the process of appeal, the execution of the challenged judgment is suspended, although cautionary measures can be taken.

After the filing of the appeal, it must be prosecuted within a month. This is made by sending the superior tribunal a copy of the challenged judgment together with a request stating the reasons why it should be amended. In the meantime the inferior tribunal will send all the acts of the case to the superior tribunal before which the appellate trial will be held. An appeal filed by one party also holds for the other parties who must therefore be called to intervene in the process.

The trial is carried out like that of the first instance, but in the second level the question posed to the tribunal can only be whether the challenged judgment should be confirmed or revised. Other questions not proposed in the first instance cannot be admitted.[141] New proofs can be produced only if there is a serious cause or if all the parties consent to it.

In cases of matrimonial nullity (which are the majority), when the judgment of the first instance declares the nullity, there must always be a decision in the second instance that confirms it. This is like an automatic appeal, so to speak: the tribunal which pronounced the affirmative judgment sends the acts *ex officio* to the appellate tribunal even if none of the parties ask for it (c. 1682). The parties are able to contract a new marriage only after the confirmation of the nullity on the part of the appeals court.

*Adjudged Matter (*res iudicata*)*

It is said that judgment is closed when appeal is no longer possible. This can happen because it is not permitted or because the parties renounce it or allow the available time to

141. Nevertheless, in annulment cases, a new *caput nullitatis* (a new reason why it is felt that the marriage was null) may be proposed; if the court of appeals admits it, it must be tried as if it were the first instance.

elapse, or when two concordant judgments are pronounced on the same petition (for example, if the judgment of the second level fully confirms the first).

The adjudged matter (*res iudicata*) settles the issue between the parties and can be immediately executed. As a rule, it cannot be submitted to a new trial according to the principle *ne bis in idem* (the same thing cannot be judged twice). However, there are some exceptions, since cases regarding status of persons (cleric, married, single, etc.) can always be reopened if new and serious reasons arise which were not considered before (c. 1644). As we shall see, there can also be *restitutio in integrum* against the *res iudicata*.

B) Complaint of Nullity (cc. 1619–1627)

The *querela nullitatis* is another recourse against a judgment. What is put in question here is not the decision on the merits of the points under debate, but the formal validity of the judgment pronounced, by reason of some irregularity in the process.

One can request the nullity of a judgment because it is vitiated by irremediable nullity or by remediable nullity. Among the former (mentioned in c. 1620), the following can be mentioned: the judgment has been pronounced by a judge who is absolutely incompetent, deprived of power or coerced by force or grave fear; procedural incapacity of one of the parties; one of the parties has been denied the right to defense; the judgment was totally incongruous (it did not define the controversy). Remedial defects (c. 1622) include, among others: that the required number of judges were not present; that the judgment fails to contain the reasons for the decision; that it fails to contain the required signatures or the date and place where it was pronounced.

The complaint is to be filed, within the established time limit (c. 1623), before the same judge who pronounced the challenged judgment; he can decide the recourse according to the procedure of an oral process. The judge can also retract the judgment or correct it *ex officio*.

C) Total Reinstatement (*restitutio in integrum*) (cc. 1645–1648)

This recourse is given against a judgment which has become a *res iudicata* only if there is clear proof of its injustice for one of the reasons specifically listed in c. 1645 § 2: the judgment was totally based on proofs later discovered to be false; the discovery of documents which demand a contrary decision; fraud of one of the parties; the judgment goes manifestly against the prescription of a law which is not merely procedural or a judgment which has become an adjudged matter.

Restitutio in integrum must be requested within three months of the discovery of the reasons on which it is based. According to the reason for which it is invoked, it can be requested of the same judge who issued the challenged judgment or a judge of appeal. If the *restitutio* has been conceded, it belongs to the judge to decide again on the merits of the case.[142]

5. The Execution of the Judgment (cc. 1650–1655)

Once the judgment has become an adjudged matter, and thus is no longer subject to appeal, it can be executed. The judge orders the execution of the judgment by decree. In certain cases, this decree can be included in the judgment itself that is to be executed. In other cases, the judge will issue a corresponding decree of execution.

Administrative execution of the judgment is the responsibility of the bishop of the diocese in which the judgment of the first level was issued. He can do this himself or by means of others. However, if he does not wish to do so, or if he is negligent, then the authority charged with executing the judgment is the bishop of the appellate tribunal.

If the judgment establishes that something belongs to the petitioner, this must be consigned to him immediately. If, on

142. See A. BETTETINI, *La restitutio in integrum processuale nel diritto canonico*, CEDAM, Padua, 1994.

the other hand, it is determined that the respondent must accomplish a specific obligation, the executor establishes a time limit for its accomplishment.

6. The Oral Contentious Process

This is an ordinary process that is simpler and quicker, in which—once the terms of the controversy and the object of contention have been defined in the normal way—the other stages are carried out in audience before the judge.

In the audience, the parties present their requests orally, proofs are collected (interrogation of the parties, witnesses and experts; presentation of documents, etc.), and an oral debate is held. Afterwards, the judge, separately, decides the case and communicates his verdict to the parties. Subsequently, he will write out the judgment with the corresponding motivations.

The oral process is carried out, in the first instance, before a single judge and can be used in cases for which it is not excluded by law (cases of matrimonial nullity and all those which require a collegiate tribunal are excluded). If one of the parties requests it, the case must proceed according to the ordinary written procedure.

7. Special Processes

Special processes are those which depart in some aspect from the ordinary process. The most important are matrimonial processes, regarding either the nullity of the marriage,[143] separation of the spouses or dissolution of the bond.

a) The object of the marriage nullity process is to declare whether or not the nullity of a marriage is evident. It does not annul the marriage, as it is frequently and incorrectly said,

143. The Inst. *Dignitas connubii* is a kind of vademecum orderly presenting the rules to follow in handling those matrimonial processes.

since a valid marriage cannot be annulled by anyone (if it is ratified and consummated it cannot even be dissolved). Therefore, it is a matter of examining whether, for the reasons introduced by the petitioner, the marriage was null from the beginning.

Among the special features of the process, it should be mentioned that only the spouses have the capacity to challenge their marriage (except for the promoter of justice when the nullity has already become publicly known, c. 1674). After the death of one of the spouses the marriage can normally no longer be challenged (c. 1675).

In the formulation of the doubt (the question posed to the tribunal), it is not sufficient to ask whether the nullity is evident, but the ground or grounds of nullity must be indicated. In other words, it must indicate the reason or reasons on the basis of which it is being requested (for example, because one of the parties was already married or was incapable, etc.).

Logically, in these cases the defender of the bond must intervene because a public good is at stake. If the nullity is requested for impotence or for mental illness, recourse must be made to the technical opinion of experts (c. 1680).

In order for the parties to pass to new marriages, the nullity must be declared by two concordant decisions (that is, substantially coinciding with regard to the motivations). Therefore, after a first affirmative judgment, there is a kind of automatic appeal to the superior tribunal which will decide whether or not the first judgment is to be confirmed. In certain cases confirmation may be decided by decree.

When documents not subject to exception show with certainty that there was an impediment that was not dispensed, or the lack of the legitimate form, or that the marriage was celebrated by a proxy without a valid mandate, the documentary process can be followed. On the basis of these documents, the judge, after having heard the parties and the defender of the bond, can declare the nullity of the marriage by a judgment, leaving aside the other formalities of the ordinary process (cc. 1686–1688).

b) The cases of separation of the spouses are characterized by the fact that they can be defined by decree of the diocesan bishop in addition to a judgment by the judge. In such cases, the oral process is followed. In addition, in certain cases, the diocesan bishop can also authorize that the cause of separation be presented before a state tribunal instead of an ecclesiastical one.[144]

c) A third type of matrimonial process is that for the dispensation from a ratified but not consummated marriage. In reality, it is a procedure rather than a process or trial, since it does not end with a judgment but with a dispensation (or not) from the marriage, conceded by the Pope. However, this procedure for the dispensation is carried out in a manner similar to a trial (cc. 1697–1706).

In fact, as c. 1142 states, the dissolution or dispensation from a marriage that is ratified and not consummated belongs to the Roman Pontiff, for a just cause, and on the request of one or both parties. The procedure therefore has the purpose of judging on the fact of non-consummation and on the existence of a just cause. This judgment, according to c. 1698, is the competence of the Holy See, and concretely of the Congr. for Divine Worship.[145]

The request for dispensation must be presented by at least one of the spouses to the diocesan bishop of their own domicile. The bishop, if he thinks that it is well founded, entrusts the tribunal (or a suitable priest) to instruct the

---

144. W. H. WOESTMAN, *Special Marriage Cases: Non-Consummation, Pauline Privilege, Favour of the Faith, Separation of Spouses, Validation, Sanation, Presumed Death*, 3rd ed., Saint Paul University, Ottawa, 1994.

145. See *Pastor Bonus*, art. 67. Regarding the way to proceed, the Congr. has given instructions in the Circular *Congregatio pro sacramentis*, December 20 1986: *Communicationes* [1988] 78– 84; EV 10/1012-1044.

process, which is carried out as in cases of matrimonial nullity (citation of the parties, intervention of the defender of the bond, collection of proofs, argumentation in favor of the request).

Once the instruction is completed, the instructor submits the acts to the diocesan bishop together with his report.

The bishop transmits the acts, with the observations of the defender of the bond, to the Apostolic See, adding his own opinion concerning the truth of:

- the fact of the lack of consummation;
- the existence of a just cause for the dispensation;
- the opportuneness of granting the favor.

The Congr. for Divine Worship will decide whether the non-consummation and the other requisites have been established, and if that is the case, it will propose the dispensation to the Holy Father.

d) Still in the area of marriage, there is also the process in the case of the presumed death of a spouse (c. 1707), which has the purpose of declaring the death of one of the spouses when this cannot be demonstrated by an authentic document (state or ecclesiastical).

The surviving spouse cannot be considered to be single until the presumed death of the other has been declared by the diocesan bishop. He will make such a declaration only after an accurate investigation which brings him to moral certitude of the death, based on witnesses, hearsay, or other indications. The sole absence of the spouse, even if prolonged, is not sufficient.

e) Another special process is what aims at the declaration of nullity of sacred ordination. Here also, as in marriage, we are faced with a declarative trial: it is a matter not of conceding the nullity, but of seeing whether the ordination for some specific reason was null from the beginning.

The competence to deal with these cases belongs to the Congr. for Divine Worship[146] which, however, can entrust each individual case to another tribunal designated by it.

By law, the validity of ordination can only be challenged by the interested cleric and by the Ordinary to whom he is subject, or in whose diocese he was ordained.

The process follows for the most part the ordinary procedure but, as in matrimonial cases, the defender of the bond must intervene, and the rights and duties of the clerical state cease only after a second decision which confirms the nullity of the ordination declared in a first judgment.

A) Penal Processes (cc. 1717–1731)

Penal processes are those whose purpose is to establish whether criminal acts were committed, determining the responsibility and inflicting the corresponding punishment.

Among the special features presented by these trials, the most important is the preliminary investigation. The Ordinary who receives information about the commission of an offence, must first of all make (by himself or by means of someone he assigns) a prudent investigation which does not endanger anyone's good name.

Only after this investigation, if sufficient elements have emerged, will the Ordinary decide whether it is possible or appropriate to proceed in a penal manner against someone, and how: by extra-judicial decree or by a true penal process.

If he decides to proceed by decree (if the law allows it), it is a matter of an administrative procedure and not a true process. However, this procedure demands that the accused party be given the possibility to defend himself, making known to him the accusation and the proofs against him. The decree must contain the reasons of law and of fact on which it is based.

146. Ibid., art. 68.

If, on the other hand, the Ordinary determines that a penal process is to be initiated, he submits the acts of the investigation to the promoter of justice so that he may formulate the accusation before the judge.

The penal process is carried out like the ordinary contentious process, with the following characteristics:

- the accused must always have an advocate, selected by him or named by the judge;
- during the process, the Ordinary can, as a preventive measure, impose the prohibitions or injunctions that he sees fit, in order to avoid scandal or safeguard the course of justice, having heard the promoter of justice;
- in the discussion of the case, the accused always has the right to speak or write last (personally or through an advocate or procurator);
- since a penal trial puts the good name of the accused in jeopardy, if he is considered innocent, he has the right that everything be done to arrive at a judgment which fully absolves him.

Finally, the possibility is given to the party injured by an offence to ask for reparation of damages. Also the accused who was found to be innocent can ask to be compensated according to c. 128.

8. Administrative Justice (cc. 1732–1739)

When a person considers himself to be injured by an act of the ecclesiastical authority, the procedures for claiming his proper rights follow the administrative rather than the ordinary path. The "administration" (in generic terms), enjoys certain prerogatives (and has certain duties) because in principle it works for the public good and its activities are initially presumed to be correct and impartial. This means, as stated in c. 1400 § 2, that recourse against an administrative act can only be presented before the hierarchical superior of the authority which issued the challenged act or before an administrative (not ordinary) tribunal.

As for all conflicts which arise in the Church, one must first seek peaceful paths of resolution to avoid, if possible, the development of a heated controversy (c. 1733).

A) The Administrative Recourse

For the above-mentioned reason, a person who considers himself to be injured by an administrative act must first of all present the petition of revocation or correction before the same organ which issued the contested act, within 10 days. In this way, the possibility is given to the author of the act to review it before recourse is made against him. He has 30 days to reply, after which the response is presumed to be negative, in that silence is interpreted as refusal of the recourse (cf. c. 57).

Only after the negative outcome of this petition for revision, the interested party can have recourse to the hierarchical superior of the author of the act, within 15 available (or canonical) days after the negative response. This hierarchical administrative recourse can be presented before the author of the act himself, who must transmit it to the superior with the necessary documentation.

The superior that is competent to receive the recourse is the superior of the authority who issued the challenged act. For example, against the acts of the diocesan bishop, one must have recourse to the Holy See, whereas recourse is to be made to the diocesan bishop against the acts of an authority subject to him (vicar, pastor, superior of an institute of diocesan right).

All individual administrative acts (decrees, precepts, rescripts) are subject to recourse, but not those of general normative or judicial character. Logically, no recourse can be made against the acts of the Roman Pontiff and an ecumenical council, although one can ask for the favor that an act issued by them be reviewed.

Administrative recourse can be filed by any subjects (physical persons or corporate bodies) who consider themselves to be burdened by an act, and for any just reason (c. 1737).

Hierarchical administrative recourse is not of a judicial nature. In it, the superior administrative authority simply evaluates whether an act of an inferior authority is to be confirmed, revoked, annulled, or at least corrected.

B) Contentious Administrative Recourse

This is the administrative recourse that is presented before an administrative tribunal. The only administrative tribunal currently existing is the Apostolic Signature, to whom it belongs to deal "with controversies [...] which arise from an act of ecclesiastical administrative power" (c. 1445 § 2).

The singular administrative acts issued or approved by a dicastery of the Roman Curia can be challenged. This means that against acts issued by an inferior of the Roman Curia, one must first have recourse to the corresponding dicastery (in the administrative path), and then, if the dicastery confirms the act, the party who has recourse will have to go to the Tribunal (in the contentious path) against the act of confirmation.

Recourse cannot be made for any reason whatsoever, but only when "it is contended that the impugned act violated some law either in the decision-making process or in the procedure used" (*Pastor Bonus*, art. 123 § 1). The petitioner can also ask the Tribunal to adjudicate the reparation of damages incurred.

The process before the Apostolic Signature is carried out according to the special norms of this tribunal. A characteristic of this process is that in the preliminary stage, the Signature must decide whether or not the recourse is admissible.

Chapter XIII.

Relations Between the Church and the Political Community

In this chapter we shall examine the juridical principles that govern relations between the Church and other social groups, especially political communities.[147]

From the beginning the Church has presented herself not only as a community of believers and baptized persons, but also as a juridically structured society, founded by Christ, and which has received from Him the mission of continuing His work of salvation in history.

"The work of Christ's redemption concerns essentially the salvation of men; it takes in also, however, the renewal of the whole temporal order. The mission of the Church, consequently, is not only to bring men the message and grace of Christ but also to permeate and improve the whole range of the temporal by means of the spirit of the Gospel" (*AA* 5).

The awareness that the Church has of herself, of her foundation, organization and mission, makes it impossible

147. On this subject, see S. Z. EHLER, J. B. MORRALL, *Church and State Through the Centuries*, Biblo and Tannen, Dublin, 1954; E. CAPARROS, L.-L. CHRISTIANS (eds.), *Religion in Comparative Law at the Dawn of the 21st Century / La religion en droit comparé à l'aube du 21e siècle*, Bruylant, Bruxelles, 2000; G. DALLA TORRE, *La città sul monte*, 2nd ed., A.V.E., Rome, 2002.

for her to identify or confuse herself with any other society. However, this poses the problem of her relations with other organizations and the ways and means she should use in order to carry out her mission. In fact, in the world in which the Church was born 2,000 years ago, the fact of belonging to a people also determined the fact that one would belong to its religion. There was a unity or confusion between the political community and the religious community, and thus between their corresponding authorities.[148]

From her first steps, the Church knew herself to be called to bring together a people for God composed of peoples of every race, nation and culture. She is called to build up the Kingdom of Christ, which is not of this world and thus does not intend to enter into competition with the kingdoms of the earth, but is present in and acts in this world to attract the nations to the light of the faith.

1. Christian Dualism

Christianity thus introduced a historical novelty in the relations between religion and politics, and more specifically between the Church and civil society. This novelty is called Christian dualism. The Church is autonomous and independent in the realization of her religious mission, and in this sense she is sovereign with respect to any other entity. Her relations with political societies throughout the centuries have been built on the basis of this dualism.

The problems that this dualism poses concern not only the balance between two centers of power but above all, the individuals who, as citizens and members of the faithful, belong to

148. Religion was, as Leziroli states, "a fact pertaining to politics and not to conscience, as we are used to considering it today" (*Relazioni fra Chiesa cattolica e potere politico*, Giappichelli, Turin, 1994).

two societies at the same time and must accommodate their behavior to the demands of both. In fact, Christian dualism distinguishes but does not separate or confuse the temporal with the religious sphere, and establishes their relations.

The first Christians, basing themselves on the deeds and words of our Lord, interpreted this dualism very well. They knew that it was necessary to "render to Caesar the things that are Caesar's, and to God the things that are God's" (Mk 12, 17; cf. Mt 22, 21). They considered themselves citizens of the Empire equal to others (not segregated or different) and, therefore, while they submitted themselves to the legitimate laws and commands of the state authority, in their religious and moral life they obeyed God and His Church.

This was the cause of the first conflicts, since the Christians refused to obey the commands of the imperial authority which had a religious character or were in any way contrary to the divine law. For the ancient world, on the other hand, religion and politics were both subject to a sole authority (monism): it was held that religious life entered into the competence of the political power. The attitude of Christians before this dilemma is clearly synthesized in the response of Peter to the Sanhedrin: "We must obey God rather than men" (Acts 5, 29; cf. 4, 20). This was a source of the persecutions and accusations against the Christians.

Tied together with dualism is the problem of the freedom of the Church. In every moment she has always claimed the right to freely organize and carry out her mission, by means of preaching, worship, and works of charity.

2. Historical Interpretations of Dualism

Although the principles are clear, the doctrinal and practical interpretations of this dualism which have followed one another throughout the centuries reflect the changing conditions of every period. On the one hand, the Church herself penetrates her own mystery more and more, and discovers new possibilities and methods to carry out her mission. On the other hand, these possibilities and methods depend in a certain way on the concrete social and political configuration of the civil community, and on its attitude with regard to religion and the Church.

a) As soon as it emerged from the catacombs, with the end of the persecutions and the Edict of Milan (313) promulgated by Constantine and Licinius, Christianity quickly became the official religion of the empire which, however, claimed to put the Church in the place of the ancient pagan religions. This meant that she would be not only under the protection of the empire, but also under its competence.

The Christian emperors, although favoring the development and the spread of the Christian religion, attributed to themselves, as formerly, the role of religious leaders: they convoked councils, settled dogmatic disputes and named bishops. This vision of the relations between the Church and the empire has been called cæsaropapism, in that the political power attempts to substitute itself for Church power. The pastors reacted to this abuse to defend ecclesiastical liberty.

A commonly used example of this struggle is the letter from Pope Gelasio I to Emperor Anastasius I (494), which is the first magisterial formulation of the dualism:

> There are indeed, augustus Emperor, two powers by which this world is chiefly ruled: the sacred authority of the Popes and the royal power [...] although you have the chief place in dignity over the human race, yet you must submit yourself faithfully to those who have charge of Divine things, and look to them for the means of your salvation. You know that it behooves you in matters concerning the reception and reverent administration of the Sacraments, to be obedient to the ecclesiastical authority rather than to control it. So in such matters you ought to depend on ecclesiastical judgment, instead to seeking to bend it to tour own will. For if in matters pertaining to the administration of public discipline, the Bishops of the Church, knowing that the Empire has been conferred on you by Divine instrumentality, are themselves obedient to your laws, lest in purely material

matters contrary opinions may seem to be voiced, with what willingness, I ask you, should you obey those to whom is assigned the administration of Divine mysteries?[149]

Cæsaropapism ended by becoming established in the East, contributing not a little to the division of the Church (schism of the East), and has influenced relations between Orthodox Churches and the state power up until the present time.

In the West, the triumph of the Germanic invasions and the decline of the empire created moments of chaos and social regression, and it seemed that the Church was the sole survivor. However, she still had to defend her freedom with great effort.

b) In the feudal Middle Ages, civil society and ecclesiastical society were confused in one homogeneous *respublica christianorum* or *christianitas*, within which the secular and ecclesiastical powers were intertwined, and contended for supremacy. Ecclesiastical offices were often also political positions: bishops and abbots were princes and lords in their domains.[150] The choice of suitable persons to fill these positions became a political issue in which the secular princes sought to intervene at the expense of the freedom of the Church. Thus arose the famous controversy of investiture, in which—on the level of ideas—Gregory VII (1073–1085) triumphed.

Within Christendom, the relations between the two powers came to be identified with the clergy–laity relationship in the Church. Both clergy and laity cooperate in the attaining the same ideal: conserving and extending the Kingdom of God. However, the secular power was to be guided by the priestly power as an instrument in their

149. MIGNE L, LIX, col. 42; English version: S. Z. EHLER, J. B. MORRALL, *Church and State Through the Centuries,* Biblo & Tannen, Dublin, 1954, p. 11.

150. The Roman Pontiff himself was also a territorial ruler, and remained one until the end of the Papal States (1870).

service, "because as the spiritual life is more worthy than the earthly and the spirit more than the body, so the spiritual power precedes the worldly or secular power in dignity and honor."[151]

In this way, a system of relations was formed in which the priestly power had the primacy. The dualism of powers was not denied, but the dualism of societies within which each of them operated was obscured. In the confrontation between the two authorities, whose relations were in fact established within the only Christian Kingdom (*respublica christianorum*), which was identified with the Church itself, it was logical to affirm the superiority of the spiritual over the earthly authority.

It always belongs to the Church to judge over everything that presents an aspect of sin in the life of men (what is not in harmony with the Gospel). However, in the medieval context, this judgment could not avoid having more or less direct political repercussions. One of the most important of these was that of excommunication, which has the same effect as a deposition because it dissolves the bond of fidelity of subjects towards the excommunicated monarch or emperor. By means of this path of moral judgment (*ratio peccati*), the Pope was called to resolve conflicts between Christian princes, or to ask for their collaboration in the struggle against heresy and paganism.

At the end of the Middle Ages there was, on the one hand, a strong crisis of the prestige of the papacy, while the need for a profound reform of the Church was felt to be ever more imperative. On the other hand, there arose new theological and political ideas which contested the hierarchical nature of the Church (especially the primacy of the Supreme Pontiff) and affirmed ever more strongly the power of princes. From this ferment there arose, in the 16th century,

151. HUGH OF S. VÍCTOR (1096–1141), *De Sacramentis christianæ fidei*: MIGNE L, CCXVII, col. 418.

the dismembering of the Church due to the Protestant reformation, and the dismembering of the Holy Roman Empire into many absolute monarchies jealous of their unlimited sovereignty, also in ecclesiastical matters.

c) In the modern period, the relationship between politics and religion was in fact resolved into a predomination of the temporal power, summed up in the formula *cuius regio eius religio,* with which the religious wars were ended. It signified that it is the prince who chooses the official religion in his kingdom, to the exclusion of other religions. The existence of a State religion went together with considering it as a factor of political unity. This led therefore to the repression of other forms of worship, which only slowly acquired certain degrees of tolerance.

In the States in which Protestantism triumphed, monism was restored. The reformed community became the State Church, whose head, in one way or another, was the prince. In Catholic States, dualism was interpreted in different ways. On the part of the State, although still remaining faithful to dogmatic principles, there was the tendency to intervene in ecclesiastical affairs through what has been called "an administrative heresy":[152] jurisdictionalism in its various national forms (French Gallicanism, German Febronianism, Spanish and Portuguese Regalism, Austrian Josephinism, etc.).

Jurisdictionalism is a sort of modern cæsaropapism which broadly interpreted the competencies of princes in ecclesiastical matters, obtained on the basis of ancient or new pontifical privileges, or in return for the work of defending the faith and evangelizing the newly discovered lands. At root, however, there was always the idea of the absolute sovereignty of the monarch, founded (along the lines of that of the Pope) on titles of divine right. This sovereignty was also considered to extend to religion, and thus over the life and organization of the

152. A. DE LA HERA, C. SOLER, "Historia de las doctrinas sobre las relaciones entre la Iglesia y el Estado", in *Tratado de Derecho Eclesiástico*, Eunsa, Pamplona, 1994, p. 69.

national Church, whose relations with the Holy See were more or less monitored by the State bureaucracy.

The practical consequences of jurisdictionalism were various, and differed in intensity from country to country. In general, they were made concrete in what has been called *iura maiestatis circa sacra*: intervention with regard to new circumscriptions and ecclesiastical appointments (monarchical patronage); subjecting the publication of ecclesiastical documents (especially pontifical ones) to the *placet* of the monarch; control and taxation of ecclesiastical goods; control of ecclesiastical tribunals by state ones, etc.

On the ecclesiastical side, this tendency was resisted on two different levels: doctrinal and practical. In the first, the medieval arguments on the supremacy of the spiritual power were further developed, interpreting this in a way more in harmony with social dualism and determined by the consolidation of the nation–States. In this way, the doctrine of the indirect power (*potestas indirecta*) of the Church over temporal questions was proposed.

According to this doctrine, the State and the Church appear as societies that are diverse and autonomous in their own sphere, guided by their respective authorities. However, since the Church has a mission transcending that of the State, her jurisdiction is not limited to purely ecclesiastical affairs, but also extends to temporal things which indirectly regard the good of souls, in order that state institutions may not only not impede, but also contribute to the spiritual task of the Church.

On the practical level, however, the Holy See frequently ceded to the jurisdictionalist claims of the Catholic princes, conceding them, in the form of pontifical privileges, those competencies that the kings claimed to possess by their own right. From this political interplay were born the modern concordats. Roman diplomacy played a prominent role in these agreements.

d) The revolutionary period beginning at the end of the 18th century brought with it great changes in civil society and in its relations with religious confessions. Enlightenment rationalism inspired the idea of a liberal State in which the exercise of power is limited, divided and regulated by a political constitution which guarantees equal rights to citizens, among which the right to freedom of worship is included. With regard to religious confessions, liberal principles required the abandonment of State religions and the separation of the Church and State.

Nevertheless, the practical realization of these premises proceeded in various ways in the different countries, both in time and in their modalities, according to their history and traditions. The American and French Revolutions are the two paradigmatic examples. The North American colonies had the ideal of constructing a free and open society, in which every person could practice the religion that they considered most suitable for themselves, with a total but respectful separation between the State and the Christian religious groups then present in the colonies, whose freedom was guaranteed.[153]

The French Revolution, which then inspired those of Europe and South and Central America, began instead from a spirit of reprisal against everything that was represented by the Old Regime. The close alliance between the monarchy and the Catholic Church was also an object of this hostility. The ideals of religious liberty and of separation were frequently interpreted in an anticlerical way, as meaning to exclude religion from social life and to subject the Church to the political power.[154]

---

153. The *Virginia declaration of rights* (1776) says "that religion, or the duty which we owe to our Creator, and the manner of discharging it, can be directed only by reason and conviction, not by force or violence; and therefore all men are equally entitled to the free exercise of religion, according to the dictates of conscience; and that it is the mutual duty of al to practice Christian forbearance, love, and charity toward each other" (Section 16).

154. The *Déclaration des droits de l'homme et du citoyen* of 1789, art. 10 reads: "no one should be molested because of his opinions, even religious opinions, in as much as its manifestation does not alter the public order established by Law." See J. HERVADA, J. M. ZUMAQUERO, *Textos internacionales de derechos humanos,* Eunsa, Pamplona, 1978, p. 50.

This mentality led to the suppression of the religious orders, the confiscation of ecclesiastical goods, and the suppression of Catholic schools and other Catholic works.

The response of the Church Magisterium to the revolutionary events and to the tenets of liberalism could not but be negative. In addition to deploring the disorders and excesses of the revolutions, the Roman Pontiffs condemned the liberal ideas: religious indifferentism which denied the existence of an objective moral order and consecrated the freedom of worship, of thought and of the press; the agnostic State which excluded religion from social life; the secularization of marriage and schools; the separation between Church and State translated into anticlerical laws which denied the freedom of the Church. There was also the problem of the Papal States, combated within and without by the liberals. Pius IX summarized the condemnation of liberal principles in various fields in his Syllabus (1864).[155]

Thus began what later came to be called the social doctrine of the Church. In the face of liberal utopias which tended to base the State on purely rationalist principles and no longer on an objective moral order, the Magisterium proposed those principles which reflect the divine plan regarding the order of human society, applying them to the new and various questions arising in each historical moment.[156]

Among other questions, Leo XIII (1878–1903) developed the characteristics of the Christian State and its relations with the Church.[157] On the basis of evangelical dualism, the Catholic

155. On the origin and significance of this document, see G. DALLA TORRE, entry under "Sillabo," in *Enciclopedia del Diritto*, vol. XLII, Giuffrè, Milan, 1990, pp. 575–581.

156. The liberal revolutions and the State model that stems from them, indicate the purpose (first in the facts and then in doctrine) of a dualism understood as a distribution of competencies; the Church will more and more follow the Magisterium route, that of the formation of consciences and always less that of claiming jurisdiction over temporal matters.

157. Especially in the encyclicals *Immortale Dei* (1885) and *Sapientiæ Christianæ* (1890).

Church and the State are two perfect societies, willed by God, which must mutually recognize the freedom and autonomy of each in their own order. However, since the same persons are the subjects of both orders, their legislation must be in harmony with the principle that everything in relation with the moral order and the salvation of souls falls under the competence of the Church.

Furthermore, the religious dimensions of man must also be manifested in social life; this is the reason why the State must act according to Christian principles. As a result, both Church–State separation and freedom of worship were condemned. The latter, inspired by indifferentism, put the Catholic religion on an equal level with other religions. Non-Catholic religions were to be tolerated, however, in the extent that this was fitting to protect peace in social intercourse; and of course, one must always distinguish between the sin and the sinner, who must always be treated with respect.

Leo XIII did not fail to realize that many nations were by then very far from these principles. Therefore, he called Christians to be present in the political life of their countries so that, as far as possible, the values of which they were the bearers would be received by the State.

e) In the first half of the 20th century, the doctrine of Pope Leo XIII was repeated, with nuances of circumstance, by his successors up until Pius XII. They had to confront new problems, especially those provoked by the historical realization of different totalitarian ideologies (Marxism, Nazism, fascism). Although ideologically distant one from another, all of these systems are tied to the thought of the Enlightenment and present a totalitarian conception of the State which (confused with the only official party) sees it to be the exclusive protagonist absorbing all aspects of social life. The individual is significant only as a part of the community (nation or class) and is entirely in its service. Several times, Pius XI (1922–1939) had to condemn these deifications of the State which leave no room for religion, especially in the encyclicals

Non abbiamo bisogno (1931) against fascism, *Mit brennender Sorge* (1937) against Nazism, and *Divini Redemptoris* (1937) against communism.

The disasters caused by these ideologies led the Magisterium to reflect more deeply on the dignity of the person and his rights, on the basis of arguments not only from Revelation, but also from natural law which could be understood and accepted by all men of good will, to whom the social doctrine is now explicitly addressed. Furthermore, the importance of the lay apostolate has come to appear ever more decisive for the Christianization of a secularized and pluralistic society.

Faced with the carnage of World War II and the need for reconstruction, Pius XII defended a national and international order of Christian inspiration, based on respect for the rights of the person and of peoples. Although he did not admit religious liberty, the Pontiff enlarged upon the doctrine of toleration for all forms of worship, and spoke of the legitimate lay character of the democratic State in an ever more heterogeneous society.

The pontificate of Blessed John XXIII marked an important turn in the relations between the Church and civil society, which can be traced to the Magisterium of the same Pope and to the teaching of the Second Vatican Council convoked by him. In his Encyclical *Pacem in terris* (1963), John XXIII made a positive evaluation of human rights, based on the fact that "every human being is a person, that is, his nature is endowed with intelligence and free will." Among the rights listed in the encyclical, there is the right "to honor God according to the dictates of one's upright conscience, and therefore the right to render private and public worship to God." Thus recognition is given to religious liberty on the basis of natural law and not on the basis of liberal relativism.

3. The Second Vatican Council

In the wake of the preceding Magisterium, the last council found greater possibilities for dialogue between the Church and the other communities. This was done, on the one hand, by reflecting more deeply on the nature of the Church itself, and on the other, by taking seriously the reality of a society ever more sensitive to respect for the rights of the person.

The Church sees herself as a people of God gathered in Christ, a unique reality in which human and divine, earthly and heavenly, visible and spiritual elements are intertwined in a mysterious way, in the image of the mystery of the Word incarnate (*LG* 8). Her mission is the continuation of that of Jesus, "to make all men partakers in redemption and salvation, and through them to establish the right relationship of the world to Christ" (*AA* 2a).

The mission of the Church, in fact, "is not only to bring men the message and grace of Christ but also to permeate and improve the whole range of the temporal by means of the spirit of the Gospel" (*AA* 5). This is not a matter of an abstract and external preaching, but of making the Gospel take flesh in the various historical circumstances and in human affairs. Thus the Church is called to undertake a relationship with all earthly realities (culture, politics, religion, science, etc.) with the purpose of elevating and perfecting them. These relations are amply dealt with in the conciliar Const. *Gaudium et spes*.

Since "in the Church there is diversity of ministry but unity of mission" (*AA* 2), all the members of the faithful, in virtue of baptism, are called to participate in this mission, each according to his own condition. From our point of view, it is relevant to define briefly the nature of the mission possessed by the Church with regard to the world, the relations this mission determines with regard to the world, and how this mission is to be realized.

The mission Christ has entrusted to His Church is exclusively religious, not temporal: she does not claim to reach a dominion of a political, economic or social type over earthly realities (*GS* 42).

Given these premises, the Council has spoken of Christian dualism on various planes and perspectives:

a) There is a distinction and a relationship between the temporal and the religious orders. The Const. *Gaudium et spes* (n. 36) specifies the way in which the proper autonomy of earthly realities should be understood:

> If by the autonomy of earthly affairs is meant the gradual discovery, exploitation, and ordering of the laws and values of matter and society, then the demand for autonomy is perfectly in order: it is at once the claim of modern man and the desire of the Creator. By the very nature of creation, material being is endowed with its own stability, truth and excellence, its own order and laws [...]. However, if by the term 'the autonomy of earthly affairs' is meant that material being does not depend on God and that man can use it as if it had no relation to its Creator, then the falsity of such a claim will be obvious to anyone who believes in God. Without a Creator there can be no creature.

At least two considerations can be deduced from this:

- the laws and proper order of earthly things and the moral order not only are not in opposition to each other, but rather they form part of one and the same divine plan for all of creation, including man. For this reason, the correct use of things of the earth implies respect for the principles and values proper to both orders: "Consequently, methodical research in all branches of knowledge, provided it is carried out in a truly scientific manner and does not override moral laws, can never conflict with the faith, because the things of the world and the things of faith derive from the same God" (*GS* 36);
- the mission of the Church to lead created things to God does not imply that they fall under ecclesiastical government, but consists in guiding man, with doctrine, to a correct use of earthly realities which will lead him to perfection and to the realization of his divine vocation.

The laws and principles of a scientific or technical order which rule nature and society do not, in fact, form part of Revelation. However, this cannot be said of the laws and principles of a moral order according to which earthly things are to be used and ordered (*DH* 14c). It is these ethical foundations of human life (individual and social) that the Church teaches with authority and truth. She proposes them to all men, aware that the problems of humanity can only find a truly human response on the basis of respect for these ethical principles.

b) Distinction and relations between civil and ecclesiastical society. At the social level dualism has been defined by the Council in terms of autonomy and collaboration: "The political community and the Church are autonomous and independent of each other in their own fields. Nevertheless, both are devoted to the personal vocation of man, although under different titles. This service will redound the more effectively to the welfare of all insofar as both institutions practice better cooperation according to the local and prevailing situation" (*GS* 76).

Therefore, there are two societies differing in nature and aim, the one being temporal and the other supernatural. Both act according to their own proper criteria, and both find their reason for being and their point of contact and cooperation in their service to man.

The Church on her part recognizes that "the terrestrial city, rightly concerned with secular affairs, is governed by its own principles" (*LG* 36), and therefore, "the Church [...] has no desire to become involved in the government of the temporal order" (AG 12c).

Likewise, in order to carry out her religious mission, the Church asks to be able to enjoy "that freedom of action which her responsibility for the salvation of men requires" (*DH* 13). Specifically, she claims her right to have "true freedom to preach the faith, to proclaim its teaching about society, to carry out her task among men without hindrance, and to pass moral judgments even in matters relating to politics, whenever the fundamental rights of man or the salvation of souls requires it." In these activities, the Church uses those and only those means which "are in accord with the Gospel and the welfare of all men" (*GS* 76).

Although their natures remain distinct, ecclesiastical and civil societies need each other in a certain sense, in that both collaborate in the perfection of man, in his personal and social, material and spiritual welfare. This corresponds to the plan of God who is the author of the natural and supernatural orders, the Creator and Redeemer of man, and his final end and happiness. The ways and paths of this cooperation will vary according to the circumstances, but they must begin from a consideration of the dignity of the person and of his rights.

On this basis the Church maintains institutional relations with many countries, and international bodies of particular relevance are the diplomatic relations maintained by the Holy See with a large number of States, with many of which it has signed international agreements. In these juridical instruments, at the same time that they define the juridical statute of the Church in civil society, its liberty, they establish the means for cooperation between it and the State.

c) Autonomy of the faithful in secular activities. The Church carries out her mission of Christianizing human society above all through the activity of her members, especially the laity, whose specific vocation is "to seek the kingdom of God by engaging in temporal affairs and directing them according to God's will." It is God Himself who calls them, "that being led by the spirit of the Gospel, they may contribute to the sanctification of the world, as from within like leaven [...]. It pertains to them in a special way so to illuminate and order all temporal things with which they are so closely associated that these may be effected and grow according to Christ" (*LG* 31).

Since ordering earthly realities according to the laws of God does not mean denying their autonomy or subjecting them to the governance of the Church, the laity have, on the one hand, the duty to "recognize the inner nature, the value and the ordering of the whole of creation to the praise of God [...] remembering that in every temporal affair they are to be guided by a Christian conscience" (*LG* 36). On the other hand, they have the right that the pastors give them "the liberty which belongs to all in the terrestrial city" (*LG* 37).

This autonomy in secular activities has been expounded in c. 227 of the CIC, in which it is noted that in the exercise of this freedom, the faithful "are to take care that their actions are imbued with the spirit of the Gospel and take into account the doctrine set forth by the Magisterium of the Church; but they are to avoid proposing their own opinion as the teaching of the Church in questions which are open to various opinions." This means that every Christian is free to maintain any temporal option that is compatible with faith and morals. The hierarchy or other members of the faithful cannot impose particular choices or strategies on them, nor can they present themselves as representatives of Catholics in temporal affairs.

The Gospel message contains, in fact, the necessary teachings for the salvation of men and for the organization of the Church. However, it does not contain a program for the political, economic, or cultural organization of civil society: in these matters many different types of projects may be in harmony with the Gospel.

The Catholic citizen, since he enjoys this freedom, must assume responsibility for his actions in civil life, without claiming to involve the Church in his personal options. Following the invitation of the Council, "the faithful should learn to distinguish carefully between the rights and duties which they have as belonging to the Church and those which fall to them as members of the human society" (*LG* 36). It would not make sense, for example, to claim from the hierarchy religious freedom, which is a civil right, nor would it make sense to claim from the state courts a right they have in the Church.

Likewise, one must clearly distinguish "between the activities of Christians, acting individually or collectively in their own name as citizens guided by the dictates of a Christian conscience—in which action they are free and responsible—and their activity acting along with their pastors in the name of the Church", which must be performed in obedience to the guidelines of the ecclesiastical authority, by whose mandate they act (*GS* 76).

Religious Liberty

One of the most important documents of the Council is the Declaration *Dignitatis humanæ* (*DH*) on the right of religious liberty. This is a civil right which has as its foundation "the very dignity of the human person," and which means "that all men should be immune from coercion on the part of individuals, social groups and every human power so that, within due limits, nobody is forced to act against his convictions nor is anyone to be restrained from acting in accordance with his convictions in religious matters in private or in public, alone or in associations with others" (*DH* 2).

From the moral perspective, every man has the duty of seeking and living the truth, "especially in what concerns God and his Church," but this obligation can only be realized in freedom, since "truth can impose itself on the mind of man only in virtue of its own truth" (*DH* 1). For this reason, in civil society, neither the State nor any other authority or group within is competent to determine the religious choices of the citizens in a coercive way.

The Church and the other religious confessions, comprised of the citizens belonging to the same religion, are also the subjects of civil religious freedom. They have the right to organize themselves according to their own norms, to practice worship, to support the religious life of their members, promote institutions and initiatives with a religious purpose, spread their doctrine, etc.

Religious liberty must be protected and promoted by the state authority in the same way as the other human rights, without discrimination. However, it has limits, which are those necessary to guarantee peace, justice, public morality, and the rights of all. This is summed up in the notion of public order, rightly understood.

Christian dualism finds a valid support on the basis of religious liberty. Even a government which defines itself as secular and does not recognize the Church "as a spiritual authority founded by Christ the Lord" (that is, by a title of divine right), must recognize that the religion of its citizens does not lie within its competence, and it must thus respect their freedom and that of religious confessions, including the Catholic Church. Therefore, the Council affirms: "When the principle of religious freedom is not just proclaimed in words or incorporated in law but is implemented sincerely in practice, only then does the Church enjoy in law and in fact those stable conditions which give her the independence necessary for fulfilling her divine mission" (*DH* 13).

4. Various Aspects of the Mission of the Church with Regard to the World

The religious mission of the Church in itself is profoundly human: above all it has to do with man, created by God, redeemed by Jesus Christ, and called to sanctification in the Holy Spirit. "It is man, therefore, who is the key to this discussion, man considered whole and entire, with body and soul, heart and conscience, mind and will" (*GS* 3). It is Christ, the new Adam, who "in the very revelation of the mystery of the Father and of his love, fully reveals man to himself and brings to light his most high calling" (*GS* 22).

Continuing the work of her Founder, the Church intends to promote the dignity of the person and serve his vocation. She does this through her ministry of truth and charity, and "is to be a leaven and, as it were, the soul of human society in its renewal by Christ and transformation into the family of God" (*GS* 40).

Proceeding from the faith, the Church knows that "there is no human law so powerful to safeguard the personal dignity and freedom of man as the Gospel which Christ entrusted to the Church" (*GS* 41). It enters, therefore, into her mission to proclaim and promote human rights with her preaching and with works of charity "for the benefit of all men, especially of those in need."[158] She does not claim to "exercise with purely human means any exterior dominion" (*GS* 42), but offers to all the force of the Gospel for the purpose of healing the wounds of sin, the origin of all personal and social injustice, since true freedom can only be realized in the truth.

In carrying out this and other more specific conciliar goals, the pastors of the Church, especially the Popes, have repeatedly dealt with problems regarding the rights of the person: the right to life from conception until natural death, religious freedom, peace and the development of peoples, marriage and the family, the rights of women and children, schools, etc. While they encourage various initiatives in favor of the person, they have also vigorously condemned violations and threats undermining human dignity.

In doing so, the Church has not strayed from her proper task, as it is claimed by some who envision Christianity not incarnate in society. On the contrary, as stated in c. 747 § 2: "To the Church belongs the right always and everywhere to announce moral principles, including those pertaining to the social order, and to make judgments on any human affairs to the extent that they are required by the fundamental rights of the human person or the salvation of souls." All the faithful, guided by their Christian conscience, must contribute so that the law of the Gospel may always be respected in social life.

158. On the Church as a "community of love," see BENEDICT XVI in the second part of the Enc. *Deus caritas*, February, 22 2007.

Index of Particular Canons

Canon	Page
7–22	28
8	31
9	32
10	31, 46
11	28, 48
12	30
13	30
14	31
18	262
20	30
23	33
23–28	33
24	33
24–26	33
25	33
26	34
27	34
28	34
29	32, 35
30	32
31	35
31–33	35
32	35
33	34, 35
34	34, 35
35	40
35–47	39
36	38, 39, 262
37	39, 40
38	39
48	40
49	41
50	40
51	40
52	40
54	40
55	40
56	40
57	39, 40, 289
59	41
60	41
63	41
64	42
65	42
76	42
85	39, 42
86	42, 45
87	64, 125, 266
87–89	43
88	125
90	43
94	35, 36, 37, 51

Canon	Page	Canon	Page
95	37, 38	225	83
96	48	226	83, 163
96–112	48	227	83
96–123	48	228	84
97	206	229	84
97–98	49	230	85
100–107	49	231	86
107	49	232	87
108	66, 70	232–264	198
109	66	233	87
111–112	62	234	89
112	49	235	87
113	50	236	88
113–123	49	237	88
114	50, 51	238	88
115	51, 252	239	64, 88
116	52, 242	239–240	89
118	53, 66, 70	240	64
119	38, 52, 73	242	89
120	51	243	38, 89
121	51	244–258	89
122	51	246	64
123	51	259	88
124	45, 46	262	88
124–128	44	263–264	88
125	45	264	247
214	62	265	90
215	62	266	90
216	62	267–269	90
217	63, 84, 171	271	91
218	63	273	91
219	63, 66	273–289	91
220	64	274	70, 92
221	64	275	92
222	64, 241, 244	276	92, 229
223	65	277	92
224	82	278	92
224–231	83	279	93

Canon	Page	Canon	Page
280	93	327–329	97
281	93	330	108
282	93	331	111
283	93	332	68, 113
284	94	333	111, 112
285–289	94	335	113
288	94	336	68, 110
290	95	337	110
291	43, 95	338	37
292	95	340	110
293	95	341	111
294–297	119	344	37
295	37, 72	361	115
298	95	362–367	116
298–329	62	368	71, 117, 118, 121
299	96, 99, 100	369	118
301	52, 98	370	118
302	97	371	118
303	97	372	119
304	96	373	117
305	97, 100	374	117
307	97	375	67, 120
309	38, 100	380	234
310	100	381	69, 72, 121
312	97, 98	381–402	120
313	98	385	122
314	99	386	160
315	99	387	122
316	99	393	53
317	99	401	107, 123
318	99	403–411	123
319	99	412	123
320	99	416	123
321	100	431	133
322	97, 100	432	133
323	100	433	50, 134
325	100	434	134
326	100	435	133

Canon	Page	Canon	Page
436	133	590	143
439	134	603	142
440	134	604	142
441	38, 134	605	141
442	38, 134	607	145
443	134	631	38
444	135	632	38
446	135	646–653	147
447	135	654–658	147
448	135	665	147
449	136	667	147
450	136	668	148
451	136	669	148
454	136	670	148
455	136	671	148
459	137	672	148
460–468	124	684–685	149
462	38	686–687	149
469–474	124	688–690	149
475–481	125	691–693	149
492–493	125	694–704	149
494	107, 126	705–707	148
495–501	126	710–711	150
502	127	712	150
503–510	127	713	150
511	128	714	150
511–514	128	715	150
515	128	716	150
515–552	128	731–746	151
522	107	747	154, 310
528	160	748	48, 155
530	236	749	156
532	53	750	157, 158
538	107	751	158
553–555	131	752	158
556–563	131	753	159
564–572	132	754	159
566	74, 132	755	160

Canon	Page	Canon	Page
756–757	160	828	172, 173
758	160	830	173
759	161	833	159
762	161	834	175
762–772	161	835	85, 176
763	161	838	176
764–765	162	841	177
766	85, 162	842	31, 178
767	162	843	178
773	163	845	177
775	163, 172	849	178
776	163	851	48
782	164, 165	861	85, 179
784	165	865	180
788	48	869	179
790	165	870	179
793	166	871	179
794	166	874	180
797	167	875–878	181
799	167	879	181
800	166, 168	880	183
801	168	883	74, 183
803	168	889	182
804	167	891	182
805	167	892	183
807	166	893	183
808	169	894–896	183
810	169	899	184
811	169	900	184
812	170	902	185
815	170	905–906	185
816–817	170	907	184
821	171	908	185
822	171	910	85, 186
823	172	913	187
825	172	914	187
826	172	916	187
827	164, 168, 173	917	187

Canon	Page	Canon	Page
921	186	1006	195
922	186	1007	195
923	188	1008	67, 196
934	188	1008–1009	58
938	188	1009	196
939	189	1010–1011	199
940	188	1012	196
941–942	189	1013	197
943	189	1015	197
944	189	1024	197
945–958	189	1025–1052	198
948–950	70	1055	200
952	133	1057	202, 204
959	190	1059	201
960	193	1060	203
961–963	193	1061	204, 221, 277
964	64, 192	1063–1072	225
966–975	191	1073	213
967	74, 191	1074	213
968	74	1075–1077	213
969	74	1076	33
976	74, 95, 191	1078	43, 125, 217
977	192	1078–1082	214
978–983	191	1079	43, 74
983	64	1080	43
984	64	1082	74
985	89	1083	215
986	192	1084	28, 215
987	192	1085	215
988	192	1086	216
989	192	1087	31, 92, 216
991	64, 192	1088	217
992–997	194	1089	217
998	194	1090	217
999	195	1091	217
1000	195	1092	218
1003	195	1093	218
1004–1008	195	1094	218

Canon	Page	Canon	Page
1095	206	1189	231
1096	207	1190	232
1097	208, 209	1191–1193	232
1098	210	1191–1204	232
1099	208	1192	232
1100	208	1194	232
1101	210	1195	233
1102	211	1196	43, 233
1103	212	1199–1200	234
1107	208, 224, 225	1200	234
1108	219	1201	234
1111	74	1208	236
1112	85, 219	1212	235
1121	235	1213	235
1121–1123	220	1214	235
1125–1126	216	1215	236
1131–1133	220	1216	236
1134	220	1217	236
1135	48, 220	1218	236
1137	204	1219	236
1137–1140	221	1221	235
1141	221	1223	236
1142	221, 285	1224	236
1143–1150	222	1225	236
1151	223	1226–1229	237
1152	223	1230	237
1153	223	1231	237
1156–1160	224	1232	237
1161–1165	225	1233	237
1166–1172	227	1235	237
1170	48	1236	237
1172	229	1240–1241	238
1173–1175	229	1241	238
1176–1185	229	1244	238
1183	48	1245	238
1186–1190	231	1246	239
1187	231	1247–1248	239
1188	231	1249–1251	239

Canon	Page	Canon	Page
1252	239	1324	256, 260
1253	240	1326	256
1254	241	1328	256
1256	242, 249	1329	257
1257	242	1331	257
1259	244	1332	257
1260	244	1333	257
1261	65, 241	1334	257
1262	65	1336	258
1262–1266	245	1339	258
1263	65, 247	1340	258
1264	133, 246	1357	74, 261
1267	245, 246	1364	158, 260
1272	248	1364–1369	262
1273	249	1366	166
1275	249	1367	260
1276–1279	250	1370	260
1277	126, 127, 250	1370–1377	262
1280	250	1371	157, 158, 159
1282–1289	250	1372	259
1290	251	1374	62
1292	127, 232	1376	235
1295	252	1377	232, 252, 259
1296	252	1378	260
1297	252	1378–1389	262
1301	252	1382	197, 260
1303	52, 252	1383	197
1304	253	1388	260
1311	255	1390–1391	262
1312	257, 258	1392	94
1314	260	1392–1396	262
1315–1318	255	1394	92, 256
1317	258	1395	92
1319	41	1396	94
1319–1320	255	1397–1398	262
1321	256	1398	260
1322	256	1399	263
1323	256	1400	288

Canon	Page	Canon	Page
1401	266	1532	234
1403	266	1540–1546	276
1404–1405	266	1547–1573	275
1405	267	1562	234
1408	272	1574–1581	276
1417	266	1582–1583	277
1420–1422	267	1584–1586	277
1423	269	1598–1606	278
1424	268	1607–1618	278
1425	268	1619–1627	281
1426	279	1620	281
1427	267	1622	281
1428	268	1623	281
1430	268	1628–1640	279
1432	268	1644	281
1437	268	1645	282
1438	269	1645–1648	282
1444	267	1650–1655	282
1445	290	1673	272
1452	273	1674	284
1457	272	1675	284
1465	272	1680	276, 284
1481–1490	271	1682	280
1501–1525	273	1686–1688	285
1504	273	1697–1706	285
1505	273	1698	285
1526	274	1707	286
1526–1586	274	1717–1731	287
1527	274	1732	39
1530–1538	274	1732–1739	288

Subject Index

A

Absence 286
Abuse 122, 256
Accomplice 256–257, 259
Administration 125–126, 146, 148
Administration of ecclesiastical goods 248–250
Administrative act 38–43, 289–290
Administrative recourse 289–290
Administrative silence 39, 289
Admission 89, 146, 197–199
Age 28, 49, 122–123, 198
Aggregate of persons 51–52
Alienation of ecclesiastical goods 251–252
Anointing of the sick 194–195
Apostasy 158
Apostolic See 115, 266–267
Apostolic Signatura 267, 290
Appeal 279–281
Association 95–97
    private 99–101
    public 98–99
Auditor 268
Authority 25
    of Church and State 291–302, 308–309
    of college of bishops 109–111
    of ecumenical councils 110–111
    of individual bishops 120–123
    of institutions of the universal Church 113–116
    of Magisterium 155–159
    of Pope 111–113, 266–267
Auxiliary bishop 123–124

B

Baptism 28, 48, 82, 176, 177, 178–181, 222–223
Bishop 9, 15, 29, 120–123
Books 171–173

C

Cæsaropapism 294–295, 297
Calumny 64
Candidate 87–89, 196–199
Canon law 1–46
    history 7–20
Canonical provision 105–107
Capacity 45–46, 47
Cardinal 111, 114, 266
Catechesis 163–164
Catechumen 78
Catholic (title) 62, 168
Catholic education 166–171
Catholic persons 77–78, 307–308
Catholic schools 168–169
Censure 257
Chaplain 132–133
Christian dualism 292–302
Church (building) 188, 235–236
Circumstance 48–49, 256
Cleric 78–79, 86–95, 97, 286–287
Codex canonum Ecdesiarum orientalium 18–20
Codex iuris canonici 13, 16–17
Coercion 212–213, 308
College of bishops 6, 14, 29, 59, 107–109, 109–111, 115, 156–157, 158–160

College of consultors 127
Communication 171–173
Community 33
Complaint of nullity 281
Compromise 106
Concordia discordantium canonum 10
Conference of bishops 135–137
Conferral of office 105–107
Confirmation 181–183
Conflict of competence 267
Consent 45, 179, 202, 204–213
Constitutional principles 56–59
Council
 ecumenical 110–111
 particular 134–135
 pastoral 128
Council of Trent 11
Culpable 255, 256
Custom 7–8, 33–34

D

Damage 288
Deceased 229–231
Deceit 210
Decree 33, 40
Defense 270–271, 278
Diaconate 88, 94, 162, 196
Diocesan curia 124
Diocesan synod 124
Diocesan vicar 125
Diocese 117 118, 120–133, 251, 266, 267, 269, 282
Dismissal 94–95, 149
Dispensation 42–43
Divine law 5–7, 28, 42–43
Document 276
Domicile 49, 64
Doubt
 concerning reception of sacraments 177, 179

E

Eastern Church 18–20, 119
Ecclesiastical goods 241–253
Ecclesiastical office 105–107, 295
Ecclesiastical province 133
Ecumenism 159–160
Education 163–164, 166–171
Election 106, 111–113
Episcopal vicar 125
Erection 97–99
Eucharist 178, 183–190
Excardination 90
Excommunication 257, 259, 261
Execution of judgement 282–283
Expert 276–277
Expiration 107, 149

F

Faithful 48, 56–59, 60–65, 95–101
Family 83, 163, 198, 202, 223
Fear 212–213, 256
Feast day 238–239
Fidelity 92, 211
Formation 63, 84–85, 87–89, 93, 146
Freedom 61, 63, 83–84
 of the Church 296, 308–310
 of worship 298–302, 307–309
Funerals 229–231

G

Good
 common 25–27
 public 268, 271, 272
Governance 77–78, 103–137
Gratian 10
Gravity of crime 263

H

Heresy 158
Holy day 122, 130, 238–239
Holy orders 86–95, 196–199, 216, 286–287
Holy See 115, 266–267
Holy Spirit 6, 27, 153–156
Human law 5–7, 28

I

Ignorance 207, 256
Impediment 106–107, 213–218, 223–224
Incapacitating law 31
Incardination 90–91
Indulgence 194

Infallibility 12, 157–159
Institute of consecrated life 142–151
Instruction (in a process) 268, 269, 278, 285–286
Instruction (norm) 35
Interdict 257
Interrogation 275–276
Invalidating law 31

J

Jesus 4, 5–6, 77, 141, 153, 155, 175, 176, 183, 188, 196, 200, 291, 303
Judicial act 43–46
Judicial confession 275
Judicial vicar 268
Juridical case 265–290
Juridical person 49–53, 241–244
Justice 1, 5–7, 33

L

Laity 15, 81–86
Latin Church 18–20, 119
Law 1–20, 27–32
Liturgy 175, 176
Liturgy of the hours 229
Local Ordinary 43, 125
Loss of clerical state 94–95

M

Magisterium 6–7, 155–159
Mandate 40
Marriage 199–227, 283–286
- canonical form 218–220, 225–226
- conditional marriage 211–212
- convalidation of a marriage 223–225
- defect of consent 205–213, 224
- defect of form 225
- dispensation of non-consummated marriage 221
- dispensation of ratified but non-consummated marriage 285–286
- dissolution of the marriage bond 221–223
- doubt of validity 203
- error 208–209
- impediment 213–218
- incapacity 205–207
- marriage by proxy 204, 227
- marriage nullity 205–207, 280, 283–285
- pastoral care 225–227
- putative marriage 204
- renewal of consent 224–225
- retroactive validation 225
- separation 223, 285
- simulation 210–211

Mission Church 164–165
Motu proprio 9

N

Negligence 256, 262
Non-baptized person 48, 216, 222–223
Non-Catholic person 77–78, 187, 220, 302
Non-Catholic religion 297–302
Norm 21–38
- administrative 34–35
- canonical 25–27
- custom 32–34
- law 27–32
- rule of Order 35–38
- statute 35–37

Notary 268
Notification 40
Nullity 45–46, 268
Nullity of sacred ordination 286–287
Nun 147
Nuncio 116

O

Oath 232–234
Obreption 41
Occult impediment 224
Oral contentious process 283
Oral testimony 275–276

P

Parish 128–131, 188
Particular Church 107–109, 116–120
Party 268, 270–272, 274–276
Pastor 61, 91, 163
Penal remedy 258

Penalty 256–263
Penance (days of) 239–240
Penance (penal) 258
Penance (sacrament) 187, 190–194
Perpetual vow 145, 147, 151
Personal prelature 119
Petition 41, 61, 265
Physical person 48–49
Pleading 278
Pontiff 6, 9, 107–114, 155–159, 266–267
Postulation 106–107
Preaching 154, 161–163
Precept 40–41
Presbyterate 160, 162, 196–199
Presumption 277
Priest 86–95, 160, 162, 196–199
Priest (parish) 128–131
Priesthood 86–95, 175–176, 196–199
Procedural action 265
Procedural law 265–290
Process 265, 269–279
Promulgation 27, 31
Property 148, 241–253
Publication 171–173

Q

Question in a judicial decision 278

R

Reason 28, 47, 48, 256
Recourse 39, 279–281, 289–290
Rector
  of church 131–132
  of seminary 88
Religious 145–149
Religious institute 145–149
Remission 260–261
Remuneration 93
Renunciation 148
Reparation 288
Representation 48, 52–53, 115–116
Rescript 41–43
Resignation 113, 122–123, 129
Respondent 270, 273
Retroactivity 32
Revelation 6, 158, 177
Revenue 244
Revocation 289–290
Rights 1–4, 14, 15, 310
  of clerics 91–95
  of the faithful 60–65
  of the laity 83–86
Rite 49, 57, 62
Roman Curia 11–12, 114–115, 290
Roman Rota 267

S

Sacrament 60, 62, 176–227, 257
Sacramentals 227–229
Schism 158, 295
Scripture 8, 170
Seminarian 87–89
Seminary 87–89
Sick person 186–187, 188
Simony 262
Sin 187, 190–192, 296
Society of apostolic life 151
Spouse 83, 199–204, 220, 225–227
Statute 35–37
Subreption 41
Substitution 240, 256, 259
Superior 132, 139, 145, 146
Suspension 257
Synod
  diocesan 124
  of Bishops 113–114

T

Tax 64–65, 246–247
Temporal goods 93, 241–253
Territory 133–137
Testimony 275–276
Time limit 282–283
Total reinstatement 282
Transfer 91, 148–149
Trial 265–290
Tribunal 266–269, 271–272

U

Unity
- of Christianity 159–160
- of Church 103, 109, 116–117
- of marriage 208

University 169–171

V

Vacancy 113, 123, 128
Validity 177
Vatican Council (First) 12–13
Vatican Council (Second) 14–15, 303–309
Veneration
- of Eucharist 188–189
- of saints, sacred images, and icons 231–232

Vicar 123–125
Vicar forane 131
Vicar general 123–124, 125
Violation 255, 265
Vocation 77, 81, 86, 139–141, 146, 148, 199–202, 220
Vote 106, 111–113, 134–135, 136–137, 124, 268
Vow 139, 141, 142, 145, 147, 149, 217, 232–234

W

Word 4, 61–62, 153–155, 158, 160–165
Worship 175–240
Writing 171–173

Last published / Dernières publications

HANDBOOKS / MANUELS

A Handbook on Canon Law, 2nd updated edition, J. T. MARTÍN DE AGAR, 2007, ISBN 978-2-89127-804-1.

Liturgie et droit – Le droit liturgique dans le système du droit canonique de l'Église catholique, John HUELS, Traduit par Jean PELLETIER, 2007, ISBN 978-2-89127-811-9.

NOTEBOOKS / CAHIERS

The Juridical Mind of Saint Josemaria Escriva, A brief History of the Canonical Path of Opus Dei, 2nd updated edition, 2007, E. CAPARROS, ISBN 978-2-89127-833-1.

La mentalité juridique de saint Josémaria Escriva, Un bref historique de l'itinéraire canonique de l'Opus Dei, E. CAPARROS, 2007, ISBN 9778-2-89127-834-8.

RESEARCH TOOLS / INSTRUMENTS DE RECHERCHE

Dictionnaire biographique des cardinaux du XIXe siècle, Jean LEBLANC, 2007, ISBN 978-2-89127-801-0.

ANNOTATED LEGISLATIVE TEXTS / TEXTES LÉGISLATIFS ANNOTÉS

Code de droit canonique bilingue et annoté (3e éd.), E. CAPARROS, H. AUBÉ (directeurs), 2007, ISBN 978-2-89127-768-6.

Forthcoming / En préparation

HANDBOOKS / MANUELS

Introduction to the History of the Sources of Canon Law I – The Ancient Law up to the Decretum of Gratian, Brian E. FERME, 2007, ISBN 978-2-89127-805-8.

Introduction to the Study of Canon Law, J. HERVADA, 2007, ISBN 978-2-89127-836-2.

NOTEBOOKS / CAHIERS

Fidèles dans le monde, La sécularité des laïcs chrétiens, Jorge MIRAS, 2007, ISBN 978-2-89127-841-6.

Published in 2006 / Parus en 2006

PROCEEDINGS / ACTES

Symposium on Dignitas connubii, Patricia M. DUGAN & Luis NAVARRO (Editors), 2006, ISBN 2-89127-782-1.

ANNOTATED LEGISLATIVE TEXTS / TEXTES LÉGISLATIFS ANNOTÉS

Canonical and Pastoral Guide for Parishes, Canadian Edition, Assembly of Catholic Bishops of Québec; J. PELLETIER (Editor), 2006, ISBN 2-89127-779-1.

Guide canonique et pastoral au service des paroisses. Édition canadienne, Assemblée des évêques catholiques du Québec; J. PELLETIER (directeur), 2006, ISBN 2-89127-778-3.

HANDBOOKS / MANUELS

A Critical Introduction to Natural Law, J. HERVADA, 2006, ISBN 2-89127-776-7.

Advocacy Vademecum, Patricia M. DUGAN (Editor), 2006, ISBN 2-89127-777-5.

Liturgy and Law – Liturgical Law in the System of Roman Catholic Canon Law, J. M. HUELS, 2006, ISBN 2-89127-773-2.

Other published / Déjà parus

Canonical and Pastoral Guide for Parishes, Assembly of Bishops of Québec; J. PELLETIER (Editor), 2005, ISBN 2-89127-640-X.

Incrementa in Progressu 1983 Codicis Iuris Canonici *with a Multilingual Introduction (English, Français, Italiano, Español, Deutsch, Polski)*, E. N. PETERS, 2005, ISBN 2-89127-663-7.

The Penal Process and the Protection of Rights in Canon Law, Patricia M. DUGAN (Editor), 2005, ISBN 2-89127-664-7.

Code of Canon Law Annotated, 2nd revised and updated edition, E. CAPARROS, H. AUBÉ (Editors), 2004, International edition, MTF ISBN 1-890177-44-X/Canadian edition W&L, ISBN 2-89127-629-9.

Exegetical Commentary on the Code of Canon Law; Á. MARZOA, J. MIRAS, R. RODRÍGUEZ-OCAÑA (Editors); E. CAPARROS (General Editor, English edition).

International edition 2004:
- Volume I Chicago, MTF ISBN 1-890177-34-2/Montréal, W&L, ISBN 2-89127-621-3
- Volume II/1 Chicago, MTF ISBN 1-890177-35-0/Montréal, W&L, ISBN 2-89127-622-1
- Volume II/2 Chicago, MTF ISBN 1-890177-36-9/Montréal, W&L, ISBN 2-89127-623-X
- Volume III/1 Chicago, MTF ISBN 1-890177-37-7/Montréal, W&L, ISBN 2-89127-624-8
- Volume III/2 Chicago, MTF ISBN 1-890177-38-5/Montréal, W&L, ISBN 2-89127-625-6
- Volume IV/1 Chicago, MTF ISBN 1-890177-39-3/Montréal, W&L, ISBN 2-89127-626-4
- Volume IV/2 Chicago, MTF ISBN 1-890177-40-7/Montréal, W&L, ISBN 2-89127-627-2
- Volume V Chicago, MTF ISBN 1-890177-41-5/Montréal, W&L, ISBN 2-89127-628-0

Guide canonique et pastoral au service des paroisses II, Assemblée des évêques du Québec; J. PELLETIER (directeur), 2004 ISBN 2-89127-639-6.

Code de droit canonique bilingue et annoté (2e éd.), E. CAPARROS, M. THÉRIAULT, J. THORN (†) (directeurs), 1999, 2e tirage 2003; ISBN 2-89127-460-1.

Dictionnaire biographique des évêques catholiques du Canada (1658-2002), J. LEBLANC, 2002, ISBN 2-89127-506-8.

Code of Canon Law Annotated, E. CAPARROS, M. THÉRIAULT, J. THORN (Editors), 1st edition: March 1993, 2nd printing: October 1993, 3rd printing: 1996, 4th printing: 1997, 5th printing: 2000, ISBN 2-89127-232-3 (out of print).

Governance Structures Within the Catholic Church, J. I. ARRIETA, 2000, ISBN 2-89127-518-7.

Tabulae congruentiae inter Codicem iuris canonici et versiones anteriores canonum: With a Multilingual Introduction (English, Français, Italiano, Español, Deutsch), E. N. PETERS, 2000, ISBN 2-89127-500-4.

A Handbook on Canon Law, J. T. MARTÍN DE AGAR, 1999, ISBN 2-89127-457-1.

La charge pastorale d'une paroisse sans curé, B. A. CUSAK & T. G. SULLIVAN, trad. et adaptation par M. THÉRIAULT, 1997, ISBN 2-89127-417-2.

Code de droit canonique, E. CAPARROS, M. THÉRIAULT, J. THORN (directeurs), édition bilingue et annotée, 1re édition : mars 1990, 2e tirage : décembre 1990, 3e tirage : 1994, 4e tirage : 1995, ISBN 2-89127-153-X (épuisé).

NCCB/Conférence des évêques catholiques des États-Unis. Le manuel de l'évêque, trad. par M. THÉRIAULT, 1994, ISBN 2-89127-309-5 (épuisé).

Orders to / Commander à:

WILSON & LAFLEUR LTÉE

40, Notre-Dame Est
Montréal (Québec) Canada H2Y 1B9
Tél. : 514 875-6326 / 1 800 363-2327 • Téléc. : 514 875-8356
www.wilsonlafleur.com

EUROPE

Éditions Le Laurier
19, passage Jean Nicot
75007 PARIS
Tél. : +33 1.45.51.55.08 • Fax : +33 1.45.51.81.83
e-mail : editions@lelaurier.fr
www.lelaurier.fr

USA

www.CanonLawBooks.com
2662 East Allegheny Avenue
Philadelphia, PA 19134-5115
Telephone: 215-634-2355 • Fax: 215-634-2373

Midwest Theological Forum
1420 Davey Road
Woodridge, IL 60517 U.S.A
Phone: 630-739-9750 • Fax: 630-739-9758
e-mail: mail@mwtf.org

MARQUIS

Québec, Canada